D0906405

Dayspring in Darkness

Dayspring in Darkness

Sacrament in Hopkins

JEFFREY B. LOOMIS

LEWISBURG
Bucknell University Press
LONDON AND TORONTO: Associated University Presses

Associated University Presses
440 Forsgate Drive
Cranbury, NJ 08512

Associated University Presses
25 Sicilian Avenue
London WC1A 2QH, England

Associated University Presses
P.O. Box 488, Port Credit
Mississauga, Ontario
Canada L5G 4M2

The paper used in this publication meets the requirements of the American National Standard for Permanence of Paper for Printed Library Materials Z39.48-1984.

Library of Congress Cataloging-in-Publication Data

Loomis, Jeffrey B., 1947–
  Dayspring in darkness.

Revision of the author's thesis (Ph. D.)—University of North Carolina at Chapel Hill.
  Bibliography: p.
  Includes index.
  1. Hopkins, Gerard Manley, 1844–1889—Criticism and interpretation.   2. Sacraments in literature.
3. Christian poetry, English—History and criticism.
I. Title.
PR4803.H44Z7117   1988   821'.8   87-47819
ISBN 0-8387-5138-5 (alk. paper)

for
parents, brother, students, true colleagues
and
in memory of
Barbara Spitzer
("sing . . . sweetest spells": "bónes rísen")

Contents

Preface

DAYSPRING IN DARKNESS continuously interacts with earlier scholarly work on Gerard Manley Hopkins and indeed lauds the decades of effort that have formed the Hopkinsian "interpretive community."[1] Almost all previously published study of his background influences has relevance, and his life must be understood in terms of its dialectical interplay of various forces. He was surely, and powerfully so, a Jesuit and a Scotist. But he was also a Ruskinian and an Origenian, a speech theorist and a rhetorician, a reader of most major world literature, and a man well acquainted with his contemporary Victorians, both sacred and secular. He was, as we tend to forget, at first an Anglican convert to Roman Catholicism, and he was also a long-term practitioner of Augustinian-Origenian methods of biblical exegesis—methods that he importantly transferred to his own sacramentalist poetics.

In this book, by detailing for the first time many dimensions of Hopkin's "husk-kernel" sacramentalism, I present what should become a work of helpful revisionism worthy of being added to the collection of Hopkins studies. Augustine's and Origen's "husk-kernel" paradigms help explain a great deal we have never recognized, or at least have not fully understood, about Hopkins. These paradigms seem to explain: (1) why Hopkins the sacramental transubstantiationist coined, along with the famous term *inscape*, a term like *outscape* that has been hitherto unexplored; (2) why he emphasized the contrasting poetic textures of outer "overthought" and inner "underthought"; (3) why he set the external experiences of the "affective will" against the internal choices of the "elective will"; and (4) why he alternated exuberant externalist nature poetry with poetic monologues about the spiritually struggling internal soul. Once one recognizes that this receptive transubstantiationist valued inner sacramental *substance* more than accidental outer *species*, it seems no wonder that he also valued *inscape* more than *outscape*, "underthought" more than "overthought," "elective will" more than "affective will," and the spiritually self-sacrifical human soul more than even the loveliest natural vistas. It seems, after such discoveries have emerged, somewhat illogical still to concentrate (as many psychologistic critics have in every Hopkinsian generation) on this poet-priest's superficial laments over external personal difficulties. These do not seem at all the key signs by which we should define his life—or even his difficult last years. These are mere outer, not inner, signs and hence no necessary denial of the power he had long sought to develop within—a *substantial* spiritual "dayspring."

Acknowledgments

AFTER YEARS OF STRUGGLE with the gray obscurities of language, this book has finally come to birth due to many nourishers. I acknowledge, celebrate, give thanks for their plenteous contributions.

Knowing that the manuscript they read required much modification before it could develop into this study, my 1980 dissertation committee at the University of North Carolina at Chapel Hill (Alfred G. Engstrom, Eugene H. Falk, C. Carroll Hollis, George Lensing, Diane Leonard, Christoph Schweitzer) guided patiently my earliest Hopkinsian research and argumentation with sensitivity and a zeal for intellectual breadth. Reading early and later versions of my work, Leslie Banner and Frances Widman (Duke University), Bruce and Margaret Graver (Providence College), Susan Betts Landstrom (University of North Carolina at Chapel Hill), and C. Douglas Murray (University of Alabama at Huntsville) helped to water those seeds of intuition and thought that the original guiding professors had helped to plant.

Just as much as Hopkins, I have also throughout my writing of the manuscript "need[ed] encouragement as crops need rain." I have received that nurture partly from genial Hopkinsians throughout the United States, in Canada, and even in Northern Ireland and Japan. And I have daily been blessed with collegial partners in teaching (Sarah Adams, Carol Campbell, Mary Ellen Molinaro, Robert Newman, and James Dean in West Virginia; Grace Burton, Robert and Leili Burton, Pamela Clements, Dennis Goldsberry, Kathleen Haney, Anne Hawkes, Michael Jenson, and Jeffrey Porter in South Carolina). These folk—along with my parents, my brother, and my students—have proved that I, again like Hopkins, "in all removes . . . can / Kind love both give and get."

Research for this work has led me to meet and receive bounteous help from library personnel at Duke, Emory, and Georgetown universities, at the University of North Carolina at Chapel Hill, the University of Pittsburgh, the University of South Carolina at Columbia, and the University of Tennessee at Knoxville. Especially helpful were the interlibrary loan and periodicals officers at the College of Charleston in South Carolina: Veronique Aniel, Tom Gilson, Helen Ivy, and Norma

Jenson. I must also surely thank that college's Research and Grants Committee, which in 1985 awarded me with released time from teaching and helped me progress toward completion of my writing.

I am of course deeply grateful to Professor Mills Edgerton and his staff at Bucknell University Press, as well as to the staff at Associated University Presses and especially my copy editor Lauren Lepow. Throughout the pages that follow, my deep debt to the wide-reaching Hopkinsian "interpretive community," as well as to theologians and other scholars of many variations, should be readily apparent.

Finally, abounding thanks go to those three fine typists and splendid persons who produced the final version of this book's manuscript. Only with steady fingers and stalwart hearts like those of Susan Bogdanowicz, Mary Goldsberry, and Cheryl Graves could a product like this have finally emerged.

*   *   *

Dayspring in Darkness

1

The Sacrament of the Soul

You will do well to attend to [the scriptural words] as to a lamp shining in a dark place, until the day dawns and the morning star rises in your hearts.
—2 Peter 1:19

IN HIS INTRIGUING LIFE AND WORK, Gerard Manley Hopkins strikingly manifested the sacramental impulse in multiple ways. First of all, he certainly revered the seven official Roman Catholic sacraments as "permanent, sensible, rite[s] instituted by Christ to confer grace efficaciously."[1] Indeed, in his poetry he even *narrated* his ardent immediate experience of these seven sacraments. Especially did he do so during his early Oxford Anglican years (the mid–1860s) and during the several years following his 1877 Jesuit ordination.

Yet Hopkins was doubtless also familiar not only with influential Scholastic and Tridentine definitions of these *seven* sacraments, but also with the much earlier basic Augustinian definition of *any* "sacrament" as "a holy sign (image, symbol, expression) through which we both perceive and receive an invisible grace."[2] Hopkins repeatedly sought to demonstrate how "invisible grace" could sacramentally penetrate, transubstantiate, the outer matter of many "holy sign[s]"—both traditional "ecclesial sacraments" and further experiences that he and others deemed "sacramentals."[3]

Much as the earliest Christians and their later medieval counterparts called "sacraments" many rites that the Church does not call sacraments today ("including the sign of the cross, the conferral of ashes on Ash Wednesday"),[4] so Hopkins seemed to extend his sacramental theology outside the bounds of the seven "ecclesial" Christian mysteries. Because he so firmly believed that "In the beginning was the Word, and the Word was with God, and the Word was God. . . . All things were made by Him, and without Him was not anything made that was made" (John 1:1–3), Hopkins often appeared to believe that Christ had instituted sacramentality within language (human words or logoi) and within nature (which Christ as Logos had created).

Thus it seems that for Hopkins language and nature did—at least at times and to some degree—appear "efficacious" means for Christ to use in transmitting "actual grace."[5] For example, Hopkins's poems of the 1870s largley concentrate upon what I would call the *visible sacrament* he found available in "sensible" natural scenes. There he felt he could "perceive" hints of Christic Real Presence and "receive" what he hoped his readers might also "receive." That was nothing less than a gracious sacramental urging to self-sacrifice, to imitatio Christi.

In both these 1870s poems and in his even-denser works of the 1880s, Hopkins strove to order words tautly so as to reveal "invisible grace" emerging even from the limitations of language. He surely knew that "words" of institution were called the "form" joined to the "matter" in official "ecclesial" sacraments,[6] and that Augustine had thus termed any sacrament a "*verbum visibile.*"[7]

Hopkins surely also knew that the biblical prophets "were genuinely persuaded that God's word on their lips not only announced but determined the course of history in an infallible way—not because they spoke but because God spoke through them."[8] In his own poetry, Hopkins as a sacramentalist wordsmith sometimes even seemed impatient with linguistic and audience-perception barriers. After all, he wished with great earnestness to make his art transcribe quasi-prophetic theophany. Yet ultimately, in those late poems that are probably his greatest spiritual contribution to the world, he more limitedly declares a rather humble sort of *verbal sacrament*. His writing now confirms—hermetically and quietly—the internalization of his sacramental faith.

Emphasizing in these late poems the sanctifying *effects* of a sacramentalist life (one that has sought "invisible grace" everywhere, both in the "holy signs" of "ecclesial sacraments" and in all devout human experience), Hopkins demonstrated how "sanctifying grace," available to human beings through sacraments,[9] "infuses supernatural life into the soul," "life essentially superior to natural life."[10] He thus seemed to recognize a principle central to the teachings of the Apostle Paul. Christians, Paul proclaims, "must become 'new creatures,' and must 'put on Jesus Christ.'"[11] They need a principle today also strongly voiced in post–Vatican II theology: they need sacramental empowering for life in Christian community.

G. M. A. Jansen writes that Christ "had to give," in the Eucharist, his "body . . . to his Apostles in order that he could act through the mystical body which he thus formed."[12] Bernard Cooke, like Jansen a post–Vatican II theologian, declares the "experience of Christian discipleship . . . sacramental of Christ's presence" and adds that "What Jesus did to bring about this situation, that is to 'institute the [sacrament of the] church,' was to become the risen one and to share . . . as risen Lord his . . . Spirit of new life."[13]

As Cooke further recalls, "In the johannine description of Jesus' last supper with his disciples, Jesus tells the disciples that he is the true vine and that they are the branches."[14] Thus, Cooke declares, "the people who . . . are the Christian community act as 'body' to locate the risen Christ in space and time." And therefore, says Cooke, "all the activity of Christian communities is sacramental, even though certain actions, the sacramental liturgies, may be more formally and explicitly singled out as 'sacraments.' "[15]

In Hopkins's great archetypal Christian biography sonnets of the 1880s, he affirms—eighty years before Vatican II, but in the clear light of nineteen Christian centuries that had already spoken of a large "variety of sacraments"[16]—that the individual disciple in the Christian community can most marvelously become sacramentalized as a "branch of Christ." He or she can share, through the sacramental Church, in his or her Lord's "mystical body." Hopkins indeed pictures such a person as one who germinates Christ within the soul, proving his or her own outer self to be a dark "husk," but still only a "husk" surrounding a hidden divine "kernel" of sacramental grain.[17] To Hopkins, God seems always both transcendent and immanent—but most fully immanent in a sacramental, because a spiritually fruitful, soul.[18]

* * *

Hopkins's desire for meaningful ecclesiastical worship led him early in life "to embrace the Catholic doctrine of the Real Presence of God in the Eucharist, the 'Half-way House' of God in this world, as Hopkins called it in his poem of that name."[19] Although he also was following John Henry Newman in the quest for reliable church authority, an ardor for the doctrine of transubstantiation surely motivated considerably this young Oxonian's conversion from Anglicanism to the Church of Rome.

Secondly, Hopkins's quest after Christ's sacramental Real Presence led him to seek that Presence in nature as much as in the Church. He affirmed belief that "it is within God's power to make the Body of Christ really present *universaliter*, anywhere or everywhere in the universe."[20] Thus he rejoiced in "accepted example[s] of sacramental nature," like Saint Winefred's Well,[21] and in Scotist and Ignatian perspectives that declared nature a partial dwelling place of Christ.

Still, he would not, any more than would Augustine, a forebear historically predating Scotus and Loyola, grovel in "a servitude under useful signs, but rather . . . [would] exercise . . . the mind . . . toward understanding them spiritually."[22] Thus Hopkins could agree with a modern sacramentalist priest that agape love emerges fully only "at the core of the universe."[23] Hopkins believed that he could experience a transubstantial Eucharist and write sacramentalist nature poetry because his Ignatian-Scotist contemplativeness allowed him, at least for brief periods, to deemphasize all negative outlooks on reality. On the other hand, he sometimes largely agreed with the modern view that "reality, the universe, the cosmos, life, call it what we will, seems most of the time to be absurd, capricious, random—and occasionally downright ugly and vindictive."[24]

Hopkins surely sought, with an impressive optimism about natural Christic Presence, to write truly priestly nature poems. With extraordinary homiletic and sacerdotal energy, Hopkins in the 1870s used poetic portraits of visible nature in order to beckon sacramental sacrifice. Along with Daniel Harris[25] and Rachel Salmon,[26] Jerome Bump rightly sees what has rarely been noted before—this true priestly urgency of much Hopkinsian art. He judges Hopkins's occasional addressing of his audience as "clearly intended to be the delivery of a 'writ' for [their] conversion,"[27] and he deems that even Hopkins's more meditative works, like "The Windhover," wish "to effect . . . change" in readers.[28]

"The Windhover," however, calls for such change rather quietly, and to me it appears the key transition poem to another kind of sacramental expression in Hopkins. It seems vital for readers to notice a sacramentalist priestly assertiveness (if not aggression) in some earlier Hopkins poems of *visible sacrament*. Only then will we notice (as Bump does in a limited way) the important contrast in Hopkins's later and more humbly purposive poems of internalized *verbal sacrament*. Around 1880, his religious verse ceases to focus primarily on summoning others affectively to sacramental participation. Rather, his later work most dominantly, if more limitedly, declares Hopkins simply to will an elective personal sacramental engagement, to express personal inner resurrection "at very profound levels of the personalit[y]."[29] No other poet has ever expressed with such power the Roman Catholic doctrine of transubstantiation, but Hopkins actually most powerfully voices this doctrine in the very poems of the 1880s that verbally focus—after perhaps his own "cold loneliness of existential doubt"[30]—on the internal sacrament of the soul. Such an emphasis on personal elective sacrament he encountered even as a young man—in the Anglican Eucharistic doctrine of receptionism.

Thus this poet-priest, even long after he had become a consecrated Roman Catholic Jesuit and a practitioner of Augustinian-Origenian poetry, seems to have restricted his field of sacramental fervor during the last decade of his life, and to have done so in order to voice his primary *receptive* wish for transubstantiation in his soul. Whereas all nature had seemed to his Tractarian predecessor John Keble "almost sacramental"[31] and in Hopkins's own practice had signaled "in a sense" or "somehow" the instrumental transubstantiation of Christ even into human words,[32] by the 1880s "The 'worldwielder' who had been perceived as God in 'Hurrahing in Harvest' is identified quite differently in Hopkins's more orthodox notes on Ignatius's *Spiritual Exercises:* 'Satan . . . the worldwielder . . . [is] as it were constricting [nature] to his purposes' (S 98–99)."[33] Hopkins now sometimes treated nature as if it were approximately what an Anglican of his youth would have called a virtualist sacrament—only "effectually" and not "substantially" transmitting divine grace.[34] Since he most often spoke thus about nature in sermons directed at average English men and women, he was perhaps deliberately speaking to them in their own dualistic language. Still, he all but constantly deemphasizes visible signs of Christ in the external world during this period.

My purpose in this study is to examine these complexities in Hopkins's sacramentalist vision, demonstrating that they form a constant dialectic of perspectives throughout his writing. A large number of critics have not been willing to allow for a purposive turn in his dialectic after 1880, a turn involving a "more orthodox sense of nature as unredeemed, subject to the Fall."[35] J. Hillis Miller, for instance, has bemoaned this change in Hopkinsian focus as the poet's "giv[ing] up everything positive, everything natural, and liv[ing] without growth or productivity, except for brief spasms of poetic creation."[36] Other critics, sometimes of highly diverse philosophical stances, are ready to proclaim even the "spasms of poetic creation" cries of near despair. They see Hopkins "being destroyed by his [antipoetic Jesuit] 'counterpoise' but believing this all he had to offer";[37] his "refus[ing] the ceremony of the poem, collapsing back into . . . pain";[38] or even his having an "inability. . . to identify the true object of his poetry."[39] A refreshing counterargument comes from Robert Boyle's essay in *Readings of "The Wreck,"* where he perceives the late Hopkins of "The shepherd's brow" as "more mature and manly," "condemning with a truly Browningesque honesty . . . [his] youthful pretentiousness."[40]

In downgrading the brash youthful Hopkins of *The Wreck of the Deutschland*, Boyle sees him at that time "bowing to a dogma which may or may not be operative for every human, rather than expressing the movement and the multileveled counterpoint of the heart, to which every human can respond."[41] Boyle finds the Jesuit of the 1870s striving "with the confidence of a dogmatist . . . , with the mere meanings of human words, to break through rational bounds to boundless mystery."[42]

And, indeed, the Hopkins of the 1876 *Wreck* nearly claims that his ode might even save readers from damnation. He almost dares say this because he has already dared to see the "tall nun" whom the ode memoralizes as baptizing damned travelers on the storm-stricken *Deutschland* by her faithful and firm declaration of Christ. Hopkins knew his ancient Origenian precedent for belief in universalist apocatastasis. By his last years, however, he seemed to find "reestablishment" of all creation in Christ[43] a less certainly tenable doctrine. He wrote, in an 1883 "prayer . . . for protestants" sent to Robert Bridges, of "trembl[ing] at [God's] power and threatened punishments," of "hop[ing] . . . never more to sin against thee," and only after "living thus, at our deaths, . . . hear[ing] God's sentence of mercy."[44] These hardly seem to be universalist (or only "protestant") statements, given their apparent emphasis on needed repentance and good works.

More important, Hopkins eventually seems far from willing to believe that *mere poetry* can accomplish universal salvation. Hopkins surely became a priest partly out of fervor to offer sacraments to worshippers, yet in *The Wreck* he may want to be a potent *scribe*-priest who can baptize all his readers into Roman Catholic Christianity—just as he is poetically imagining (or fancying?) the "tall nun" in her crucial confession of faith miraculously baptizing shipwrecked seagoers on the *Deutschland*.

Hopkins did not, as David Downes wrongly asserts, become "destroyed"[45] by later suppression of his poetry. Indeed, I do not believe that he ever at heart suppressed his poetry at all (although he did consider it, along with his specific priestly activities, less vital than sainthood). The poems of his last years are such intricate artifacts that they could not result from enforced suppression of energy. Yet these poems do have a new limited goal. They testify, in taut and multivalent complexity, only to personal strivings after Christic imitatio.

While he, like all the Christians he now humbly represents, fights against the potential hell of personal guilts and doubts, Hopkins's late poetry still declares that his soul is a receptive sacramental center for indwelling Christic Real Presence, through the aid of the parenting Holy Spirit and Blessed Virgin. Hopkins's consciously Augustinian poetry never proves that the spiritual doubts of his own late letters and journals were not perhaps the final sad truth about cosmic reality. His late work is a dramatized would-be spiritual *biography*,[46] not an *auto*-biography of realized victory. Yet he does witness that he felt he "kn[ew]" that Christ was he in "whom he [had] believed," and that he was "persuaded"—even if with some painful tentativeness—that Christ was "able to keep that . . . committed unto Him against [the apocalyptic] day" (2 Timothy 1:12).

* * *

Writing about John Ruskin, but meanwhile comparing him to Gerard Manley Hopkins, Alison Sulloway declares that "the dark side of [his lifelong] schema is related to the joy": "For even when it is joyous, 'the Ruskinese point of view' is filled with paradoxes and contradictions, in imitation of the complex world of fact and value he surveyed."[47] What Sulloway has affirmed for Ruskin is surely true of the Jesuit poet Hopkins whom he so strongly influenced, and it is unfortunate that more critics have not joined Sulloway in recognizing the constancy of diversity within Hopkins's thought. If others had perceived this truth, there would not still exist the regrettable tendency to divide his life into discrete periods of confused preparation, flashing conquest, and debilitating defeat. Such is the basic wrongheaded critical pattern for many: the standard opinion seems to be that Hopkins's youthful writings live only "on the surface of religious experience,"[48] that his middle period of nature lyrics is a "great systematic effort . . . to construct and render within . . . poetry a sacramental vision of nature,"[49] and that his last years are a sad time when he loses his Newmanesque will to assent, producing instead verses which "suggest the impossibility of answer."[50] Unable to perceive "that complete conversion does not completely change the earthly self,"[51] that a sensitive poet's "Victorian Catholic imagery" may address a God revealing both "necessary light" and also "darkness [that] is a mode of light,"[52] the majority of critics still fail to find unity within the diverse foci of Hopkins's life. Because he sometimes starkly expressed his fear of apparent divine darkness, while on the contrary chanting elsewhere with extreme jubilation his bliss before deific lights in nature, some assume that only the period blessed by ample light shows him triumphing. Often the oversimplified reading of Hopkins's life and poetry results simply from theological ignorance; theological knowledge makes Boyle, for instance, see the curve of the Hopkins life and its vision much more insightfully than do many. Yet even Boyle has sometimes oversimplified matters somewhat, in his sometimes fierce disdain for "pagan" critics who see some tinges of an apparently Protestant dualism expressed in Hopkins's Roman Catholic poetry.[53] Few critics have followed Wendell Stacy Johnson who, twenty years after its initial publication, reiterated his view: even though Hopkins writes "his major work as a Roman Catholic," he never completely leaves behind "his beloved Herbert, his native [Anglican] communion, and—to some extent—his own [Victorian] age."[54]

Yet proper understanding of Hopkins depends on exactly such openness to his intellectual and theological diversity. Otherwise, the poet's work becomes too easily attached to the individual critic's own evident special pleading, even if that be the dazzling logic of agnosticism (Miller) or the supposed primacy of aestheticism (Michael Sprinker). Neither of these ideas goes far in explaining Hopkins.[55]

Gerard Manley Hopkins is a sacramental poet. That statement has indeed been made many times before with an apparent belief that no further definition of his sacramental impulse is needed. Yet the term *sacramental* has surely not meant the same to each Hopkins scholar who has used it. The diversity of meanings they have attached to the term is only to be expected—and not merely because they no doubt each intuit and define sacrament from personal life-perspectives. It is also true because Hopkins—a far more multifaceted contemplative person than he often receives credit for being—saw the sacramental experience at various stages of his life (and sometimes simultaneously) from variant perspectives. For him, authentic contemplative openness superseded dogma.[56]

Hopkins was raised and educated in an English church where the Tractarians were seeking to create a "comprehensive Anglicanism" that would define the proper meaning of the sacraments for a church of historical "continuity and catholicity," rather than simply reinforcing the sacramental definitions established during their own denomination's relatively short history.[57] The Tractarians had much reason to seek after universal meanings, for their church's own unity was by 1830 already tenuous and by 1870 deeply fissured. Anglican Evangelicals often held Zwingli's memorialist hypothesis of the sacraments as mere "memorials" of "grace."[58] High Church Anglicans, meanwhile, usually held either the virtualist hypothesis (that the elements only "effectually" and not "substantially" transmit divine grace) or the receptionist theory that Christ is "present wherever two or three are gathered in His name," and that the communicant's faithful reception of Christ at the altar makes that communicant, rather than the bread and the wine, the center where Christic Real Presence is most fully known.[59] The Tractarians did mostly gravitate toward the Roman Catholic doctrine of transubstantiation—although slowly, with many stops and starts. Hopkins, who entered Anglican Oxford at a time when the remaining Tractarians were being challenged by the newest and fiercest opposition camp, the *Essays and Reviews* liberals,[60] seems to have expressed a notable vocal fervency in support of the transubstantiation doctrine, showing little of the doubt that had sometimes characterized Newman, Pusey, and Keble as they debated Eucharistic dogma.[61] We see Hopkins's firmness in "The Half-way House," where he disdains the memorialists for distancing Christ by declaring him only *symbolized* in the sacrament. Hopkins instead chooses the transubtantial Christ—who is *bodily present*, here and now, in the Eucharistic meal:

> Love I was shewn upon the mountain-side
> And bid to catch Him ere the drop of day.
> See, Love, I creep and Thou on wings dost ride:
> Love, it is evening now and Thou away;
> Love, it grows darker here and Thou art above;
> Love, come down to me if Thy name be Love.
>
> My national old Egyptian reed gave way;
> I took of vine a cross-barred rod or rood.
> Then next I hungered: Love when here, they say,
> Or once or never took Love's proper food;
> But I must yield the chase, or rest and eat.—
> Peace and food cheered me where four rough ways meet.
>
> Hear yet my paradox: Love, when all is given,
> To see Thee I must see Thee, to love, love;
> I must o'ertake Thee at once and under heaven
> If I shall overtake Thee at last above.
> You have your wish; enter these walls, one said:
> He is with you in the breaking of the bread.[62]

Even though he does perceive greater variety in Hopkins's total vision of life, Johnson shows how "The Half-way House" clearly points "beyond typology to the Real Presence of Christ as a literal and daily feeding of faith not to be 'interpreted' [as by receptionists, virtualists, and memorialists] in a spiritual . . . sense [alone]."[63]

The doctrine of transubstantiation, maintaining that the Eucharistic sacrifice transforms "the entire substance or basic reality of the bread and wine into the body and blood of Jesus Christ,"[64] surely came to dominate Hopkins's entire world view. Writing later in his life of a "world . . . charged with the grandeur of God," of sky and earth "hurrahing" over Eucharistic potential for divine "harvest," and, most dazzling of all, of a human "heart" that experiences hypostatic union with the bloodstream of the Sacred Heart of Christ, Hopkins voices beliefs in transubstantial sacraments that extend far past the boundaries of chapels, altars, and sacristies. The poetry of his youth already shows him striving to envision nature as a divine sacramental vessel. By the 1870s, with Duns Scotus's theological aid, he had applied the Pauline doctrine of Christ's kenosis to his understanding of Christ's role as a creative Logos who through a transubstantial Great Sacrifice shares his substance with earthly creaturehood.[65] And, after 1879 especially, he richly envisions the possibility that at least some men and women, those who with their elective (or receptive?) wills choose fervently to follow Christ, can become transubstantial Christic saints.

Yet it is telling that Hopkins's later poetry, emphasizing the necessary choice of Christ by what Scotus and Hopkins saw as the human elective will, not only bears great affinity with the transubstantial doctrine of sacrament, but also still utters forth the receptionist attitude on which Hopkins had been reared. Even when he was experiencing his first tremblings of Roman Catholic ardor and was enraptured by the splendor of transubstantiation dogma, Hopkins still could sound almost equally devoted to receptionist perspectives. If, in "The Half-way House," he firmly announces with the words "To see Thee, I must see Thee," his need to experience a transubstantial Eucharist, he adds the receptionist's acknowledgement of his own required devotion: "to love, love." To be sure, the potentially transubstantiationist averral "God shall strengthen all the feeble knees" provides closure for "Easter Communion," a sonnet of Lent 1865. But the poem has nonetheless given almost all its previous attention to the receptive penitents kneeling at the altar: "Pure fasted faces" (1), "Lenten lips" (2), "sergèd fellowships" (7), "vigil-keepers" (8), "scarce-sheathed bones . . . weary of being bent" (13). In "Barnfloor and Winepress" (1865, P, 247), early stanzas do stalwartly end with Hopkinsian exultation over transubstantial Real Presence: "on a thousand altars laid, / Christ our Sacrifice is made!" (9–10); "Now in our altar-vessels stored / Is the sweet Vintage of our Lord" (19–20). Yet the final stanza culminates in a recognition that the partaker of sacrament must be receptively devout to the point of consciously practicing the imitation of Christ:

> We scarcely call that banquet food,
> But even our Saviour's and our blood,
> We are so grafted on His wood.
>
> (31–33)

The youthful scribe whose poem is of the same length in lines as Christ's life was in years surely seems to be conscious here of his need to identify himself receptively with his Divine Master. Otherwise he could not ultimately know the Real Presence, which *completes* his "graft[ing] on[to Christ's] wood."

Hopkins's most famous, and perhaps greatest, poem ultimately focuses quite strongly on a form of advanced receptionist devotion. While others of his Scotist nature lyrics ("Spring," "The Starlight Night") seem deliberate emulations of the ritual order of the Eucharist, by which Hopkins first describes nature as a sacramental experience and then calls his readers to respond to it, "The Windhover" suggests the more obviously receptionist sacrament of confirmation. Hopkins does not seem directly to call others to the sacramental scene, but instead to focus on his own reverent response to it.[66]

"The Windhover" does not function as pure Anglican receptionism, however, but rather as a highly complete example of *Jesuit* meditative principles. In this sonnet the bird's "achieve" and "mastery" surely point ultimately to the Christ who created it (8), but not without ambiguities. Here the true Jesuit Hopkins *tests* his natural vision; is it from the good or the evil angel?

The kestrel hawk's militant power as a hero of the air might suggest to a Jesuit soldier of Christ (and to a reader of Ephesians 6:10–18) the Christic power of the "whole armor of God" that one should wish to "buckle" on.[67] The bird's descent to earth may also have reminded Hopkins of Robert Southwell's *Meditation 56*:

O princely Hawk, which camest down from Heaven into the bowels of the Blessed Virgin, and from her womb unto the earth . . . and from the Cross unto hell, and from hell unto Heaven . . . is it much that Thou requirest our heart for reward . . . ?[68]

Indeed, as Alfred Thomas points out, the bird's downward "buckl[ing]" may have directed the poetic speaker in "The Windhover" to see other earthly symbols that more clearly reveal Christ's self-humbling crucifixion: coals that "Fall, gall themselves, and gash gold-vermilion" (like Christ who " 'fell' three times, was offered 'gall' to drink, and [was] 'gashed' by the spear of a Roman soldier").[69] The meditative Hopkins, in watching these many sensory cues to Christ's affinity with nature, may even have imagined himself, refreshed now by his spiritual perception, as able to rise with a power (Christ-transubstantiated?) like the windhover's, having become one of those who "wait upon the Lord [and] renew their strength . . . [to] mount up with wings as eagles" (Isaiah 40:31).[70]

Yet for all these hints of Christ's substantial being in nature (hints that at least a *receptive* partaker of sacrament, like Hopkins, could garner from the scene), Hopkins does ask a question which the meditating Southwell also asked: "What [earthly] hawk ever made such a brave flight, or lost so much blood in the pursuit of her game, as the salvation of our souls hath cost Thee, our God and our Lord [?]"[71] Hawks are always creatures; they are not fully their Creator Christ. Thus it does not seem to some readers quite fitting to say that this depicted bird always will suggest a Christ who fights against the "powers of the air that rule [Satan's] world of darkness."[72] According to the innate ambiguity of symbols, the windhover's "Rebuff[ing of] the big wind" ("The Windhover," 7) could also suggest a contrarily Satanic scorn for the "wind" of the Holy Spirit (Acts 2:2) or for the "whirlwind" of God the Father (Job 38:1). Likewise, its being "king- / dom of daylight's dauphin" ("The Windhover," 1–2) may make it ambiguously either "darling of morning, the prince of the kingdom of heaven . . . the kingdom of daylight"[73] or (with more direct Biblical evidence) a symbol of Lucifer, the spiritually *fallen* "son of the morning" (Isaiah 14:12–14).[74] Because of these ambiguities, one can say that "The Windhover" might seem to certain readers a poem treating nature much like a virtualist sacrament: nature's images, they might say, perhaps may direct us "To Christ our Lord," as the poem's epigraph reads, but only indirectly. To Hopkins nature sometimes reveals Christ by showing its spiritual limitations.

While Johnson can see, in a discussion of "The Windhover," that Hopkins surely there attempts to write a transubstantiationist theodicy in religious poetry wherein "every man is a vicar and every thing is sacramental,"[75] the same critic can also observe that "Temporal images" are to Hopkins sometimes both "earthly things" and "*like* sacramentals" (emphasis mine).[76] Given Johnson's definition of even a full "sacramental" as "a natural object *not transformed* but *given* special sacred meaning, as medals, holy water, and palm leaves may be,"[77] he surely appears to hint that Hopkins's nature reveals Christ but is not itself fully Christic. Without question, after "The Windhover" Hopkins's nature poems are not so anxious as they had been earlier to move directly from summoning the reader's affective responses before natural beauty to summoning that same reader's elected Christian abnegation. Even as Hopkins does not completely cease, in such works as "Heraclitean Fire" and "My own heart," to express a belief that Christ resides within nature, the priest-poet does at least once call natural things (although admittedly through the words of a somewhat ironic narrator) "the sots and thralls of lust" ("Thou are indeed just, Lord," 7). Hopkins in the 1880s is centrally concerned not with nature theodicies but with directly urging humankind, and especially his own human self, to the process of elective pentience that spurs sacramentalization of the *soul*.

*   *   *

The theologian Yngve Brilioth declared, in 1930, ". . . [W]e ought to abstain from the attempt to find in the Scripture one normative liturgical type [of Eucharist]. In this sphere as in others we ought to seek in the Scripture less a system of doctrine than a life; life in its apparently inconsistent variety, rather than a standard form. We must take pains to appreciate the richness and manifoldness in the New Testament evidence; otherwise we shall miss the fullness of the Divine revelation, and take as a substitute some one-sided expression of fragmentary aspects of it."[78] Brilioth asks us to study sacrament more as life than as dogma, and with Gerard Manley Hopkins, ultimately, that is what we must do.

Why did Hopkins become a Roman Catholic? To gain intellectual confidence through religious authority—like Newman? To enjoy aesthetic satisfaction in the beauty of the liturgy—like Ruskin in Saint Mark's?[79] His letters from Oxford do reveal these to have been his partial and intermittent motivations, and actually the quest for religious authority is rather decisive. Already among the Anglican tractarians, Hopkins could find the satisfying doctrine of Eucharistic transubstantiation, but he could not find the security of a group that truly held sway over doctrinal opponents. With the Jesuits, by contrast, when he joined their order as a Roman Catholic convert, he found relative success; Roman Catholics in general were a minority in England, but the Jesuits, at least, were an advancing camp of influence within the minority body.[80]

Yet, as Hopkins told his friend E. H. Coleridge, for instance, on 1 June 1864, "The great aid to belief and object of belief is the doctrine of the Real Presence in the Blessed Sacrament of the Altar. Religion without that is sombre, dangerous, illogical, with that it is—not to speak of its grand consistency and certainty—*loveable*. Hold that and you will gain all Catholic truth."[81] It is the desire to experience an authentic sacramental encounter with God that best defines Hopkins's entire life, not only its first years. What varies are his authentic investigative attitudes, both explicit and implicit, about what sacraments are and mean.

Miller was one of the first to emphasize the young Hopkins's exultant response to the Roman Catholic belief in a Eucharistic transubstantial Real Presence. For example, Miller cites [82] part of the following passage in Hopkins's letter of 16 October 1866 to his father: "I shall hold as a Catholic what I have long held as an Anglican, that literal truth of our Lord's words by which I learn that the least fragment of the consecrated elements in the Blessed Sacrament of the Altar is the whole Body of Christ born of the Blessed Virgin, before which the whole host of saints and angels as it lies on the altar trembles with adoration. This belief once got is the life of the soul and when I doubted it I shd. become an atheist the next day."[83]

Miller also shows how study of Parmenides had already focused, long before he read Duns Scotus, Hopkins's metaphysical belief that "Being . . . holds nature together, and makes language and our knowledge of nature possible."[84] Believing that Christ is "creat[or]" of "all things"[85] already helped Hopkins form "a Catholic version of the Parmenidean theory of being . . . [and a] means by which [to] . . . unify nature, words, and selfhood."[86]

Miller surely does define with point the immanentist religious perspective of the young Hopkins. Meanwhile, however, he exaggerates Hopkins's desperation to flee from what Miller treats merely as Protestant theories of religous transcendence. Without truly comprehensive evidence, the author of *The Disappearance of God* maintains staunchly that Zwinglian memorialism (which we have already seen was not the only sacramental vocabulary of Hopkins's youth) produced for Hopkins a "thinning of the meaning of the communion service" and a consequent "diminish[ing of] the divine meaning of the whole world."[87] Miller may be partly correct, as our examination of Hopkins's Eucharist poems has shown, but he does overstate his case.

Even though he worthily highlights the idea of the passional Christ in the late Hopkins, Miller does not want to see such a doctrine contributing to the poet's early work. As modern theologian Gordon Lathrop avers, this passional Christ is the crucified victim who is to mere immanentists, like Jesus' contemporary Jews, a "disappointment"— "one . . . cruelly executed . . . for charges that still remain not entirely clear," one in whom it is hard to put "trust that there is in him the Messianic for us all."[88] Surely, especially in his early poetry, the young Hopkins does not make the mistake of these mere immanentists. As a man already prepared to practice imitatio Christi, he may lament a transcendent God's distance ("My prayers must meet a brazen heaven"), but he also intuits that Christ in his Passion provided an example for those who sensed the Father's distance. Much later, in 1885, he directly "echoes the agonized words of the dying Christ" in the "(my God!) my God" of "Carrion Comfort."[89] Yet he seems to sense even earlier that "My God, my God, why hast thou forsaken me!" was fittingly taken from Psalms 22:1 to express Christ's despondency at his Father's apparent darkness.[90]

Christ's words express continued mystic *faith* in God, whether or not they can easily proclaim firm *beliefs* about the rationale for God's self-enshrouding. As Antonio De Nicolas eloquently declares, "Beliefs are handed out freely, at no cost; they are easily interchangeable and their supply is unlimited. Faith guarantees mobility, even in the dark, that is, in the absence of beliefs and their concomitant sensations. This inner mobility is the hidden spring we all need to travel the discontinuous paths of life."[91] Faith, therefore, arises from, and itself further instills, a dayspring for the soul that encounters trials of darkness.

Hopkins at Oxford gained beliefs in how divine transubstantiation came from *inside* sacraments that as "outward appearances (species, accidents) . . . are unaffected."[92] But he also could see that the Zwinglians did have a point: God is not always, in "unaffected" *outer* "appearances," at all clearly visible. Even the Bible, his chief tool for heaping irony on disconsolate narrators, expressed to him, as to others, a common human spiritual "thirst" amid "disappointment."[93] Not only Zwinglians but also the writer of the Epistle to the Hebrews record belief that "faith is the substance of things hoped for, the evidence of things not seen" (Hebrews 11:1).

Most critics, including Miller, for many years ignored detailed analysis of Hopkins's early poems. As a result, such critics attribute to the more apparently somber Hopkins after 1885 none of the irony he had already long before practiced, but rather a constant sentimental sense of a new and personally defeating "isolation and destitution."[94]

Yet the young author of "*Nondum*" ("Not Yet") illustrates throughout his life that "The Christian is not rescued from the ambiguity of the immediate future through the eucharist [or any sacramental devotion], but he is rescued from the terror of ultimate meaninglessness by the coming into the present of the ultimate future. . . ."[95] Miller surely laments far too strongly over Hopkins's ultimately being "sustained by nothing but the comfort of the Resurrection."[96] Despite his many never-quite-quelled doubts, Hopkins's sacramentally receptive life, especially as its ironic lessons took form in poems, repeatedly evoked a Christ who was to him "interpersonally present,"[97] although hidden by Time's imperfection. Even Miller is forced to admit that such an attitude places Hopkins among others throughout Christian history, not only among his own contemporaries.[98] Like others throughout Christian history, Hopkins was always both a transubstantiationist *and* a receptionist, one who sensed both God's immanence *and* his transcendence.

To be sure, he still wanted, perhaps too fiercely, to see immanent divine blessing poured out on him: he wanted a "happiness spread over . . . life" in outward sacramental signs.[99] Yet he did not ever deny that the blessing of God might remain, even to a religious servant, partly transcendent (or *inwardly* substantiated) and thus nearly invisible: it might be but "a spark or star in the dark."[100] The most poignant passage in his prose comes as he cries out, in January 1888, "What is my wretched life?"[101] Yet that lament, although emerging from "a course of loathing and hopelessness" which occurred rather frequently in his late years, does not exist without the lustrous counterforce of the prose passage's climax: "I wish then for death: yet if I died now I should die imperfect, no master of myself, and that is the worst failure of all. O my God, look down on me."[102]

During the 1860s Hopkins wrote six poems about the immanent spiritual joy he found in the Eucharist. Yet he also wrote at least one full poem, "The Habit of Perfection," in which the speaker aspires to partly transcendent spiritual gains, in the sacrament of Holy Orders.[103] From the first, Hopkins sought to perceive the *visible* Real Presence of God within incarnate vessels; but he also sought, in the soul, God's *invisible* (although also, according to *receptive* faith, His still-*transubstantiating*) Real Presence. He chose "the way of perfect obedience" and, even if "grace" did not seem visibly to "descend," this does not mean, as Miller opines, "the failure of grace."[104] The poet-priest kept believing, and even implied, in his last poems and prose, that the power to choose such obedience was grace made manifest. His assured sacramental receptionism always made Hopkins himself appear, especially in his poetry, the "outward and visible sign" of "inward and spiritual grace."[105]

* * *

Downes has written that "Hopkins' creative, Romantic imagination found it possible [in his late poetry to communicate] . . . experiences of 'dark' graces . . . with as much power and perfection as he was able earlier to produce [in nature] poems expressing . . . 'light' graces."[106] Downes calls these late poems of the soul "not spiritual breakdowns, but breakthroughs to greater and richer religious consciousness."[107] His judgment, shared by Bernard Bergonzi,[108] is incontrovertibly correct. Even Harris (who throughout his volume on Hopkins so distorts the " 'dark' graces" of the "Terrible Sonnets" as almost to accord with Miller and make them appear to be blasphemies against grace of any kind) does tacitly admit that Hopkins's "Thou art indeed just, Lord," at least, achieves a spiritual breakthrough from the apparently grim spiritual state of the "Terrible Sonnets."[109]

One feels awe at how unified Hopkins's spiritual vision eventually proves. The "Terrible Sonnets," in the midst of their " 'dark' graces," do argue for a very real incarnation of Christ. They portray the Marian Hopkinsian soul, through strenuous birthpangs, letting Christ take flesh within it. The passional human will thus engages in almost unstinting struggle. Yet any Hopkins scholar who confronts all, and not just some, of the evidence available can see that all the poet's work, at every stage from his first verse writing at age sixteen to his death not quite three decades later, commands a personal confrontation with the Passion. As Paul Mariani eloquently summarizes, "Christ's last words, the lance, the gall, wood, nails, the outstretched arms and buckling body: all point toward the right reading of all that Hopkins sees in the fact of creation about Him."[110] For the Passion, "the primal theological drama of sacrifice," is in Hopkins's view central to any *complete* incarnational theology.[111]

What Hopkins termed Christ's "great sacrifice," as Downes well explains it, "designated a kind of triple [or quadruple] heroism in Christ."[112] First came His pre-Creation willingness to assume "creaturehood" and hence his subsequent partial immanence in all creatures.[113] This Christic immanence was not "cloud[ed]" before the Fall of Eden ("Spring," 12), and it is, according to Hopkins, still oftentimes glimpsed (if only glimpsed) in creatures.

The next step in the "great sacrifice" came through Christ's heroic "incarnation" as a human being in Mary's womb and through his eventful earthly life.[114] "The "triple heroism" of the "great sacrifice" culminated in the supreme self-sacrifice of Christ's "crucifixion,"[115] and it resulted, finally, in his eternal heroic triumph (introducing actually a fourth stage in the complete process that his "sacrifice" enables):

> Let this mind be in you, which was also in Christ Jesus,/ who, being in the form of God, thought it not robbery to be equal with God: / But made himself of no reputation, and took upon him the form of a servant; and was made in the likeness of men: / And being found in fashion as a man, he humbled himself, and became obedient unto death, even the death of the cross. / Wherefore God also hath highly exalted him, and given him a name which is above every name: / That at the name of Jesus every knee should bow, of things in heaven, and things in earth, and things under the earth, / And that every tongue should confess that Jesus Christ is Lord, to the glory of God the Father. (Philippians 2:5–11)

Saint Paul's explanation to the Philippians of Christ's kenosis is the crucial biblical statement upon which Hopkins based his own sacramental theology and its call to Christic imitatio.[116] Because nature in his poems often becomes the "outward . . . sign" revealing the "inward . . . grace" of both the incarnate and the crucified Christ, his nature imagery fuses, along with *eschatological promise,* all three earthly heroic stages of Christ's "great sacrifice": *creaturehood, incarnation,* and *crucifixion.* Even in his last years, when Hopkins's poetry most assertively attends to eschatological sacramental fulfillment, he focuses upon the three heroic stages of the earthly "great sacrifice" as parts of the process leading to the essential fourth stage, the great *eschaton* of eternal heroic victory.[117] In "That Nature is a Heraclitean Fire and of the comfort of the Resurrection" (1888):

Man's soul, like Christ, is "immortal diamond."	(creaturehood)
Christ "was what I am."	(incarnation)
"*Across* my foundering deck Shone a beacon, an eternal *beam*"; therefore "World's wildfire, *leave* but *ash.*"	(crucifixion, on a "beam" of a leaved ash tree)
"Enough! the Resurrection!. . . In a flash, at a trumpet crash, I am all at once what Christ is."	(eschatological heroic triumph)

In the 1860s Hopkins had already assimilated—through traditional Biblicism, knowledge of creedal and patristic faith, and much reading in previous Christian poetry—the firm devotion to Christ's human incarnation and crucifixion that could guide him in his own chosen imitatio Christi. But he was not yet constantly satisfied that Christ was in creatures—although in the phrase "Speak! . . . / One word," from "*Nondum*" (49–50), he shows that he could sense the Logos Christ, the Creator of creatures, to be the key to solving this dilemma.

In the 1870s, having gained that sense of Christ's partial immanence in creatures (and rarely, if ever, exaggerating that sensed immanence), he used nature, as contemplative Ignatian poet and man,[118] to provide a special type of sacramentalist guidance of his own self-sacrifice.[119] Then, in the 1880s, he turned to chronicling the struggle of the human soul to become "a new creature" in Christ (2 Corinthians 5:17).

Nature images symbolizing Christic *creaturehood* are occasionally part of the late Hopkinsian lyrics. His Scotist natural theology had not completely collapsed.[120] Yet nature imagery in the 1880s poems is relatively rare, and Hopkins's parish sermons at the turn of the decade repeatedly emphasized nature's spiritual limitations.

At least once, although only in a brief and speculative passage,[121] Hopkins even expresses, to the subsequent shock of some misguided readers,[122] what is actually a normative Scotist position: that only with difficulty can one perceive the linkage between the "universal" and the diffuse human "self." According to Christopher Devlin's translation of Scotus, this difficulty of anagogical perception results from "intrinsic limitation," or "*carentia entitatis*," of the universal within the individual.[123] If late in life he could indeed voice such honesty about the hiddenness of Christic reflections in human beings, Hopkins had for much longer revealed that, even for a Scotist, nature sometimes only seemed to reflect Christ by "analogy."[124] Thus it is no wonder that his late poems continue to hint that the Edenic Fall limits affective observations of creaturehood as ideal sacramental experiences.

Hopkins's theology, however, is always ultimately incarnational, in the fullest sense, for it records human sacramentalist *reception* of Christ's total *transubstantiating* Incarnation. That total Incarnation demands especially the experience of dark passional rebirth before eventually blazing Apocalypse. To Hopkins, Downes so rightly perceives, "out of the rage of grace comes a new self, filled and flooded with the Presence of Christ. This is . . . [the] way back to fulfillment in God forever."[125]

* * *

Like many critics, Geoffrey Hartman proves unable to see in Hopkins's late poems their still vital sacramentalist affirmation. Yet even Hopkins's writing of those very powerful poems in itself contradicts Hartman's belief that Hopkins in 1880s Dublin only lived "passive suffering."[126] Hartman writes that Hopkins should have rebelled against passivity by proving himself capable of even potential "scandal" through "a new vocation."[127] In response, John Warner has already rightly criticized Hartman for "assum[ing] . . . that Hopkins is a 'real' poet only when he abandons the dogmatisms of his religious faith and allows the mysteries of his [poetic] craft to override him." To Warner, "such analysis seems to reflect more the critic's despair than [Hopkins] the poet's vision."[128] That vision, however much it accepts suffering as a part of life, is not passive but *active*.

Yet in "Poetry and Justification" Hartman does at least perceive better than many critics Hopkins's poetry-initiating sacramentalist motivations. Indeed, Hartman's most adept insights truly could have helped him understand masterfully the ways in which Hopkins' poetry functions. Hartman's chief discovery is that the "obscurity difficult to remove" from Hopkins's poetic texts is not so much the product of " 'Romantic' individualism," that "scapegoat" to which Yvor Winters assigns blame. Instead, Hartman says, Hopkinsian "obscurity" results from "something very different from Romanticism: Hopkins' desire for an impersonal and esoteric discipline . . ., his urge towards a [sacramentalist] sacrifice of [consecrated?] intellect and a true religious anonymity."[129] Such statements indicate that Hartman might have fully understood the key to Hopkins's entire canon had he been able to see that by poetic acts of sacramentalist "sacrifice" Hopkins was during almost all his adult life specifically composing a Victorian version of Augustinian-Origenian poetry. In such poetry Hopkins deliberately hid, within "obscurity,"[130] sacramental secret "kernels" of faith-filled consolation, kernels that emerged "from the husk" of a confusing, and thus often a faith-testing, world, in order to serve "as nourishment for charity."[131]

Understanding of this Augustinian-Origenian "husk-kernel" principle as the main force behind all Hopkins's art seems to me centrally important. Such understanding might conquer for many what Hartman seems to feel is their inevitable "defeat" in undertaking "exegetical activity" with Hopkins's poems.[132] At least my own rather recent discovery of Origen and Augustine as sources for Hopkins's sacramentalist vision of religious wordings has made me understand why my linguistic structural "exegetical activity" with his work has almost from the beginning revealed a "husk-kernel" /"overthought-underthought" structure in lyrics from throughout his adult life—even though he first specifically defined "overthought" and "underthought" only during his last decade.[133]

Clearly—despite the strong early influence he derived from poets of his own century like Keats, Arnold, Tennyson, and Browning—Hopkins is already demonstrating medievalist "husk-kernel" sacramental theology in some of his best youthful poems. Ironic undertexts contradict, in "*Nondum*" and the spy soliloquy, the overattention of illogical narrators to earth's depressing "husk," rather than to the "kernel[s]" of hope in divine glory that words of faith promise them. Hopkins also seems to reveal such "husk-kernel" theology, although slightly differently, in his early poetic portraits of Saint Dorothea's martyrdom-release from the "husk" of sinful earth into the "kernel[led]" opening spaces of Heaven. His Oxford readings—both of Origen[134] and, most likely also of the Augustine who highly influenced his later work[135]—blended certainly with Hopkins's ardor for transubstantiationist faith in the Eucharist. Such combined impulses, both of which spurred him toward seeking *visible* sacramental signs, joined together with his sacramental receptionist willingness to devote himself to *verbal* faith, even if it lacked visible consolations.

In the 1870s the Scotist-influenced Hopkins seems to have found a confidence, elsewhere lacking in his works, that sacramental revelations consistently emerge from the viewing of nature. But close analysis shows that the "husk-kernel" pattern operates in these 1870s lyrics also. It is not a mimesis of natural "overthought" that here reveals the central Hopkinsian message of four successive Christian sacramental stages (creation, incarnation, crucifixion, eschaton). No, even these exuberant poems only reveal sacramental messages through symbolic "underthought," an "underthought" that controls the overt mimesis but itself is a linguistic undercurrent sacramentally *interpreting* the mimesis.[136]

To be sure, the sacramental "underthought" seems closer to the surface in the 1870s poems than it is in the 1860s works. It is also closer to the surface than in works of the 1880s (which dimly sketch the gestation—beneath the outer "husk" of an imperfect human self—of a Christic "kernel," an inner sanctified soul). Still, even if Hopkins demonstrated in the the 1870s great assurance that he could communicate an anagogical sacramentalism envisioning Christ as the readily perceivable "underthought" of things, he did not proclaim, at this period or any other, that Christ was pantheistically present *as* things. The world's "husk," more strongly sensed as an obscuring barrier at other periods of his life, he still considered a somewhat obscuring barrier even during these years. For that reason, the poems of the 1870s sometimes express their insights through images that can be read dualistically—reflecting Hopkins's continued respect for such Calvinist thinkers as Ruskin (and for Calvinist members of Hopkins's own potential reading audience) almost as readily as they display his ardor for the seemingly less dualistic thought of Duns Scotus. At heart, they may most of all reflect the *quiet* dualism of Loyola.

The "husk-kernel" pattern of sacramental revelation thus holds force throughout Hopkins's entire canon.[137] However, the central three chapters of this book will examine, as is appropriate, his decade-by-decade chronological development. Each of these three chapters will be divided into three segments. The first segment of each chapter concerns Hopkins's developing attitudes about *art*, the second examines his developing attitudes about *nature*, and the third treats his developing attitudes about human beings' *inner spiritual life*.

During the 1860s Hopkins as poet was finding that a sacramental type of *art* was the ideal means by which he could fuse his love for resplendent visible signs with his conviction that all earthly resplendence was ephemeral and in need of ultimate rejection for higher spiritual goals. In the 1870s his Scotist poetic vision seemed to permit him to employ natural symbols with a faith that they, in God-given *physical* beauty, could grant readers anagogical revelations of *spiritual* beauty.

However, Hopkins in his 1870s enthusiasm occasionally may overtrust the communicability of anagogical revelation to readers; he may perhaps have failed to heed Augustine's admonition about scriptural exegesis: "[S]ome things are taught for every one in general; others are directed toward particular classes of people, in order that the medicine of instruction may be applicable not only to the general state of health but also to the special infirmities of each member. For what cannot be elevated to a higher class must be cared for in its own class."[138] With this sort of admonition apparently more firmly in mind, he writes in "The Windhover" a poem that seems to speak variant theological messages to various types of readers, although all the messages are still designed to promote self-sacrifice.

In the 1880s Hopkins uses his art more humbly, with chief attention to his personal sacramental life. At the same time he emphasizes more trenchantly than before the supremacy of the self-sacrificial elective will. Placing himself in the lineage of great medieval forebears like Dante and Chaucer, he announces in his last poems that what he had always believed is surely true: art must be deemed hierarchically less important than spirituality. At the point of human death, after all, art, unlike spirituality, must be left behind.

The poems of the 1860s in their treatment of *nature* predict both the natural visions of the poems that Hopkins created in the 1870s and those more somber natural visions which he presented in the 1880s. He obviously wanted from the first to show, as he did in the 1870s, visible natural signs proving themselves sacramental. But he also sensed that such a practice was not always possible or necessary—that a darkened nature could still become the "husk" out of which the human soul would elect to follow the "kernel" of inner faith. One did not evidently need to rely on "outward and visible signs" so much as one needed to rely on "inward and spiritual grace."

The poems about Hopkins's *inner spiritual quest*, from the beginning of his canon until the end, more consistently resemble each other than do his poems about art or his poems about nature. This assertion does not mean that the subject matter of the spirituality poems does not vary. The inner spiritual questing of Hopkins especially produces, during the 1860s, dramatic monologues about spiritual doubters (although this type of Hopkins poem returns also to prominence in the 1880s). Later, Hopkins makes himself, in works written from 1878 to 1881, a poetized character in portraits of a public priest's life. He still later creates, through "esoteric discipline," an allegory of archetypal Christian biography in the "Terrible Sonnets" of the mid- to late 1880s,[139] as well as in other poems of his last decade. All these poems about inner spirituality, however, clearly resemble each other because they are all the work of a receptionist believer in imitatio Christi. This receptionist also wants consistently to have his soul transubstantiate Christ.

By the end of his life, despite a "husk" of apparent strong doubt that to some looks like "passive suffering," Hopkins truly evidenced active belief that Christ's Presence was producing more than a mere "kernel" of transformation within his soul. He surely had found in that soul, which flickered with inner confidence even amid what looked like dark outer terror, that his entire life was in essence only a humble "strain" toward faith."[140] Yet that life was still—always—a sacramental sign:

> Of her flesh he took flesh:
> He does take fresh and fresh,
> Though much the mystery how,
> Not flesh but spirit now
> And makes, O marvellous!
> New Nazareths in us,
> Where she shall yet conceive
> Him, morning, noon, and eve. . . .
> ("The Blessed Virgin compared to the Air we Breathe" [1883],
> 55–62)

2

Hopkins at Highgate and Oxford

... If still in darkness not in fear.

—Hopkins, "*Nondum*"

BOTH PERSONALITY and historical situation led Gerard Manley Hopkins, from the very beginning of his writing career, to emphasize conflict and unification between the physical and the spiritual, the natural and the supernatural, the aesthetic and the ascetic. He thus illustrated a sense of basic opposition between visible and hidden, illumined and dark—a sense familiar in the history of Christian thought. Hopkins certainly found others, both in his own age and in the further reaches of Christian history, who potently expressed the same tensions.

In the prayer "Lead, Kindly Light, amid the encircling gloom," Hopkins's own mentor Newman had stated the same paradoxes we find in the young Hopkins's sense of partially darkened and partially illumined deity. Similar paradoxes appear within Saint Paul's speech to the Athenians, recorded in Acts 17:24–25. God, says Paul, "gives to all men life and breath, and everything" (i.e., he is immanent within life), yet God "does not live in shrines made by man" (i.e., he is transcendent). Likewise, the New Testament epistles include both the Johannine tenet that "God is light and in him is no darkness at all" (1 John 1:5) and the Petrine doctrine that the historical accounts of Christ's life shine as a limited "lamp . . . in a dark place, until the day dawns and the morning star rises in your hearts" (2 Peter 1:19).

As influential as the Bible upon Hopkins's way of viewing the world's light within darkness was the full historical Roman Catholic tradition, and to that tradition Newman and the other Oxford tractarians first directed him during the 1860s. Imagery of outer dark hiddenness and inner illumination was common in that Roman Catholic tradition.

Much like his compatriot Juan de la Cruz, who wrote of "Love's Living Flame" reaching "the deep cavern of the senses,"[1] the Spanish founder of the Jesuits, Ignatius Loyola, was "convinced that . . . inner space may be revealed, opened, touched, by . . . meditation."[2] Conrad of Hirsau spoke in the high monastic era, much like Saint Peter in the early Christian centuries, of "the soul who believes, who hopes for rest after labor, [and] buries deep within him, at the beginning of his pilgrimage, the word of God as if it were the 'repository of his hope.' " In adding to that biblical hope, the soul, says Conrad, pursues the "philosophical disciplines," in order that it might "inculcate divine love, the cult of the invisible. . . ."[3]

Even earlier in history, and perhaps more dramatically than these figures, Saint Augustine had prefigured Hopkins's eventually declared sacramentalist poetic method of "overthought" and "underthought."[4] Augustine is "the most frequently mentioned of the church fathers in Hopkins's writings,"[5] and in *On Christian Doctrine*, a work of the early fifth century, he proclaimed that "figurative . . . secrets" from the Scriptures are "to be removed as kernels from the husk as nourishment for charity."[6]

Acting especially strongly to influence even the Hopkins of Oxford student years was the rich spiritual writing of the third-century Alexandrian church father Origen. His texts in Greek were translated into Latin early in the Christian era, and they were especially influential during both the Carolingian Renaissance and the Cistercian twelfth century—periods that also knew "vast" influence from Augustine and the "Latin patristic tradition."[7] To Origen both "this world" and "holy scripture" contain "seen and unseen things"—as in the Scriptures' "body, . . . the visible letter [;] . . . soul [,] . . . the meaning found within it [;] and . . . spirit [,] by which it also has something of the heavenly."[8]

Origen anticipates, and even amplifies, Augustine's treatment of inner and outer layers in religious texts (such as the sacramentalist poems Hopkins was to write as if in imitation of Origen's concepts). The Alexandrian church father discusses "the first glimpse of the letter" as "the bitter rind of a nut," then moves on to discuss "the protective covering of the [inner] shell" that "designate[s]" the "moral doctrine," and finally postulates the "hidden and concealed . . . sense of the mysteries of the wisdom and knowledge of God." These last mysteries are revealed, he says, only when the level revealing "moral doctrine" is itself "smashed and broken through."[9]

To Origen "the light . . . called God dissolves all darkness and ignorance of sin" and "send[s] its own rays without hindrance to those . . . being enlightened."[10] This ancient Alexandrian Christian genius was probably the first strong noncontemporary influence upon Hopkins. As an Oxford student in 1865, the Victorian English youth already found Origen's work able to elicit from him deep sympathy, "real feeling."[11]

And Origen argues with more optimism than Augustine about spiritual light's fully demolishing spiritual darkness.[12] Augustine sees the external world to be "not food for men but for swine" if they, like pagan idolaters, worship it too much for itself alone; they should rather realize, he says, that "This husk shakes sounding [spiritual] pebbles" not outside, but "inside its sweet shell." He admonishes that "it is a carnal slavery to adhere to a usefully instituted sign instead of to the thing it was designed to signify."[13] Origen, however, believes more confidently than Augustine in the inevitable triumph of spiritual perceptiveness:

> . . . [T]he light is the truth. When untruth and every kind of deceit—this is the darkness—persecutes the light, it is dissolved and dispersed when it approaches what it persecutes. . . . [W]hen the darkness is distant, it persecutes the light, but when it approaches in order to overcome the light, it disappears. . . . God has permitted evil to exist, that the greatness of virtue might be demonstrated.[14]

Hopkins too, as befits his early influence from Origen, often shares Origen's confidence that human blindness to the spiritual messages of word and world will inevitably be overcome. On the other hand, he is also careful, like Augustine, to urge readers to look "inside" the "sweet shell" of word and world, for his mature sacramentalist vision of earthly reality will not ultimately tolerate in himself or in others mere "carnal slavery" to a simple "usefully instituted sign." In the 1860s he may have been weighing the views of both these thinkers against each other, while he seems more Origenian in the 1870s, more Augustinian in the 1880s. Yet in his work there is always something of a balance between Origen's confidence and Augustine's caution.

Surely a desire for visible divine signs inspired much of Hopkins's poetic work—and understandably so, since he lived after Darwin, in an age when Christianity was spurned by many who believed it lacking in visible proofs.[15] But even when he was young Hopkins felt, like his biblical and earlier Christian forebears, that the most important truth did not abide in the visible, whether in this world's art, its nature, or its religious activity. His titling of the poem "*Nondum*," as well as his ironic treatment of its vision-hungry narrator, already clarifies that to Hopkins, as to Augustine and Origen, full truth always was believed to await in his future and eventually in his eschatological resurrection—but that it was not now fully known, "not yet."

A. The Art of "Gloom" and "Glories": Resignation, Resplendence, or Sacral Mystery?

There is a massy pile above the waste
Amongst Castilian barrens mountain-bound;

A sombre length of grey; four towers placed
At corners flank the stretching compass round;
A pious work with threefold purpose crown'd—
A cloister'd convent first, the proudest home
Of those who strove God's gospel to confound
With barren rigour and a frigid gloom—
Hard by a royal palace and a royal tomb.

With these seemingly stern words Hopkins composed the first stanza
of "The Escorial"—an effort with which, in 1860, he won the poetry
prize at London's Highgate School.[16] The poem closes fifteen stanzas
later with a somewhat timid declaration that the building, now "barren," reflects a majesty more satisfying than the majesty of physical
resplendence. The "barren" ruin now imitates the "barren rigour" of
that religious fervor to which it was originally dedicated.

This conclusion emerges, although it is not boldly declared, as the
poem's narrator reflects upon the gradual removal of artistic relics from
the Escorial. Long before 1860, because war and storm had threatened
the fortress, Spanish rulers had taken its art treasures back to a safer
Madrid (st. 15). The narrator assesses the results:

        . . . Since which no more
Eighth wonder of the earth, in size, in store
And art and beauty: Title now too full—
More wondrous to have borne such hope before
It seems; for grandeur barren left and dull
Than changeful pomp of courts is aye more wonderful.

                                                   (st. 15, 4–9)

Hopkins thus frames his poem with opening and closing stanzas that
examine austerity in both religion and art. He somewhat affirms the
worth of these austerities by writing with considerable energy about the
austere martyrdom of Saint Lawrence, to whom Spain's Philip II dedicated this fortress: "that staunch saint still prais'd his Master's name /
While his crack'd flesh lay hissing on the grate" (st. 3, 1–2). And he also
describes the single picture, of all those formerly held in the Escorial,
that recalls the fertility of life. While "Ceres there / Raves through
Sicilian pastures many a mile" (st. 11, 3–4), the other paintings recall
the deaths of Christ (st. 10, 7–8), of Hyacinthus (st. 11, 5–8), and of the
Python in the Belvidere Apollo (st. 11, 8–9), as well as Paris's "fatal"
choice of Venus's "envied fruit" (st. 11, 2). Both in its framing ideas and
in some of its details, "The Escorial," one would say, sees death as the
inevitable conclusion to human life in the physical world, and the
poem deems "barren" religion and art partially appropriate responses
to this natural death.

Yet this poem is not entirely sober and opposed to life's sensuous richness (the Ceres description, for example, and even the sketch of Lawrence's "hissing" death, show a taste for just such sensuous richness). In the middle stanzas, while the narrator tries to deny any primary devotion to sensuous abundance, he cannot do so, any more than Philip could subdue completely his taste for splendor, which would provide Saint Lawrence's memory the "richest [of] gift [s]" (st. 2, 6), the "pride of faith" (st. 8, 9; emphasis mine). Even as Hopkins's narrator prepares for a specific description of the Escorial's severe Italian classicism—which he appears ready to proclaim far superior to the "flowing tracery engemming rays" (st. 6, 2) of "Gothic grace" (st. 6, 1), the "golden fillets and rich blazonry" (st. 7, 6) of the "Doric mood" (st. 7, 2), and the "Splendid . . . phantasies aerial" (st. 8, 2) of the Moorish Alhambra—he cannot refrain from devoting an entire stanza apiece to each of these supposedly inferior architectural modes. Even the fortress's designers were "not all / Unmindful of [the] grace" of Moorish structures (st. 8, 4–5), and it would seem that Hopkins's narrator is attracted to the graces of all these styles. For instance, he hesitates to accede with complete certainty to the notion that the paintings once part of the Escorial have fittingly been removed. It "seems," he says, that the "changeful pomp of courts" is to be less revered than the "grandeur barren left and dull" (st. 15, 8–9). Yet, given his enthusiasm for the sensuous splendor now lost to the building, he would perhaps most like to see the primary "grandeur" and the "changeful pomp" reunited.

Hopkins's first known poem thus appears ideologically inconsistent. He frequently seems to side with Philip of Spain in that ruler's judgments concerning the proper form which a religious monument should take, but neither he nor Philip can maintain a constant taste for such "frigid gloom" (st. 1, 8). And indeed, if one reads the opening stanza carefully, one will note that Hopkins the lover of the world and its physical beauty sees how the zealously rigorous Spaniards did "confound" or "confuse" (*Oxford English Dictionary*, hereafter *OED*), "God's gospel" with their "barren rigour" (st. 1, 7–8). But Hopkins does not consistently deride Philip in this way, either, and so one must judge that the poem's inconsistencies are the inconsistencies in thought of the youthful poet himself. Hopkins's career as an artist will show him developing toward an almost perfect consistency between his reverence for the life of self-sacrifice and the use of art as a sacramentalist activity wherein he declares his loyalty to sacrificial action. But progress to that final consistency of thought involved some tension.

Hopkins in 1860 was soon to begin university studies at Oxford. There he would not only gain such friends as the poet Robert Bridges and the aesthetician Walter Pater, but he would also participate in intense theological discussions and sessions of prayer with such men as Edward Bouverie Pusey, H. P. Liddon, and Cardinal Newman.[17] He would find Newman's often stern orthodoxy especially convincing intellectually, although troubling to his own sensuous nature.[18] Thus, although he would become "more ascetic," in his personal religious habits, than most Oxonians,[19] he would also, at Newman's Littlemore Chapel, respond with pleasure to its "altar and reredos," which were— he said in a letter of 22 April 1863 to his mother—"exquisite."[20] Roman Catholicism provided, in its ritual, satisfactions not only for his spirit of self-denial, but also some satisfactions for his aesthetic sensibility.

We thus are not surprised to find Hopkins, once he had entered Oxford, seeking better methods than he had used in "The Escorial" for blending religious themes and sensuous richness. One could see his "For a Picture of St. Dorothea," written in 1864 (P, 249), as an imitation of the liturgical incantation and visual ceremony. But the poem paradoxically suggests, through its very delicate music and ethereal images, the necessary evaporation of all earthly things into an invisible heavenly incense.[21] Now Hopkins does not write at so much contradiction with himself; both his theme and his method have become surer than in "The Escorial."

The events of Dorothea's martyrdom are purported to have occurred as follows:

> . . . St. Dorothea was a Christian virgin of Caesarea, tortured by the Governor (Sabricius or Fabricius) for refusing to worship idols and marry. Condemned to be beheaded (c. 303), she exclaimed that in the garden of Paradise grew roses and apples (quinces, 1. 9). Tauntingly asked to bring him some by Theophilus the protonotary, she agreed. And though it was winter, presently a fair angel (Hopkins suggests St. Dorothea in angelic form) appeared bringing them in a basket. Theophilus was converted by the miracle and was himself martyred. . . .[22]

This angel seems to speak in Hopkins's poem:

> I bear a basket lined with grass;
> I am so light, I am so fair,
> That men must wonder as I pass
> And at the basket that I bear,
> Where in a newly-drawn green litter
> Sweet flowers I carry,—sweets for bitter.
>
> Lilies I shew you, lilies none,
> None in Caesar's gardens blow,—
> And a quince in hand,—not one

Is set upon your boughs below;
Not set, because their buds not spring;
Spring not, 'cause world is wintering.

But these were found in the East and South
Where Winter is the clime forgot.—
The dewdrop on the larkspur's mouth
O should it then be quenchèd not?
In starry water-meads they drew
These drops: which be they? stars or dew?

(1–18)

Knowing that human beings demand visible signs of God, the angel
gives Theophilus heavenly flowers and thus makes the transcendent
immanent. Yet the angel also urges him to forsake an excessive reliance
on visible signs, saying that each "dewdrop" of earth (15) strives toward
a heavenly evaporation into "starry . . . meads" (17), where it is
"quenchèd" (16).[23] Theophilus, too, the angel may imply, should strive,
as Dorothea's witness, to reach Heaven through self-sacrifice like hers.
The angel's implicit argument is successful. Theophilus is converted,
and he may be the dazed speaker of the poem's last stanza:

Had she a quince in hand? Yet gaze:
Rather it is the sizing moon.
Lo, linkèd heavens with milky ways!
That was her larkspur row.—So soon?
Sphered so fast, sweet soul?—We see
Nor fruit, nor flowers, nor Dorothy.

(19–24)

Theophilus is definitely the final speaker in a revision of this poem,
which is titled "Lines for a Picture of St. Dorothea" and is undated but
potentially even as late as 1868 in composition.[24] In the second version
a subtitle names "Dorothea and Theophilus" as paired speakers. Theophilus again is seen to be powerfully affected by the visible miracles of
the heavenly flowers and Dorothea's translation into Heaven. But this
Theophilus much more strongly recognizes his need to sacrifice himself
in order to reach union with the invisible God. He even suggests his
own potential martyrdom:

Ah dip in blood the palmtree pen
And wordy warrants are flawed through.
More will wear this wand and then
The warpèd world we shall undo.

(37–40)

He is ready to question all "wordy warrants," probably meaning most specifically the edicts demanding executions of Christians like Dorothea (and, soon, of him as well). He believes that the "palmtree pen" of martyrdom provides a statement of power far surpassing any "flawed[-]through" human words. Perhaps he derides, from a distance, even "wordy" poems.

The "wordy warrants" Hopkins seems to critique are perhaps also "wordy" because they are too impersonally formal, i.e., because they ae written instead of spoken discourse. As Bump notes, "Theophilus, himself the Protonotary, writer of writs, [is] now converted by the spoken rather than the written word."[25] Bump contributes valuable evidence that Hopkins came firmly to believe, during the 1860s, in a strongly aural form of at least *potentially* sacramental poetics.

Bump traces the intellectual roots of Hopkins's emphasis on aural poetry to the young Roman Catholic convert's study of ancient rhetoric; to his acquaintance with and translation of Thomas Aquinas's hymn "Adoro Te Supplex" ("How says trusty hearing? that shall be believed"—Hopkins, "S. Thomae Aquinatis Rhythmus" [6]); and to the German and English Romantics' "praise . . . [of] music as the non-mimetic, expressive art to which lyric poetry should aspire."[26] Most important as influences, probably, because of their association with Hopkins's particular sacramentalism, were his likely sense of a sacramentarian atmosphere in Victorian gatherings for "communal" reading of literature[27] and his awareness of biblical texts in which the patriarch, king, psalmist, prophet, Pauline convert, or the Lord himself "perform[s]" a spiritual "word."[28] Not only contemporary Pre-Raphaelite poetic practice, then, but also a long list of influential traditions, especially the biblical, made Hopkins aware that "word-music was designed to convey that sense of the possibility of a radically different order of time and experience that is one of the goals of most religions."[29] That "sense" on earth "of a radically different order of time and experience" truly can make some sounds, some music, suggest mystical silence.[30]

Bump offers many citations from Hopkins's own prose that verify lifelong commitment to a speech-oriented sacramentalist art. Intriguingly, however, Hopkins's most aurally dynamic poems are those of the 1870s; in their content, as opposed to their form, these poems emphasize the *visible* signs of nature. Meanwhile, his poems with densest hermetic sentences—which paradoxically thus require long pondering of their semantics' visual print—emphasize *verbal* utterances that can withstand the darkening of vision. Hopkins is thus always both a visual and a verbal sacramentalist, although he mixes the two modes of expression in complex ways.[31]

He seeks both visual and verbal evokings from the poetic craft of the

Dorothea poems, and he has most certainly adopted a firmly sacramentalist purpose. Even while he is using language richly in order to suggest the visible events of two martyrdoms and an angelic visitation, he seems convinced in the Dorothea poems, as he was not fully convinced in "The Escorial," that religious art must deny its own importance as mere art—mere structured and beautiful human statement. Religious art speaks, in a "warpèd world" ("Lines for a Picture," 40) about how that "world is wintering" ("For a Picture," 12).

Thus, despite their aesthetic complexity (the second poem is indeed Hopkins's first specimen of sprung rhythm), these Dorothea poems seem in keeping with Hopkins's mood as he briefly renounced beauty for Christ in 1865,[32] and poetry for Christ in 1868.[33] Both poems show strong belief, as Hopkins's renunciatory actions themselves did, that only a human being's interior sanctification can "undo" the "warpèd world."

The two works, do, however, develop a special religious function for art—a function akin to evangelism, as Hopkins reports two evangelists' messages in a poetic context. To be sure, Hopkins does not directly tell us, as an evangelist might, how we should live. Yet his poem is offered like a sacramental vessel that might enlighten us, bless us, inspire us to self-sacrifice.[34] Other poems from his Oxford years do show him nonetheless wanting more direct spiritual visions than any words could guarantee. He wanted the "warpèd world" itself to *show* him God.

B. Hopkins's Earliest Creaturehood Symbols

In a poem of 1865 "Where art thou friend?" Hopkins expresses the sad uncertainty resulting from lack of an immediate blessed vision. He wishes a human friend, ultimately, to live righteously for the sole sake of "Christ." Yet only in the poem's last lines does he relinquish his own desire to witness visibly that friend's spiritual growth.

As the poem begins, he is ruing the loss of his friend's physical presence. He feels desolate when his own physical eye cannot perceive spiritual virtues; his mind, from a spatial distance, can only conceive their present continuation or cessation. Thus he grieves:

> Where art thou friend, whom I shall never see,
> Conceiving whom I must conceive amiss?
> Or sunder'd from my sight in the age that is
> Or far-off promise of a time to be . . . [?]
>
> (1–4)

Although he does eventually resign to Christ's will his own desire for the friend's physical presence, he does not do so easily. He wants to see his friend, to see "Christ" in the friend, and to see this blessing now instead of in the "far-off promise" of Heaven.

Only the Eucharist, especially when sensed as transubstantial, seems to Hopkins, at this point in his life, a fully satisfying visitation of God's earthly presence.[35] In his words, the man or woman who is "weary of being bent" in penitential self-chastisement ("Easter Communion," 13) can find truly "strengthen[ed] . . . feeble knees" (14) at the Eucharistic altar, when "God comes all sweetness to . . . Lenten lips"(2).

Precise Roman Catholic definitions of the transubstantial Eucharist obviously gave Hopkins a stronger sense of specific sacramental power than did those imprecise Anglican definitions of sacrament that he had heretofore known. (We have heard him tell his father how he believed in transubstantiation even as an Anglican.)

Anglicans still in this century have defined "sacrament" as a "sign conveying what is signified," "both a symbol and an instrument" of divine grace.[36] That definition suggests some experience of Christ's immanent presence within an active "instrument"; it is not, for instance, a Reformed Protestant Zwinglian theory of the Eucharist as a mere "symbol" or memorial meal. Yet the modern Anglican definition still offers no exact definition of how a sacrament like the Eucharist is specifically more than a "symbol," how it becomes an actual "instrument" of grace. Indeed, almost from its very dawn as a discrete religious body, Anglicanism has emulated the paradoxical qualities of "independence of mind" and "appeal for unity" that belonged to Henry VIII's archbishop of Canterbury, Thomas Cranmer, the first "church father" of the Anglican tradition.[37] Peter Brooks judges that "Cranmer was not a great theologian, and perhaps for that reason he thought Reformed agreement in the matter of the Sacrament both possible and essential." At the same time, however, his "long years of careful Scriptural study, intimate Patristic knowledge and a remarkable familiarity with the main writings of the Continental controversies, enable[d] him to adopt the main principles of Reformed eucharistic understanding while ignoring the divisive details of particular interpretations."[38]

Cranmer, forecasting such later eclectic Anglicans as Hopkins's contemporary Tractarians,[39] redefined his theology of the Eucharist several times. In a letter of 1533, he scorned the "heretical" John Frith who "thought it not necessary to be believed as an article of our faith, that there is the very corporal presence of Christ within the host and sacrament of the altar."[40] By 1538, however, he, like his contemporary Martin Luther in Germany,[41] had "come to regard the scholastic idea of transubstantiation as an 'opinion' that can be denied" without the denial's causing "simultaneous abandonment of Real Presence doctrine."[42] Both he and Luther, whose German writings about the Eucharist are often directly translated into the Latin of Cranmer's Commonplace Books,[43] had come to believe that "a miracle *ipso facto* defies any [Aquinian-Aristotelian] explanation."[44]

Cranmer gained freedom to become a still more creative theologian after the 1547 death of Henry VIII.[45] By 1551 Cranmer was thus expressing a vaguer doctrinal stance than before on the Eucharist; his statements indeed resemble the later Anglican position of virtualism: ". . . I teach not . . . that the body and blood of Christ is contained in the sacrament, being reserved, but that in the ministration thereof we receive the body and blood of Christ; whereunto if it may please you to add or understand this word 'spiritually', then is the doctrine of my Catechism sound and good in all men's ears, which know the true doctrine of the sacraments."[46] In the 1548 debate on the sacrament in the House of Lords, Cranmer sounded more like what later in history would be called a receptionist. He declared there that "They be twoo things to eate the Sacrament and to eate the bodie of Christ. / The eating of the bodie is to dwell in Christ, and this may be thoo a man never taste the Sacrament."[47] Cranmer was very concerned at this time in his life to insist, like many receptionists of later centuries,[48] that "Onely goode men can eate Christ's body."[49]

To Anglicans, of course, the imprecision of their official Eucharistic definition has the virtue of representing a via media between Rome and Protestants.[50] But Gerard Manley Hopkins, the fervent truth-seeking Oxford undergraduate, did not want a via media. In part he simply wanted a doctrinal authority for sacramental meaning, and he knew that the Roman Catholic tradition had declared transubstantiation offical dogma in the Fourth Lateran Council of 1215 (although only after lengthy quarrels between symbolical memorialists and the debate-winning realists).[51] Yet Hopkins also wanted more than the intellectual pacification that came to him with devotion to church authority. He wanted, most of all, a sensory pacification, a confidence that full divinity was dwelling inside the physical sacramental species that he could touch and see: "I must o'ertake Thee at once and under heaven / If I shall overtake Thee at last above" ("The Half-way House," 15–16).[52]

Halfway between allegiance to Canterbury and allegiance to Rome, Hopkins declares his reason for changing his loyalty. It seems even to him a "paradox" ("The Half-way House," 13) that in order to dedicate himself to a seemingly transcendent God he must "see" that God immanently (14), "o'ertak[ing Him] at once and under heaven" (15). Yet the doctrine of the transubstantial Eucharist announces to him that the "paradox" need not remain "paradox," that his desire for divine immanence can be fulfilled "in the breaking of the bread" (18). (It is a quite different paradox that he is here using allusions—as he does in "Let me be to Thee as the circling bird" [*P*, 251], inscribed in that same month—to George Herbert's via media Anglican poetry about "Love" [Christ] and the Eucharist. Like Herbert, Hopkins seems eventually to learn more fully the limitations of sensible signs.)[53]

One of Hopkins's earliest poem fragments, "Il Mystico" (*P*, 297), which he sent to his friend E. H. Coleridge in September 1862, foreshadows the way in which his desire for powerfully visible sacramental signs could extend into his view of nature. A long work analyzing somewhat vague stirrings of religious aspiration, "Il Mystico" treats three ways by which "sensual gross desires" (1) may be overcome when one rises past physical bounds by contact with the "Spirit's wings" (10). Although their experience often seems blended in the poem's descriptions, the three discrete methods involved are those three alternating focuses that I am studying in Hopkins's entire life: poetic singing, meditation upon nature, and religious asceticism in the quest for inner spirituality.

At least the first two of these suggested practices obviously do demand sense experience. Hopkins does not even completely dissociate from sense experience the third method, the asceticism of Ezekiel, who "could keep silence, tho' the smart / Yawn'd like long furrow in the heart" (63–64). Like the later Galahad, writes Hopkins, Ezekiel found "common earth and air / . . . limn'd about with radiance rare" (59–60).

The speaker of these lines indeed sings of an "inner spirit that fills / Questioning winds about the hills" (43–44). He implies that only Ezekiels and Galahads—"pure souls" (142)—can ever perceive the spirituality of nature. Yet, if one willingly becomes ascetic like such folk, one then apparently can encounter nature, and nature poetry, as sacramental tokens of God's grace.

Hopkins here reveals the incipient "program" for much of his poetry, but he also reveals some naïveté. The Greek verb *myein* means "to initiate into the mysteries," while the Greek verb *poiein* means "to make, produce, execute . . . art."[54] To the Greeks, especially Plato in his frequent scorn for poetry, the words were hardly equal. But the Hopkins of "Il Mystico" and of many later poems sometimes may have felt them to be.

Yet it is true that Hopkins was finding apparent theological justification for what could be called eccentric positions. As James Finn Cotter reports, Hopkins became drawn, while studying with Liddon, to the biblical verses from Colossians 1:16–17: "All things have been created through and into him, and he is before all creatures, and in him all things hold together." From his response to these verses, Cotter says, Hopkins made central the tenet that dominates some of his notes now at Oxford's Bodleian Library: "Christ . . . [was] the creator and end of all things.''[55] Christ, as their supernatural source, seemed to complete both sensory and abnegating experience, and this realization excited the young Oxonian. It excited him, first of all, because he felt the need to meet Christ's rigorous standards for moral behavior. But it also excited him—just as importantly for his development at this stage—because he loved the visible world of sensuous experience. Perhaps Christ, he may have thought, could be perceived in all natural beauty; perhaps nature was Christ's visible sign.

Cotter has found among Hopkins's published and unpublished Oxford notes the poet's attempts to see in the physical shapes of the natural world suggestions that created things are everywhere striving upward, reaching toward the seemingly transcendent height of God. One of these physical shapes is the "bow"[56] seen in the "rainbow" of "Il Mystico" (107, 140). Synonymous with the "bow" is the "curve" of a "horn," " a projection, . . . something sprouting up."[57] The "bugle moon" of line 15 in the 1863 poem "Winter with the Gulf Stream" (P, 247) seems a crescent-shaped horned moon: bugle shaped. As the strongest symbol of relief for the atmosphere of wintry gloom that dominates that lyric, the moon is located at a greater height than the "hoarse leaves" (5) and "clogged brook" (9), and its horn-shaped cusps meanwhile seem to arch upward to an even greater height of aspiration, such as that divine height toward which the singing bird of "Il Mystico" was ascending.

If physical shapes in nature contained for Hopkins both immanence and hints of transcendence, so, it appears, did human words, expressive signs for the poetic music that "Il Mystico" hinted was a development of nature's birdsongs. In 1868, the Oxonian Hopkins wrote that any word had "prepossession of feeling" that extended beyond its dictionary definitions.[58] He therefore surmised that "every word may be considered as the contraction or coinciding-point of its [general] definitions." Thus "prepossession of feeling" was "in fact the form" of the word, a "form" that is something greater than the word's "application, 'extension,' the concrete things coming under it."[59] Words, to this Oxford student, apparently could provide relative mimesis of human experiences and also suggest the divine forms that were hidden within those human experiences. Hopkins talks as if this purpose can be best achieved through the word's "prepossession," which he associates with its "feeling" more than with dictionary definitions of "concrete things." His own poetic practice, especially in his major poems, shows him attempting to arrive at "prepossession of feeling," "some remnant of the original power that first matched [words] with reality,"[60] by balancing various definitions of a word within a complex musical setting.[61] Variant definitions of words already provoke his etymological study in 1863 and 1864.[62] And in one of these entries, he saw the culmination of a long series of synonyms for the noun horn (*corona, cornel, grin*) to be a term of potential sacramental significance: Christ's "horn of salvation."[63]

Discussing Hopkins's sense—shared with many of his century's revolutionary etymologists and other linguists[64]—that "language [is] something separate from man that must be studied to reveal its inner mysteries,"[65] James Milroy contributes greatly to our awareness of what the early Hopkins journals clearly demonstrate: Hopkins ardently sought after language's " 'original' [word-] roots with 'original' meanings"[66] and may even have believed, along with such modern writers as the American psychologist Roger Brown, "that phonetic and metaphorical extensions of vocabulary *may* be universal and not necessarily language-specific."[67] Milroy suggests that such intuitions may guide Hopkins's lifelong fascination with integrating his poetic matrices by using "schemes of alliteration and vowel or consonant rhyme."[68] If he indeed believed that the chiming of similar sounds reflected a primal unity of linguistic meaning in the words containing such similar sounds, it is no wonder that he felt it appropriate to focus the ritual of a sacramentalist poetry (which sought to restore readers' sense of a primal unity) by means of sound chiming, a "metonymical convergence of sounds."[69]

Hopkins's study of etymology seems to bear affinity with the attitudes toward language expressed by the title figure in Plato's *Cratylus*.[70] Cratylus wanted to believe that the words of his own historical age accurately referred back to primal word origins, and so he was distressed to find such inconsistencies as conferral of the name *Hermogenes* upon a poverty-stricken fellow who hardly seems to resemble the money-endowed Hermes from whom he gained his name.[71] Much like the young Oxonian Hopkins, who wanted to revive the unpopular "onomatopoetic" theory of word origins,[72] Cratylus wanted words to have "inherent correctness."[73]

Plato's Socrates told Cratylus that words might have indeed begun their histories with a "certain correctness."[74] But by the end of the dialogue Socrates refused to consider further such relative definitions of cosmic purpose as human language gives. Much as he in the *Phaedo* repudiated nature because *it* had historically lost contact with primal forms,[75] so Socrates in the *Cratylus* eventually left his discussion of fluctuating language behind, choosing instead to contemplate the primal forms themselves: "[I]f there is always that which knows and that which is known—if the beautiful, the good, and all the other verities exist—I do not see how there is any likeness between these conditions of which I am now speaking and flux or motion."[76]

The youthful Hopkins does not seem at all ready to share Plato's stance of full-fledged irony against linguistic reflection of primal cosmic origins. Indeed, Hopkins never fully shared that irony, and Sprinker is wrong to find him ever expressing a fully nihilistic distrust of language, even late in his life. When he finds Hopkins experiencing "confusion" in a search for the origins and linkages of Greek and Egyptian mythology, in a letter to Alexander Baillie of 6 April 1886,[77] Sprinker tries to make "confusion" on Hopkins's part about *mythological* origins extend to a further confusion about *linguistic* origins.[78] But Hopkins had told Baillie, even in the same 1886 letter cited by Sprinker, that "in religion *more than in language* a thing may have no one origin."[79] Whether we consider him right or wrong in his attitudes, Hopkins did remain to the very end of his life at least a *relative* idealist about the original unity of human language.

At the same time, however, Hopkins was never a full-fledged linguistic idealist either. He never said that modern language could fully recapture original language unity. When he spoke as a youth about evoking words' "prepossession of feeling," he did not say that he could thus place Platonic forms, or Christic Real Presence, directly onto the poetic page. Occasionally, as the next chapter of this study will argue, he may have come close to making such proclamations or trying to realize them in practice. And he certainly was attracted to philosophers like Parmenides and theologians like Origen and Scotus—all somewhat anagogical thinkers, men who sensed some real human potential to "touch" primal being. Yet much of the effectiveness of Hopkins's art comes from his ability to share at least some of Plato's irony toward language and thus to feel with Augustine, another descendant of Plato, that "since language itself is constituted by the not-being of time, we cannot speak truly [or at least fully?] of the one perfect Being."[80]

Already at Oxford Hopkins clearly expressed a level of Platonic irony toward at least the divine revelatory potential of *nature*. One of his diary jottings of 1864 eloquently conveys—at least when read symbolically, not only as a physical description—his sense that nature reflects its own mortality ("shadow") more strongly than it hints at immanent unity with God:

Distance
Dappled with diminish'd trees
Spann'd with shadow every one.[81]

Although it is not the only way in which he sees nature during this period of his life, Hopkins's perception of its mortal "shadow," and even its apparent *moral* shadow, is sometimes evoked in his Oxford poems. In "New Readings" (1864; *P,* 248), ravenous field fowl are lik-

ened to soldiers who crucified Christ and also wore winged helmets.
These birds and soldiers both belong to an earthly "legion" that is
greedy for material lucre and scornful of spiritual suffering:

> Although the letter said
> On thistles that men look not grapes to gather,
> I read the story rather
> How soldiers platting thorns around CHRIST'S Head
> Grapes grew and drops of wine were shed.
>
> Though when the sower sowed,
> The wingèd fowls took part, part fell in thorn
> And never turned to corn,
> Part found no root upon the flinty road,—
> CHRIST at all hazards fruit hath shewed.
>
> From wastes of rock He brings
> Food for five thousand: on the thorns He shed
> Grains from His drooping Head;
> And would not have that legion of winged things
> Bear Him to heaven on easeful wings.

This poem exemplifies Hopkins's lifelong habit of practicing biblical
exegesis through poems based on the Scriptures. At this period of his
life such exegesis was probably especially important to him, since
Bishop Colenso and the *Essays and Reviews* liberals were fiercely
questioning scriptural authority during the years when he was an
Oxford undergraduate.[82]

In Hopkins's exegesis, the greedy Roman soldiers at Golgotha, casting
lots for Jesus' garments (John 19:23–24) are seen to serve the demonic
"evil one" (Matthew 13:19), now emblematized as a crow who steals
seed not firmly rooted in the soil. Another Gospel account depicts as
the "legion of winged things" the soldiers offering Jesus vinegar and
scoffing that he should accept "easeful wings" of escape ("New Readings," 14–15): "If you are the King of the Jews, save yourself" (Luke
23:36–37).

The Satanic bird of the poem's image system thus becomes repre-
sentative of its vile human counterparts—"easeful" petty thieves and
gamblers who scorn Christ's Way of the Cross. Yet, at the same time, the
poem does not depreciate all of nature. Hopkins, after all, "in the
manner of George Herbert, make[s] the thorns around Christ's head into
grape vines"—rich with Christ's "blood," "the wine of the sacrament."[83] Indeed, he hints that the Eucharistic wine of the centuries, by
transforming natural products into divine ones, provides the most vital
food of all.

In 1865 Hopkins wrote two poems whose nature imagery differs, foreshadowing the two different theological frameworks he would alternately express throughout his life. "Myself unholy, from myself unholy," composed in June, speaks for the Calvinist perspective uttered in Cranmer's Anglican confession prayer.[84] If to Cranmer "there is no health in us," to the nineteenth-century youthful Anglican Hopkins there also is, at least ultimately, "no health" in nature:

> Myself unholy, from myself unholy
> To the sweet living of my friends I look—
> Eye-greeting doves bright-counter to the rook,
> Fresh brooks to salt sand-teasing waters shoaly:—
> And they are purer, but alas! not solely
> The unquestion'd readings of a blotless book.
>
> (1–6)

Nature, according to this allegorical poem, contains reassuring white "doves" to contrast their seemingly ideal moral purity with the ebony-dark "rook" (3) that might appropriately symbolize moral contagion. Likewise, although nature includes murky "salt-sand" oceans as emblems of moral cloudiness, it also includes "Fresh brooks"(4). Such brooks are the very nature symbols of purity to which the psalmist compared the holiness of God; meanwhile he treated himself as a morally thirsty human version of the "hart" parched in the physically dry desert (Psalms 42:1).

Yet Hopkins's poem actually reads nature (and, more important, through symbolic extension, humanity) as still more morally imperfect than they appeared in the Psalms text. In his lyric the "Fresh brooks" are "shoaly" to the "salt-sand waters" (4)—and thus likely at any time to pollute their purity by flowing into fouler waters to which they have a natural outlet. These "brooks" are apparently morally upright human beings (the "sweet[-] living . . . friends" of Hopkins's second line), who "are purer" than the poem's speaker "but alas! not solely / The unquestion'd readings of a blotless book" (5–6). This nonliberal Christian apologist sadly discovers that human beings cannot reveal spiritual messages so surely as can a spiritually "blotless book" (6), most likely the book of the Holy Scripture (in which he has faith, like that of Saint Peter and Conrad of Hirsau long before him):

> And so my trust, confusèd, struck and shook
> Yields to the sultry siege of melancholy.
> He has a sin of mine, he its near brother;
> Knowing them well I can but see the fall.
> This fault in one I found, that in another:
> And so, though each have one while I have all,

No *better* serves me now, save *best;* no other
Save Christ: to Christ I look, on Christ I call.

The poem concludes, like so much of both Hopkins's youthful and later work, as a pledge of receptive devotion to the Savior Christ—a Christ who is *not,* according to this poem, strikingly present in either humankind or nature. "Let me be to Thee as the circling bird," written the next October, ends with the same pledge of all-important receptive devoutness. Yet this second poem does not treat nature as a Calvinist symbol of inherent corruption in the created world. Rather, the poem forecasts Hopkins's later 1870s lyrics of nature. Those poems' Scotist theology was, after all, already being formulated by his Oxford readings and reactions to Plato, Aristotle, and Parmenides.[85]

In "Let me be to Thee as the circling bird" Hopkins almost completely reverses the response he had given to nature in "Myself unholy." In "Let me be to Thee," the "bat" (2), an animal that normally does not suggest divine beneficence, to Hopkins seems just as much to reflect origins in "changeless" divinity (4) as does the "bird" (1)—a creature that had already inspired Hopkins (as well as Wordsworth, Shelley, and Keats) to meditate upon divine stasis:[86]

Let me be to Thee as the circling bird,
Or bat with tender and air-crisping wings
That shapes in half-light his departing rings,
From both of whom a changeless note is heard.

                                                                              (1–4)

The second quatrain of this sonnet seems to record Hopkins's specific efforts, during his youth at Oxford, to prove the "preferred" divine Word (8) to be the source of the "common word" (5) expressed by language, music, and creatures. At least, he judges this Word to *surpass* all the other words:

I have found my music in a common word,
Trying each pleasurable throat that sings
And every praisèd sequence of sweet strings,
And know infallibly which I preferred.

                                                                              (5–8)

He proclaims, in the third quatrain, that these multiple features of the created world all have common telos, or "end . . ." (10):

The authentic cadence was discovered late
Which ends those only strains that I approve,

And other science all gone out of date
And minor sweetness scarce made mention of

(9–12)

The old philosophical "science" of Plato, Parmenides, and Aristotle (11) apparently has best explained to Hopkins (at least until now) the interrelations between the Creator and the creation. Such "science" has, however, now been superseded for him by the "authentic cadence" (9) of Roman Catholic Christian worship; and such old "science" is of course, also deemed "out of date" (11) by Victorian-era scientists like Darwin.[87]

It is true, Hopkins also admits, that the flights and "air-crisping" music of bat and bird (1–2) are "only strains" (10), distillations from and aspirations back toward, their divine origin. They are thus limited reflections of the divine, as limited as the "minor sweetness" (12) of human romance, which may have inspired Hopkins's poem sequence "The Beginning of the End," written the previous May (P, 250). But these experiences also have helped him to find, and to symbolize, "the dominant of my range and state—/ Love, O my God, to call Thee Love and Love" (13–14).

Hopkins wishes, like George Herbert, who bequeathed him this particular personification, to call Christ "Love" in writing that expresses his ideal musical "range." Yet he also wishes to acknowledge that in his "state" of sinfulness, he must emulate, in receptively responsive actions of self-sacrifice, the will to love Christ which was expressed by the Jesuit Saint Francis Xavier in a poem that Hopkins came eventually to translate:

O God, I love thee, I love thee—
Not out of hope of heaven for me
Nor fearing not to love and be
In the everlasting burning.
Thou, thou, my Jesus, after me
Didst reach thine arms out dying,
For my sake sufferdst nails and lance,
Mocked and marrèd countenance,
Sorrows passing number,
Sweat and care and cumber,
Yea and death, and this for me,
And thou couldst see me sinning:
Then I, why should not I love thee,
Jesu so much in love with me?
Not for heaven's sake; not to be
Out of hell by loving thee;
Not for any gains I see;

But just the way that thou didst me
I do love and I will love thee:
What must I love thee, Lord, for then?—
For being my king and God. Amen.

                                   ("O Deus, ego amo te" [undated], P, 213, 324)

Hopkins even in 1865 felt that he might as a poet "call [God] Love," but
that he would not completely express his faith until the Holy Spirit, to
him the ultimate model of each "circling bird" (1), helped him act out
"Love."

Although "Myself unholy" and "Let me be to Thee" thus present
markedly different natural theologies, both poems display Hopkins's
constantly reiterated conviction that the speaker of a proper sacramental poem must bow to, not neglect, the spirit of sacrifice. To be sure,
Hopkins will draw John Robinson's ire for some blindness to human
and natural deficiency even in poems as late as "The Bugler's First
Communion."[88] But from the beginning Hopkins also has awareness of
the painful agony that accompanies the world's loveliness, and he
believes that reverential persons must "bear on [their] bod[ies] the
marks" of Christ's *redemptive* agony (Galatians 6:17).

Hopkins's poems of the 1860s thus do not all devote primary attention
to searches after visible signs of Christ. On the other hand, almost all
his youthful poems *do* emphasize Christ's Passion. Hopkins seemed to
sense that individuals participate in that Passion whenever they recognize that beauty dies, that suffering is as necessary to humankind as to
Christ, and that God restricts easy sacramental assurance because he
wishes his mystery to be revered more than are human sense perceptions. Self-sacrifice, for Hopkins, finds its fullest depths of meaning
whenever he waits upon God's will in lonely trembling—not asking for
the visible, the tangible, the ardent revelations of sense experience, but
rather seeking a God who finally transcends this dark, dry "winter
world" ("To R. B." [1889], 13).

C. The Pilgrim in Darkness: Hopkins's Conversion and Accepted
Sacrifice

Sulloway recounts how the Christ Church Tractarians Pusey and
Liddon, during the Oxford theological debates of the 1860s, tried to win
adherents for their own position: as they "comforted the troubled young
men with seminars on religious questions of the day," they also "were
able to introduce many of the distraught undergraduates to the ancient
rites of confession, contrition and penance."[89] Hopkins may have par-
ticipated in penitential fasts and perhaps in other physical chastise-

ments while at Oxford. In seemingly, autobiographical stanzas from *The Wreck of the Deutschland* in 1876,

> I did say yes
> O at lightning and lashed rod;
> Thou heardst me truer than tongue confess
> Thy terror, O Christ, O God,
>
> (st. 2, 1–4)

he surely suggests such dreadful torments, at some point in his life before 1875.[90] In the early chapters of her Hopkins biography, Paddy Kitchen exposed material from Hopkins's papers suggesting that the Oxford student, in his personal confessional notes, seemed "excited by pain and suffering."[91] Hopkins wrote to his father, on 16 October 1866, that "Those who do not pray to [Christ] in His Passion pray to God but scarcely to Christ."[92] He also wrote of Lenten penitents "striped in secret with breath-taking whips," with "crookèd rough-scored chequers," in "Easter Communion" of 1865 (3–4). Yet there is still very little evidence that declares him to believe physical torment *essential* for passional imitatio.

For instance, we do know that he remembered two famous martyrdoms in "The Escorial" and "For a Picture of St. Dorothea," but only the martyrdom of Saint Lawrence receives his physical description. Kitchen notes the admiration Hopkins expressed in his journals for the lives of Savonarola and Origen,[93] both of whom experienced physical persecution. But Hopkins proves highly influenced by Origen's theology and highly intrigued by Savonarola's lessons for Christian artists;[94] these two saints seem to inspire him by their lives more than by their modes of death. (To be sure, however, their modes of life were themselves ascetic, antiworldly,[95] and Hopkins does praise Savonarola as one "martyred in the Church.")[96]

As a poet writing an unfinished fragment about "St. Thecla," Hopkins discusses only her conversion experience as a listener to the message of Paul the Apostle. He sees even her not-yet-converted demeanor as an ascetic quality—"grave past girlhood earnest in her eyes" (20). But he does not discuss those experiences of "flames" and "wild beasts" that made her a declared Roman Catholic martyr even though God actually spared her from death (P, 309). The Hopkins poem of the 1860s that makes the strongest reference to actual physical suffering is the fragmentary "Pilate" (1864), in which the guilt-tormented protagonist plans to crucify himself in order to atone for permitting Christ's crucifixion (P, 116–19, 297–98). Even if we might impute to Hopkins an identification of his own guilt with Pilate's,[97] he left us no similar poems from the 1860s. The physical torments recorded in even *The Wreck of the Deutschland* seem primarily metaphors for an inner suffering, not autobiographical records of physical pain. At least in Hopkins's major early poems about endured suffering, the speakers suffer mostly because God is *absent* from them, not because he is present in physical torment. Christ's Passion did, after all, include both pain and what was perceived as God's absence by his crucified Son; it included darkness at noon (Mark 15:33). "My God, my God, why hast thou forsaken me?" (Mark 15:34) is a question uttered by one to whom his goal of supreme trust is no longer visible—although he is still able to voice faith in that goal with the words "My God, my God." Hopkins already knew, in the 1860s, that a Christlike Passion, expected by all persons committed to imitatio Christi, involves the experiences of God's darkness—the loss of visible signs. Two dramatic monologues, of 1864 and 1866, indicate such knowledge on his part.

The "Soliloquy of One of the Spies Left in the Wilderness," one of Hopkins's richest ironic efforts, portrays a Hebrew who apparently wants to return to visible Egypt, with its "comfortable gloom" (28). He rejects both the physical pain and the visionary uncertainty that seem required if he would reach, instead of Egypt, the land of Canaan: currently a darker place, but still a land of divine promise.

With increased theological debate at Oxford concerning the historicity of the Scriptures,[98] Hopkin's 1866 conversion to Roman Catholicism[99] resulted largely from his attempts to find for his faith some infallible authority that surpassed the evidence of the physical world. To contemporary geologists and zoologists, the physical world proved decidedly ambiguous evidence and surely no guarantee that the earth originated with a deity. Sulloway believes that the "Soliloquy of One of the Spies Left in the Wilderness" reflects Hopkins's reactions to conflicts over historicity of the Pentateuch,[100] and Hopkins surely does wish to place his own rather traditional biblical hermeneutics on record.

Yet whether or not Victorian historical disputes prompt the spy poem, its argument is this: physical evidence is relatively unimportant for the individual's pilgrimage in faith. The poem contends that a spiritual pilgrim goes forward to an invisible goal; the physical sufferings he or she meets on the way are not nearly so important as is his or her retaining faith despite the goal's current inscrutability.

From the first moments of Hopkins's poem, the speaker seems to admit, but want to deny, his slovenly ways and their limited merit:

Forget the waking trumpet, the long law.
Spread o'er the swart face of this prodigal earth.

> Bring in the glistery straw.
> Here are sweet messes without price or worth,
>   And never thirst or dearth.
>
> (44–48)

In his irrational speech the term "prodigal earth" (45) could imply ampleness of reward ("never thirst or dearth"—48) if one continues onward to the Promised Land, but the word "prodigal" may also imply the wastrel behavior of the Egyptians in their land of "comfortable gloom" (28). Also, the land he seeks is said to be "swart," or "black," and, figuratively, "sinister, evil malignant" (*OED*). Although such an adjective could perhaps befit Canaan for a frightened pilgrim, should it ultimately describe a land that God has pledged as reward for his elect? The description seems better to fit Egypt—to which the slovenly spy apparently wishes to return.

The "glistery straw" that shines, meanwhile, in this spy's imagination (46) is the base ingredient of bricks made in Egypt by the Hebrews' slave labor. The spy here appears to forget that hardhearted Pharoahs eventually denied the Israelites "glistery straw" with which to ease their hard burden (Exodus 5:7–9). Placing his values on such paltry visible treasures as this straw, and forgetting that even it was once denied him by cruel masters, he reveals his essential folly. He wants easy, known, and perhaps falsely appealing, worldly splendor.

Portrayed as irrational and ambivalent throughout the poem, he is unable to separate clearly his present "sandfield" locale (29) from either the fearsome and uncertain land of promise or from Egypt with its "easy burden of yore" (54). When he is reporting about Canaan's greenness, for instance, he suddenly stammers forth the non sequitur "Not Goshen. Wasteful wide huge-girthèd Nile / Unbakes my pores, and streams, and makes all fresh" (31–32). And his irrationality ceases only with an apparent wish for death at the poem's end. He seems to receive the extinction he had sought to avoid in the Canaan dangers: "Sure, this is Nile: I sicken, I know not why, / And faint as though to die" (59–60).

The implication of this passage and of the entire poem is that the painful uncertainty of spiritual struggle must be accepted unless one wishes an eternal mental torpor of indecision. In Numbers 14:37, it is reported that "these men who had given out the bad report about the land were struck down by the Lord and died."

The "Soliloquy" poem, for all its realistic dramatic monologue style, may also reflect Hopkins's Oxford reading in the mystical patristic theology of Origen, who would have suggested to him that the exodus from Egypt was a symbol, essentially, for Christian spiritual pilgrimage all the way from original conversion to eschatological welcome in Heaven. Origen writes that

... we must move out of Egypt . . . . [,] leaving not with reference to a place but with reference to the soul, not by moving along a road but by moving along in faith . . . . on account of certain hidden and mystical reasons . . . led from the darkness of error to the light of recognition and . . . from earthly converse to a spiritual way of life, . . . to solitude, i.e., to that state of life in which, by peace and quiet, [one] becomes practiced in the divine laws and imbued with heavenly thoughts . . . . [T]he exodus from Egypt is also a figure of the soul which leaves the darkness of this world and the blindness of bodily nature and is transferred to that other world . . . called 'paradise'. . . .[101]

In the 1866 poem "*Nondum*" ("Not Yet"), the epigraph "Verily Thou art a God that hidest Thyself" (Isaiah 45:15) introduces another speaker's protest against God's apparent absence:

> God, though to Thee our psalm we raise
> No answering voice comes from the skies;
> To Thee the trembling sinner prays
> But no forgiving voice replies.
>
> (1–4)

When human beings sense such spiritual dearth around them, says this distraught spokesman, "Our prayer seems lost in desert ways, / Our hymn in the vast silence dies" (5–6).

Hopkins's character nearly despairs here because he cannot easily reconcile God's absence with his supposed presence in nature:

> We see the glories of the earth
> But not the hand that wrought them all:
> Night to a myriad worlds gives birth,
> Yet like a lighted empty hall
> Where stands no host at door or hearth
> Vacant creation's lamps appal.
>
> (7–12)

He admits that the external world offers "glories" to the eye (7), but he seems to deny the word "glories" its origin in etymology as "the splendour and bliss of heaven" or "the majesty and splendour attendant upon a manifestation of God" (*OED*). The "glories" contain physical splendor, but no readily apparent divine splendor. Perhaps they seem mostly to reflect "boastful vainglory," another meaning of their name according to English etymology (*OED*). But we do note, in any case, that they are there. This supposedly "vacant creation" is lit with "lamps" (12).

Judging the created world both God's reflection and sometimes so blank of meaning that it looks like pre-Creation chaos (19–24), this confused fellow asks if God is immanent in nature, as the Bible says that he is, or only transcendent, like the Spirit in chaos. He does not fully know the answer to these questions, even when speaking of "life's first germs" (24) as having emerged from chaos. Besides, the poem adds protest against the human disputations of belligerent voices; these are occurring everywhere, as they reputedly have ever since God separated the builders of the Tower of Babel (Genesis 11:9). Like the Arnold persona of "Dover Beach," this speaker sees "many creeds" shouted out by "hosts" of men who "confront" each other "with flags unfurled" (32–33). And he seems to believe himself the world's sole righteous advocate of "truth . . . , with tears impearled" (35).

In the final two stanzas of the poem, however, by quieting his own sobbing complaints, he reenforces not the surface argument of the poem thus far, the bewailing of God's absence from visible signs, but rather the undercurrent of thought suggested in the poem's ironies—the argument that one's belief in God does not depend on visible signs in nature but rather on trust in the declarations of faith (e.g., faith in Creation by God)—for which the major evidence is given not in nature but in Scripture. By habitually talking of "glories of the earth" and of the Genesis Creation, the speaker seems already to have declared his belief in Scriptural revelation. Now he acknowledges that what God is—"that Thou art" (44)—will only become apparent to the person who receives "that sense beyond" (43). God, he declares by witness of his own personal faith, is "near" (44), although he can only be known fully by "patience" (45). God is both immanent and transcendent, but above all God:

> Oh! till Thou givest that sense beyond,
> To show Thee that Thou art, and near,
> Let patience with her chastening wand
> Dispel the doubt and dry the tear;
> And lead me child-like by the hand
> If still in darkness not in fear.
> Speak! whisper to my watching heart
> One word—as when a mother speaks
> Soft, when she sees her infant start,
> Till dimpled joy steals o'er its cheeks.
>
> (43–52)

The persona still wants God to "Speak!" (49), but he recognizes now that this deity's final testimony to the truth of faith comes to a "watching heart" (49) more surely than to a watchful eye. It is true that, like the child to whom he compares himself, this poetic speaker may receive visible signs of beneficence in the natural world. The mother's smiling face comforts the child at the same time as her words do, and God may comfort his spiritual child with the beautiful "glories of the earth" (7). However, these visible signs do not constitute God's only or principal means of revelation; one may need to look for primary revelation to the oft-mysterious "word[s]" of Scripture (50), as well as to the spiritual witnessings of a contrite "heart" (49). With these matters in proper perspective, the speaker of a complex poem can conclude his own verbal sign of internal contemplativeness: "Then, to behold Thee as Thou art, / I'll wait till morn eternal breaks" (53–54).

This speaker has recognized that God must come to individuals in their "darkness," although not by causing them such "fear" as he himself had heretofore been expressing (48). Finally, he has waited in silence until God spoke, with a "whisper" (49), "One word" (50). The word was a dark one, almost silent; Hopkins's entire poem had been declaring these as its conditions. But, as the poem's irony of ironies, Hopkins's speaker had uttered the word from the poem's very opening. Although the word may also be immanent Christ the Logos (John 1:1), it is, primally, transcendent "God" (Genesis 1:1; "*Nondum*," 1).

While Herbert might easily be a source for this poem's very orthodox portrait of religious doubt, it surely is also a Victorian dramatic monologue in the tradition of Browning and Tennyson. Norman MacKenzie notes its frequent Victorian imagery, rhetoric, and clear allusions to Newman, Arnold, and Tennyson.[102] The climactic lines in particular seem clearly drawn from Tennyson:

No, like a child in doubt and fear:
But that blind clamor made me wise;
Then was I as a child that cries,
But, crying, knows his father near. . . .
(*In Memoriam*, st. 124, 17–20)[103]

And perhaps, given their shared references to female as well as male parents, Hopkins may here also be recalling Teufelsdröckh's "Everlasting Yea":

. . . Sweeter than Dayspring to the Ship-wrecked in Nova Zembla: ah, like the mother's voice to her little child that strays bewildered, weeping, in unknown tumults; like soft streamings of celestial music to my too-exasperated heart, came that Evangel. The Universe is not dead and demoniacal, a charnel-house with spectres; but godlike, and my Father's![104]

The speaker of this poem, in any case, seems to represent the young intellectual Hopkins, he whom others' (e.g., Tennyson's or Arnold's) stronger doubts of historicity of Creation might at times bewilder. It reflects also the sensuous Hopkins, whose faith often seemed firmer when he could see "the glories of the earth" and believe them signs of God. Yet the poem eventually declares, by ironies leading to the final resolution, that Hopkins, in the face of Oxford theological debates, "simply reaffirmed an ancient hierarchy of values: the things of the visible world are not as important as the things of the eternal world."[105] This is the lesson a persona relearns in what I believe may ultimately be Hopkins's most powerful poem: "Thou are indeed just, Lord" (1889). But the lesson must be repeated at the end of a writing life during which Hopkins has occasionally wished that an almost unlimited visible sacramentalism were God's principal way of speaking to human beings. On the contrary, he has by 1889 truly learned that God may speak to the eye through darkness, to the ear through silence.

To Hopkins, the life of devout self-sacrifice, even though the endurance of such a life demanded acceptance of uncertainties, had already by 1866 taken some precedence over the life of palpable sense experience. Hopkins's love for rich sensation might still continue to test his declared primary commitment to that dark divine mystery beyond both words and sights. Yet through sacramentalist art and asceticism, both experiences that he dedicated to God, he sought always to reconcile his life in the known world with God's inscrutability in the unknown Heaven:

> *Elected silence, sing to me*
> And beat upon my whorlèd ear,
> Pipe me to pastures still and be
> The music that I care to hear.
>
> . . . .
> *Be shellèd, eyes with double dark*
> And find the uncreated light:
> This ruck and reel which you remark
> Coils, keeps, and teases simple sight.
>   ("The Habit of Perfection," 1–4, 9–12; emphases mine)

3

Hopkins's Preparation and Early Priesthood

Oh, morning, at the brown brink eastward, springs—
—Hopkins, "God's Grandeur"

EVIDENTLY RECOGNIZING how important beauty and the sensate world were to him, and thus believing that physical stimuli might tempt him to forget spiritual ideals of self-sacrifice, Hopkins during his novitiate briefly gave up poetry. He seems to have wanted to make sure that as a Jesuit he would only fulfill in the most clearly self-sacrificial ways Loyola's dictum "to praise, reverence, and serve God Our Lord, and by so doing to save his soul."[1] As Downes evaluates him, Hopkins as a Jesuit always "had to face up to Ignatius' own counsel about the proper use of things: the Christian use of all things must lead back to God through the imitation of Christ."[2] Thus, Downes adds, "he probably 'burned' his poetry with equanimity when he entered the Jesuit order."[3] Yet he later reaffirmed his poetry—especially that in which nature is shown sacramentally revealing Christ—as a way "to praise, reverence, and serve God Our Lord."

Hopkins's theories of *instress* and *inscape* in nature were at this time being developed astutely from his combined studies of Ruskin's aesthetics, of English linguistic etymology, and eventually, of the medieval theology of Duns Scotus. The multiple sources that thus lie behind these Hopkinsian terms produce greater complexity in their definitions and their application than has often been perceived by critics. Evidence in both Hopkins's journals and his poems suggests that Hopkins could feel with Scotus—and somewhat with Ruskin and the guidance of etymology as well—the radiance of Christic Presence sacramentally outpouring itself from nature. But he still could also sometimes sense— as a Ruskinian, an etymologist, and even a fully orthodox Scotist—a marked gap between the things of nature and God. Nature to Hopkins was wonderful—and wondrously revelatory even of sacramental truth.

But it seems that Hopkins always felt that nature visions did not easily provoke the development of the richest sort of sacramental inscape—saintliness.[4] Still, he tried—and often very brilliantly—to make nature poems become sacramental. Like Loyola, after all, he uses "signs" to guide "elections" of, "decisions" for, self-sacrificial sacramentalism in a would-be saint's soul.[5]

Hopkins came later to sense a yet-firmer demarcation between signs of physical and spiritual beauty. As a priest in parish settings, he felt forced in the clerical vocational task to direct human beings to God by showing them the debility of their souls (and sometimes, perhaps, the debility of an ugly industrial society that such souls were producing).[6] Thus, except rarely, he would not find himself addressing the congregations to which he preached after 1878, whether in poem or sermon, by pointing with cheer to a lovely and spiritually revelatory outdoors. The same poet-priest was to write in 1885, "To what serves mortal beauty | dangerous; does set danc- / ing blood" ("To what serves Mortal Beauty," 1–2, in *P*, 285). Mortal beauty only "serves" humankind, he says very forcefully here, when human citizens "wish that . . . wish all, | God's better beauty, grace" (14). During 1876–77 in rural Wales, Hopkins sometimes may have tended to believe that all other persons could share his ardor for the coexistence of sacramental inscape in both physical grace (gracefulness) and spiritual grace (graciousness). But in the 1880s, after his public priesthood had begun, he no longer seemed very often to write as if this message were easy, or even appropriate, to communicate. Physical grace, he now said clearly, might still lack spiritual grace.

It would surely be wrong to emphasize as trenchantly unilateral Hopkins's shift of focus from affectively perceived architectonic inscape toward electively willed saintly inscape. That the two visions always to some degree blend in his work is made clear by the poem "As kingfishers catch fire," for which MacKenzie's handwriting analysis and Mariani's focus on thematic parallels produce different likely dates, as early as 1877 and as late as 1881.[7] The poem sees architectonic inscape where all "Selves—goes itself; *myself* . . . speaks and spells" (7–8). Yet it also firmly argues for the supremacy of human saintly inscape, which is not innate to all humankind but elected only by the "just": "Í say more: the just man justices; / keeps grace: that keeps all his goings graces" (9–10).[8]

Ultimately Hopkins did find physical beauty and spiritual beauty in "the just man" proving more and more distinct. Thus he withdrew from any sermonic confidence in universal visible sacraments that his earlier poems might have appeared to flaunt. He turned his didactic voice to quiet teachings about essential human and natural frailty (as in "Spring and Fall," one of the poems of the parish years), and, at times, he became even more humbly and personally meditative, seeking as his goal not so much to present visible signs of external sacrament's achievement as to offer mere verbal signs of internal sacramental struggle. Hopkins's mature poetry of verbal innercentered meditativeness may actually begin to dominate his canon with the writing of "The Windhover" in 1877. Assuredly, such poetry includes works about parish life like "The Bugler's First Communion," and it reaches its apex of power in the "Terrible Sonnets" and later poems of the 1880s.

A. A Jesuit in Preparation: How "To Praise, Reverence, and Serve"?

In 1868, Hopkins began a two-year novitiate as he prepared for further stages of Jesuit education.[9] During nearly a full decade dedicated to Jesuit training, Hopkins the poet and would-be priest attempted to determine how he would mix these vocations—or, more centrally, how he would blend his love of perceivable beauty with his goals of self-sacrifice.

The first step in this process of self-discovery came as he tested his need for artistic self-expression by briefly rejecting it. Hopkins seemed to fear art as a distraction for the senses, one that would keep him from the goals of self-sacrifice that he as Jesuit novice was assuredly accepting.[10] He wrote his friend Alexander Baillie, on 12 February 1868, "You know I once wanted to be a painter. But even if I could I wd. not I think, now, for the fact is that the higher and more attractive parts of the art put a strain upon the passions which I shd. think it unsafe to encounter. I want to write still and as a priest I very likely can do that too, not so freely as I shd. have liked, e.g. nothing or little in the verse way, but no doubt what wd. best serve the cause of my religion."[11]

Even when he talks about others' art works, during the period just before the novitiate, Hopkins writes disquisitions about the moral dangers with which uncautious authors may threaten vulnerable readers. On 15 September 1867, discussing *La dame aux camélias* of Dumas fils—which Baillie recently had read— Hopkins finds the tale of an ill-fated courtesan "graceful and pathetic," for "any subject may be chosen for its art value alone." Yet he chastises Swinburne for "the proportion of [sensual] subjects" in his work, contending that "what is innocent in a writer, if it must cause certain scandal to readers becomes wrong." Then he mentions a "question of degree," deeming *Othello* "innocent" but Ovid "immoral." Hopkins finds that literature has "art value"—in its style and its presentation of universal emotions, its aesthetic grace and emotional pathos. But he still thinks that art is open to moral danger if it causes "scandal" to readers—either by offending their prudery, or, if they lack even a proper level of prudery, by tempting them to participate in "scandal."[12]

Hopkins continued writing journal entries about paintings and the theater in the months before going into novitiate at Roehampton, in mid-1868. Yet there are not many entries in these journals, for Hopkins suddenly seems reticent. Two years earlier, before officially becoming a Roman Catholic, he had penned into a newly launched notebook, "I read today the journal I kept in 1862, burning parts."[13] There also exists good evidence by which some judge that a similar burning may have occurred at Roehampton. On 11 May 1868—nine days after writing "This day, I think, I resolved" and six after declaring "Resolved to be a religious"—Hopkins reported "Slaughter of the innocents" in his notebooks.[14] Humphry House and Graham Storey sense that the cryptic phrase refers to a sacrifice of now-unavailable poems.[15]

Richard Watson Dixon, Hopkins's childhood teacher at Highgate School and later one of his major correspondents, in October 1878 received his ex-pupil's forthright declaration of such a burning: "You ask, do I write verse myself. What I had written I burnt before I became a Jesuit and resolved to write no more, as not belonging to my profession, unless it were by the wish of my superiors; so for seven years [1868–75?] I wrote nothing but two or three little presentation pieces which occasion called for."[16] Editors House and Storey appropriately note the repetition here of the key word "resolved" from Hopkins's mysterious journal comments of ten years earlier.[17]

A much earlier letter to Robert Bridges—dating from 7 August 1868, not very long after Hopkins had vowed to join the Jesuits—records how he cannot forward to Bridges the poem "Summa," since it is now ashes.[18] Here, however, Hopkins also asks Bridges to "master the peculiar beat" of "St. Dorothea." He should, says Hopkins, set its nontraditional rhythms next to the "Whý should thís desert be?" lines from *As You Like It*. Although we have already seen that the poem of which Hopkins speaks, "Lines for a Picture of St. Dorothea," is a work in which he questions "wordy warrants," Hopkins was proud of the poem, and he wanted to share its aesthetic method with another practicing poet.

Thus it is not surprising that, once he had adjusted to the regimen of his Jesuit preparation, Hopkins's initially harsh attitude toward his involvement with artistic creation quickly relaxed. Although his poetic production during this period may only have included "presentation pieces" for religious May festivals, the "Ad Mariam" and "Rosa Mystica" examined by Elisabeth Schneider,[19] Hopkins kept highly descriptive journals about his nature walks. Such journals likely resembled those earlier burned; he was, we note, already keeping a new set.[20]

Hopkins, to a rigid judge (like, on occasion, himself) was running the risks of potentially dangerous pride by keeping this personal record of sensuous impressions. While he could come to see the relevance of a worthy pride in one's unique human "self," judging that very uniqueness to be a reflection of God, its creator,[21] he also, at least by late 1881, firmly believed that "By selving, singing himself, Satan exiled himself from heaven."[22] Because Hopkins's sense of "self" was so centrally defined by his desire to subordinate personal wishes to the will of God—and hence not to mimic the "selving, singing himself" of Satan—his sometimes-testy wish for visible signs of God, both natural and poetic, surely never undid his "resolve" of self-sacrifice. Yet there are times during the 1870s when his involvement in these sensible signs may cloud his perception of, at least, the best ways for reaching his final spiritual aim.

*   *   *

Hopkins is aware of this danger. One of the poems of the 1870s clearly shows him willing to admit the supremacy of spiritual self-sacrifice over any physical experience of beauty. But the poem, "The Lantern out of Doors," still may express overconfidence that in human percipients the illuminations of physical and spiritual beauty will automatically unite.

In this poem Hopkins may also overtrust the magic of words. He seems to believe that all word games, just because they are available in the language, participate inevitably in cosmic unity. He writes thus as if he were the naïve Cratylus, who believed that all verbal definitions reflected their origin in divine truth, and not the skeptic Socrates, with his certainty that words had historically changed their meanings so as to lose almost all contact with that divine origin.[23]

Written while Hopkins was in Wales toward the end of his training years, "The Lantern out of Doors" begins with a seemingly strong awareness of the need for self-sacrifice and love for others. Hopkins says that one's fellow human beings may be viewed as sensuously or emotionally attractive objects, but that they should far more fully be loved spiritually as souls:

Sometimes a lantern moves along the night,
   That interests our eyes. And who goes there?
   I think; where from and bound, I wonder, where,
With, all down darkness wide, his wading light?

Men go by me whom either beauty bright
   In mould or mind or what not else makes rare:

They rain against our much-thick and marsh air
Rich beams, till death or distance buys them quite.

Death or distance soon consumes them: wind
  What most I may eye after, be in at the end
I cannot, and out of sight is out of mind.

Christ minds: Christ's interest, what to avow or amend
  There, éyes them, heart wánts, care háunts, foot fóllows kínd,
Their ránsom, théir rescue, ánd first, fást, last fríend.

The poem's basic statement is simple. The speaker, although dazzled by "either beauty bright / In mould or mind or what not else," understands that physical and mental beauty of "mould or mind" are transient; "out of sight" makes both of these "out of mind" for the observer. And death will extinguish every "sight," and "mind," within that observer. Only "what not else," perhaps the other person's soul, is a lasting entity. Visible beauty, which "interests our eyes," finally must fade. What we "eye after" (10) turns to "wind" (9): spirit or soul.

Christ, wiser than the speaker of this sonnet, not only sometimes but always pays attention to human souls. As he "minds" persons, he cares for them not with the senses, or even essentially with the intellect, but rather with a soul-loving soul. Whenever he "éyes them," his "heart wánts, care háunts, foot fóllows kínd." His pursuit of them (expressed by accented verbs) joins his "kínd" love for them (in the equally accented adjective "kínd," which, in one grammatical option, can modify "foot"). He, unlike us, can "be in" with them "at the end" (10).

Yet Christ, Hopkins also may imply, is humanity's incarnating source—and, hence, ever one of their "kínd." Thus Hopkins makes, in the phrase "heart wánts," the sonnet's final lines potentially change their subject. Christ, as he redemptively pursues us, seems also to spur activities within us, making us instinctively follow after Christ. When "[he] éyes them, [each one's] heart wánts, care háunts, foot fóllows [him, their] kínd, / Their ránsom, théir rescue, ánd first, fást, last fríend."

Hopkins at this point may not allow for the unresponsiveness to Christ of even one person. His latter-day Jesuit brother Boyle likewise questions "if indeed there really are" in the world any intrinsically "faithless" persons.[24] And yet, even if Christ reveals himself to all through natural creation, many will ask if most persons innately recognize this truth. Skeptics will add a query as to whether most (including those reported to have witnessed it directly) even respond with loyal discipleship after they learn of Christ's Passion. Thus such skeptics will ask if the wordplay of Hopkins's last tercet in "The Lantern Out of

Doors" (although, to be sure, it is only wordplay, and not trenchant sermon) does not try to make Origenian universalist theology too automatic. The basic thesis of the poem—Christ's rich love—is surely the center of Christian belief. But the wordplay seems to make all folk fully Christian, inevitably summoning this loving Christ with their elective wills as well as sensing him with their affective wills. Allen Tate might say that the sonnet suffers from overexaggerating symbolic intention (magical claims of its words) at the expense of logical extension (appropriateness as a response to commonsense experience).[25]

After all, the worshipper of human beauty at this poem's beginning withdrew so that Christ could take over with his wiser spirituality. Yet that worshipper of human beauty seems to have returned at the poem's end, trying to turn physically beautiful human beings into automatons of spiritual responsiveness. He is thus false even to observations in other Hopkins poems during the 1870s: "Why do men then now not reck his rod?" ("God's Grandeur," 4); "God, lover of souls, swaying considerable scales, / Complete thy creature dear O where it fails" ("In the Valley of the Elwy," 12–13).

Or *is* he false to these observations? The answer to that question clearly depends on how committed one is to seeing Hopkins as a monolithic thinker, at any point in his career, or whether one sees him as constantly involved in alternating viewpoints within a dialectic of ideas. When one carefully reads his longest poem of the 1870s, *The Wreck of the Deutschland*, one seems to meet a Hopkins who fully has worked out a theology of universal salvation consistent with the spiritual confidence of "The Lantern Out of Doors." And yet "God's Grandeur" and "In the Valley of the Elwy," along with "The Loss of the Eurydice" and other poems of several years later, seem less certain of theological universalism.[26] I believe that an increased humility, which may reveal Hopkins's lessened confidence about universal salvation, in time makes his voice as poet more compellingly human. By contrast, the boisterous confidence occasionally expressed in the early poems advertising universalism can be disconcerting.

In *The Wreck of the Deutschland*, for instance, he combines his fervor for Scotist doctrines, which emphasize Christ's incarnating activity in matter as far back as the Creation,[27] with his own Hopkinsian fervency for the Origenian doctrine of apocatastasis, which proposes universal salvation at the other extension of history: the eschaton or Judgment Day.[28] Therefore Hopkins can declare as a Scotist in *The Wreck of the Deutschland* that Christ "rides time like riding a river" (st. 6, 7)—that he is "under the world's splendour and wonder" (st. 5, 6) and in "Stroke and a stress that stars and storms deliver" (st. 6, 5) just as much as in "Manger, maiden's knee; / The dense and the driven Passion, and frightful sweat" (st. 7, 4–5). He can also write, as an Origenian, that the Logos or Word who was in Creation is also to be known in universal eschatological redemption: "Oh [Omega], / We lash with the best or worst / Word last!" (st. 8 1–3); "Hither then, last or first, / To hero of Calvary, Christ's, feet—/ Never ask if meaning it, wanting it, warned of it—men go" (st. 8, 6–8).[29]

Hopkins creates in this ode a double-structured Jesuit meditation. His work combines two separate compositions in place, as the sketched *Deutschland* catastrophe of part 2, stanzas 12–17 is, says Milward, set against the contrary locus where Hopkins himself dwells: "the chapel of St. Beuno's College."[30] Indeed, the same two settings come together briefly in part 2, stanza 24. The ode also includes extensive Ignatian moral reasoning in both its sections (pt. 1, st. 4–8; pt. 2, st. 11, 18–23, 25–31). Finally, Hopkins pairs two discrete culminating Ignatian sections of prayerful and praising colloquy with God (pt. 1, st. 9–10; pt. 2, st. 32–35).

Yet *The Wreck of the Deutschland*, albeit that its form originates in the design of Jesuit meditation, is also poetry. Hopkins is particularly anxious—perhaps too anxious—to affirm within the ode the potential spiritual power of such poetry.

He repeatedly declares in general that spiritual power exists, that the Holy Spirit providentially benefits humankind. The Spirit is known in many forms: in the "fire of stress" burning within a pentitent Jesuit theology student (st. 2, 8); in the "dovewinged" heart of that same young man which "whirled out wings that spell / And fled with a fling of the heart to the heart of the Host" (st. 3, 4–6); or in the "feathers" that were protecting the *Deutschland* dying (st. 12, 5)—even as the feathery Paraclete at first appeared to have turned into "air . . . unkind," in "cursed quarter," "Wind" (st. 13, 4, 6). This poem declares that in all these forms, even the harsh ones, the Holy Spirit works out human good.

Yet the poem also is zealous to announce that the Logos Christ, the Word, is especially active within committed spiritual utterers of words—like the nun on the *Deutschland* who as a Christ-affirming "prophetess towered in the tumult," whose "virginal tongue told" (st. 17, 8); or like the Jesuit trainee who, when he heard about her, was moved to his own ecstatic utterances of would-be prophetic poetry. He then expressed how overpowering was the musical emergence of this message her action impelled him to share, a message that united him not only with her but with the Logos Christ who reaches both forward to a "Never-eldering revel" of heavenly eternity and (because he "rides time like riding a river") backward to Creation's "river of youth" (st. 18, 7):

>   Ah, touched in your bower of bone,
>   Are you! turned for an exquisite smart,
>   Have you! make words break from me here all alone,
>   Do you!—mother of being in me, heart.
>   O unteachably after evil, but uttering truth,
>   Why tears! is it? tears; such a melting, a madrigal start!
>   Never-eldering revel and river of youth,
> What can it be, this glee? the good you have there of your own?
>
>   Sister, a sister calling
>   A master, her master and mine!—
>   And the inboard seas run swirling and hawling;
>   The rash smart sloggering brine
>   Blinds her; but she that weather sees one thing, one;
>   Has one fetch in her: she rears herself to divine
>   Ears, and the call of the tall nun
> To the men in the tops and the tackle rode over the storm's
>   brawling.
>
>   (st. 18–19)

To Hopkins the nun's essential symbolic value is that she could read, and speak, the power of Christ the Logos, a power which has been making "triumph" (st. 28, 8) even out of this cataclysm:

>   Ah! there was a heart right! ·
>   There was single eye!
>   Read the unshapeable shock night
>   And knew the who and the why;
>   Wording it how but by him that present and past,
>   Heaven and earth are word of, worded by?
>
>   (st. 29, 1–6)

We find that in presenting the nun's power to *speak* Christ, Hopkins describes her as also able to bring Christ to birth in her soul. Hopkins's own "heart" he had already seen earlier in the ode as a "mother of being" (st. 18, 4). Thus *The Wreck of the Deutschland* is making use of Origenian imagery that Hopkins must have encountered in his Oxford reading of Origen's work a decade earlier.[31] Such imagery, arguing how Christ can germinate in the human soul, later abounds, although with a different emphasis, in "The Blessed Virgin" and subsequent Hopkins poems of the 1880s. Here, in stanza 30 of *The Wreck*, Hopkins muses upon the nun's spiritual affinity with the Virgin, whose Immaculate Conception Feast was about to be celebrated:[32]

>   Jesu, maid's son,
>   What was the feast followed the night
>   Thou hadst glory of this nun?—

Feast of the one woman without stain.
For so conceived, *so to conceive thee is done;*
But here was heart-throe, birth of a brain,
Word, that heard and kept thee and *uttered thee outright.*

(st. 30, 2–8; emphases mine)

The Christ-ravished German religious sister (3–4), in her powerful as-
senting to "glory" with Christ, indeed becomes both Christic and
Marian; thus she can give Christ "new birth" in her mind. She also
seems able to bear additional Christic progeny, by "Startl[ing] . . . back"
to religious attentiveness (st. 31, 8) all others, including the otherwise-
damned, who are dying with her in the *Deutschland* disaster. The
fullsomely sacramental storm thus might be a new Christic incarnation,
and the Eucharistic grain of a new Christic Passion, *and* Christ's baptism of the lost as well: "the breast of the / Maiden could obey so, be a
bell to, ring of it, and / Startle the poor sheep back! Is the shipwreck
then a harvest, does tempest carry the grain for thee?" (st. 31, 6–8).

The Word has, it seems, been now more fully revealed than before
through the magical power (to Hopkins, the Really Present sacramental
power) of human words. "Wrack" means, in one old definition, "marine
vegetation, seaweed or the like, cast ashore by the waves or growing on
the tidal seashore" (*OED*). The "shipwrack" therefore can be interpreted
as not only shipwreck "rubbish" (*OED*), but also, at least in etymological potential, as a "harvest" of spiritual vegetation on the sea
(*Wreck*, st. 31, 8).

And so, when Hopkins, with his faith in the Word, has speculated
that the nun's faithful wording of the Logos may have saved the souls of
the company who died with her, he proclaims, "Now burn, new born to
the world, / Double-naturèd name, / The heaven-flung, heart-fleshed,
maiden-furled / Miracle-in-Mary-of-flame" (st. 34, 1–4). He assumes
that the nun, voicing the birth of Christ in her mind and heart, might
spur conviction of their need for salvation in Englishmen who hear of
her at even some temporal distance from her death. Some who might be
convinced are Hopkins's potential readers. Thus "Now burn, new born
. . ." is Hopkins's own striving to duplicate her salvific calling upon
Christ.

Such firm faith as the nun exclaimed, upon seeing her "fetch" of
Christ, allowed her to perform, according to Hopkins's evident interpretation of her act, the priestly functions for a sacramental baptism of the
doomed seagoers. She brought into their consciousness "Our passion-
plungèd giant risen, / The Christ of the Father compassionate, *fetched* in
the [baptismal] storm of the strides" (st. 33, 7–8; emphasis mine). And
so, by analogy, Hopkins at the poem's end tries to summon a baptism
into Roman Catholicism for all of England. He very directly, therefore,

imitates, with the use of the word "King" ("Our King back, Oh, upon English souls!" [st. 35, 4]), the lexicon, although not the pulse, of the nun's stammering call on Christ—which, Downes demonstrates, Hopkins as poet could himself only utter stammeringly ("*Ipse*, the only one, Christ, King, Head" [stanza 28, 5; emphasis mine]).

Downes contends that this earlier stammering pulse of the nun's poetically repeated cry proves "Hopkins' affirmation of the limits of poetry.[33] Yet there is marked incongruity between such supposed affirming "of [poetic] limits" and the final stanza of this ode, written in a confidently nonstammering rhythm and attempting to use poetry as if to evoke priestly baptism for an entire nation. Poetry's only limit for Hopkins, at this point, seems its inability to baptize *literally*.

When Hopkins later uses similar Christic germination imagery in his poems after 1883, he does so with much-increased poetic humility. The poems after 1885, in particular, show Hopkins's "heart-throe" as much less assertive than this "birth of a brain." They do not seek to cleanse all of England from sin, but simply try to rebaptize, and again to reconfirm, one Hopkinsian persona into Christianity (for Hopkins may then himself nearly have reached, like the nun here, a cliff edge of potential destruction—in his case, through emotional and physical exhaustion leading to despondency).

Surely, like these later Hopkins poems, *The Wreck of the Deutschland* is a composition rich in emotional expressions and splendid phrasing. But at the core it frequently seems an intellectually motivated poem of the Miltonic type, one that attempts conceptually to vindicate God's ways with poets and with the cosmos. In his tender but firm critique of this *Wreckster* Hopkins, Boyle remarks that the young Jesuit in his 1870s poems sounds confident about being himself fully allied with the creative power of the Holy Spirit, whom he repeatedly sketches as a Miltonic massive bird.[34] His later bird images of the Spirit, Boyle observes, are both smaller and more distant from him; he thus ceases to appear so brash as to consider his spiritual inspiration automatic and inevitably successful.[35] The later Hopkins is indeed less Miltonic than Dantesque, clearly testing concepts of faith against experience. Yet in *The Wreck*, concepts seem more self-sufficient, despite textual references to Hopkins's life in Wales. The poet, to be sure, does already use "vein-water metaphors," Virginia Ellis notes,[36] thus revealing sacramental commitment to personal baptism and to Christic indwelling within his inner Eucharistic veins. Yet his imaged bird still seems "infinit[e]" in size, like his *confidence*.[37]

The Hopkins of 1876–77, therefore, seems a poet who may trust a bit excessively in the inherent sacramentalism of words and thus also exaggerate any potential priestly powers that poetry has. On the other hand, both *The Wreck of the Deutschland* and "The Lantern out of Doors" do themselves argue for priestly, and general human, sacramental duties that constitute something more than poetic power, however much such poems exalt and revel in the aesthetic act. To Hopkins, sacrificial love for one's fellows, like that love he attributes as motive for the nun's salvific "call" to Christ, is the highest earthly "calling." Sacrificial love for humankind, after all, is, according to both these poems, the calling of Christ himself.

B. Instress, Inscape, and Incarnation: Hopkins's Wales Nature Sonnets

According to "The Lantern out of Doors," all folk may sense Christ as Savior; occasionally, according to Hopkins's Wales nature sonnets, they all would seem ready to call Christ earth's Creator. When just beginning his two-year Jesuit novitiate, however, in 1868, Hopkins would not have so daringly asserted such propositions. On 13 June 1868, he wrote to E. W. Urquhart, "The difference between a state of grace and a state of reprobation, that difference to wh[ich] all other differences of humanity are as the splitting of straws, makes no change in the outer world; faces, streets, and sunlight look just the same: it is therefore the more dangerous and terrible."[38] Even Christian conversion does not really change one's perception of nature, he says here, for nature, as perceived by *all* persons, is fairly frightening, if not "terrible."

For several years following his Jesuit studies at Stonyhurst, nature to Hopkins rarely seemed at all "terrible." At Stonyhurst, after all, "At a time when there were perhaps only two Scotists in England [J, 249], Hopkins discovered [Duns] Scotus for himself . . . through studying a valuable volume [that the Stonyhurst Jesuits] had recently acquired . . . Scotus's *Opus Oxoniense.* . . . Despite its formidable black-letter Latin text, bristling with abbreviations, Hopkins not merely understood it, but became 'flush with a new stroke of enthusiasm' [J, 221]."[39] Hopkins the Jesuit student—who had exulted, even while he remained an Anglican Oxford undergraduate, in the message of Paul to the Colossians that Christ was "creator and end of all things"—now found that in Scotus's philosophy "the personification of nature was Christ," because "nature was a real being which originated in the mind of God as an idea . . . ." He learned, too, that "Scotus allowed for . . . a kind of visionary sense experience" with "insights . . . into the . . . order of nature."[40] It surely appears definite that Scotus aided Hopkins to sense more fully that nature could reveal God—if not "*per se*," at least "*per participationem*";[41] both men sensed that nature could be—at least in some sense—God's visible sign. Thus, after he read Scotus, the earth often became to Hopkins a place "where the land and the sky are greetings the Savior flings to the seeing beholder."[42] And thereby Hopkins's more-than-Romantic "vision" could trade "tentative questioning for dogmatic knowledge, but los[t] . . . none of the delight and wonder" that gave the Romantics before him "marvellous hints that man is not alone in the universe."[43]

Many of the 1870s poems center on visible signs within nature of the fully processed Christic Incarnation of "Great Sacrifice." These particular poems were almost all written while Hopkins found himself surrounded by the natural loveliness surrounding Saint Beuno's in rural Wales, where he underwent his theologate from 1874 to 1877.[44] And they are often magnificent poems.

They are not so, however, because they reveal Hopkins as this-worldly, affirming without reserve some immanent deity in every natural thing; Miller, at least, often seems anxious to treat them as quasi-pantheist declarations. Nor do these works deserve Robinson's contrasting overly zealous condemnation on the charge that they display "fancifulness."[45] Robinson, instead, deserves much of the disdain he receives from Downes, a disdain that could perhaps be extended to the secularizing arguments of Miller. Downes writes forcefully that "the [1870s] poems face the reader with unabashed celebrations of 'Christscapes' in the real world; take it or leave it, that's what they talk about."[46]

Yet Miller and Robinson are not altogether to be blamed for misreading the poems as either pantheistic affirmations of all life or as excessively blissful celebrations of what is in reality an often-harsh nature. Perhaps Hopkins himself sometimes took his imagined readers' spiritual perceptiveness for granted, as "The Lantern out of Doors" would seem to have indicated. And in explicating his lyrics, critics have not always demonstrated, so specifically as they might have, the ways in which he mixes a continued belief in human and even natural Fall with his radical faith that Christ's Real Presence also lovingly penetrates natural vistas. Rarely do we find critical awareness that even to Scotus nature only reflected Christ "per participationem."[47] In addition, we rarely find critics fully diagraming the cues Hopkins poetically provides to signal our attention past creaturehood itself to the other steps in Christ's "great sacrifice"—historical incarnation, salvific crucifixion, and an eschaton of ultimate cosmic victory. In Hopkins's perspective, however, we must understand these stages to the full heroic Christic Incarnation before we can ever appropriate for ourselves that portion of Edenic Christic creaturehood which nature still reveals.

Hopkins's published explicators often too blithely assume that the poet's readers will clearly discriminate between Christic Eden and modern signs of the Fall in nature; but the explicators also have often delineated such differences. Mariani, whose work of explication is so sizable and helpful, sees the "strain of the earth's sweet being in the beginning / In Eden garden" ("Spring," 10–11) as "a strain, a fragment of what nature was before the Fall (for even Christ's Redemption did not restore nature to the beauty of God's first kingdom)."[48] Meanwhile, Sulloway's ability to see the bird of "The Windhover" as partly Luciferian especially provides important cautionary focus as one interprets this sonnet.[49]

Downes also has been of aid to Hopkins students, telling us meaningfully that "Natural landscapes" for Hopkins "become beatific landscapes only by virtue of the experience of faith."[50] And Downes also counters Miller's overemphasis on the immanent by reminding us that Ruskin, who is now firmly acknowledged (by Sulloway, Patricia Ball, Bump, Johnson, Harris) as one of Hopkins's major influences from mainstream Victorianism, often "lament[ed] the absence" among Victorian artists of "esthetic expressions of . . . *transcendency*."[51]

Downes's most helpful analysis comes when he sets into proper perspective the ideas of Hopkins's sonnet "The Caged Skylark":

As a dare-gale skylark scanted in a dull cage
  Man's mounting spirit in his bone-house, mean house, dwells—
  That bird beyond the remembering his free fells;
This in drudgery, day-labouring-out life's age.

Though aloft on turf or perch or poor low stage,
  Both sing sometímes the sweetest, sweetest spells,
  Yet both droop deadly sómetimes in their cells
Or wring their barriers in bursts of fear or rage.

Not that the sweet-fowl, song-fowl, needs no rest—
Why, hear him, hear him babble and drop down to his nest,
  But his own nest, wild nest, no prison.

Man's spirit will be flesh-bound when found at best,
But uncumberèd: meadow-down is not distressed
  For a rainbow footing it nor he for his bónes rísen.

Hopkins indeed seems in this poem to be foregrounding by accentuation a theme of earth's drearying limitations upon creatures both human and animal. If at a certain limited number of "sometímes" creaturely voices can chant "the sweetest, sweetest spells" ("The Caged Skylark," 6), in sum ("sómetimes") they "droop deadly . . . in their cells" (7). Against this somber picture he ultimately sets the counterexample of heavenly resurrection, where accented "bónes rísen" (14) triumph over the limitations of an earthly existence that even at its best leaves creatures "distressed" or di-stressed (13). They are on earth intensely stretched in hope up toward this bliss that only Heaven can provide them but at the same time are intensely pressed down by the limiting "barriers" of an earthly "prison" (8, 11). The birds of nature's "free fells" (3) do not, however, demonstrate the same constraints as human beings or unnaturally caged animals, so these free birds are hopeful symbols of a freedom that Heaven can eventually provide even the encaged.

For Hopkins, says Downes, "To ascend to the viewpoint of Creation through choosing Christ involved no rejection of nature or mankind: 'Man's spirit will be fleshbound when found at best / But uncumberèd.'"[52] Careful readers of the poem will know that being "found at best," according to the sonnet's conclusion, is to be radiantly alive not on earth, but in Heaven's eschatological resurrection, in the transformed flesh of believers whose "bónes" have now been "rísen." But just to be sure that readers do not think Hopkins has merely lauded earthly flesh, Downes writes, in a different location, "Time is a rope about one's neck, the body is a weight around one's spirit, and death a chain about one's heart. We are encumbered."[53]

In general, and as an immensely illogical paradox, we have rarely seen fully thorough explications of Hopkins's incredibly dense poetry. This dearth of adequately rigorous explication has been just as true of the 1870s nature poems (Hopkins's most often-anthologized and his most popular work) as of poems from the 1860s and 1880s. Therefore, for all the fine insights that have been offered into Hopkins's work by so many, the existence of much thin critical analysis of his lyrics continues to prove damaging, for it allows unprepared readers of his art to remain only semiprepared. Hopkins's Scotism would not, for instance, so often be treated as if it were mere pantheism if we more often saw how these poems show nature to be God's revelation and yet also his revelation only partially, "per participationem."

For instance, with its surface of lilting language and music, the Wales sonnet "Spring" may tantalize us into saying, as does even such a good reader of Hopkins as Mariani,[54] that it lacks any extensive, "complex underthought." On the contrary, the poem is an amazingly intricate network of theological perspectives upon Christ's "great sacrifice." No mere charming drawing of divinity spilling over into an immanent vernal setting, the fourteen lines verbalize an unsheathing of hidden Real Presence and then invite the reader to participate in this Real Presence through self-sacrifice:

Nothing is so beautiful as Spring—
When weeds, in wheels, shoot long and lovely and lush;

Thrush's eggs look little low heavens, and thrush
Through the echoing timber does so rinse and wring
The ear, it strikes like lightnings to hear him sing;
   The glassy peartree leaves and blooms, they brush
   The descending blue; that blue is all in a rush
With richness; the racing lambs too have fair their fling.

What is all this juice and all this joy?
   A strain of the earth's sweet being in the beginning
In Eden garden.—Have, get, before it cloy,
   Before it cloud, Christ, Lord, and sour with sinning,
Innocent mind and Mayday in girl and boy,
   Most, O maid's child, thy choice and worthy the winning.

Surprisingly, Harris, who often distorts other Hopkins poems, gives some keen aid in uncovering the obscured revelations of this sonnet—without, however, explaining the full Hopkinsian theology. He sees in the sonnet "the radical equation" between creaturehood and Creator that is caused ("Spring," 3) by "the suppression of the simile in 'Thrush's eggs look [like] little low heavens' "; he identifies "blue" (7) as "Mary's color"; he notes that the "echoing timber" (4) recalls the cross by "punning" upon Herbert's "seasoned timber" in "Virtue"; and he reflects that the "glassy peartree" (6) summons to our minds "the perfect crystalline transparency of the New Jerusalem (Revelation 21:18)."[55] Harris's view, if assimilated into a fuller phenomenological study of the poem, helps us to clarify four full heroic stages of what Hopkins (following Duns Scotus) saw as Christ's ongoing sacramental "great sacrifice"—His *self-emptying Creation*, in the Heaven-imaging thrush eggs; his earthly *incarnation*, in the reminder of his mother Mary; his *Crucifixion*, in the "echoing timber" (as well as, Harris believes, in the thrush itself, which "traditionally prefigures" Christ's Passion); his *eschatological cosmic victory* in the sacramental future of the apocalyptic "peartree" image.[56]

Norman White has noted that, on a naturalistic level, Hopkins simply describes the glassy texture of pear tree leaves.[57] But such an observation does not invalidate Harris's perception, in the poem's "glassy peartree leaves" image, of New Jerusalem symbolism. It also does not invalidate the likelihood that Hopkins is adding even more symbolic ambivalence by reminding us that "Both pear and pear tree are popularly associated with lust"[58]—so that they fittingly image a partially tainted creaturehood—but that glass, meanwhile, is medievally associated with the virginal Marian incarnation of Christ: "so gleam glides thurt the glas,"[59] through Mary, "as the sonne taketh hire pas / Withoute breche thorghout that glas."[60] Therefore, this one succinct "glassy peartree" image seems actually the Scotist Hopkins's radically medievalist encapsulation in a single picture of the entire Christic Great Sacrifice pattern—the "peartree" reminding us both of lusty *creaturehood* and of the *crucifixion's* tree, while the tree's "glassy" texture calls to mind both Mary's virginal role in Christ's *incarnation* and the illumined New Jerusalem of the *eschaton*.

There is present here another apparent symbol of Christ's earthly Incarnation, as the "racing lambs [like the Agnus Dei in his earthly career] have fair their fling" ("Spring," 8). Yet one would hardly call Christ's earthly life a "fling"; these lambs therefore do not seem to remember Hebrew ritual tradition or to sense their oneness with Christ as offering in an atoning sacrifice. Thus we come, in this climactic line of the sonnet's octave, to realize—as we can, indeed, throughout the poem—that nature by itself is an imperfect or unfulfilled sacrament (indeed, it could by itself not be a sacrament at all).[61] Hopkins, like Augustine, believes Christ to be "the only true 'similitudo' because His relation to God is one of genuine 'simultaneity' . . . outside of time."[62] And it is for that reason that, as the priestly narrator asks what all the apparently merely "fling[ing]" "juice and . . . joy" in nature ("Spring," 7–8) really mean, he answers that their *outward* . . . *sign* hints at a deeper *inward* . . . *grace*, the grace of Christ. That grace, and not nature, we must spiritually appropriate for the welfare of our souls. To reiterate the all-important principles offered by Downes, ". . . [W]hile in Christian consciousness, the Incarnation permeates all of Creation, as its source and exemplar . . . yet Christ as the second person of the Holy Trinity calls for a supernatural faith"; "Creation is finite"; "[there is] ontological evil in nature."[63] And it is, we thus see, only for the Christian faithful that the "juice," "joy[ous]" of nature ("Spring," 9) will ultimately accompany this poem's Augustinian "kernel" of Christic revelation, serving as true spiritual "new wine" for a sacramental Eucharist (Acts 2:12–21).

"Spring" truly conveys an appropriate sense that nature by itself cannot reveal fully its sacramental source. The quasi-Edenic "thrush" song, to be sure, "strikes like [painful, even punitive] lightnings" ("Spring," 5) upon the sin-tainted human hearer; it provides him or her a harsh, but purificatory, therapy for innate human disease, when it "does so rinse and wring / The [disease-packed?] ear" (4–5). But "Spring" also asserts that nature itself is postlapsarian; a distilled "strain" (10) of now-lost Edenic purity in nature is now "strain[ing]" (aspiring and struggling) back toward a lost creational splendor:

> For the creature was made subject to vanity, not willingly, but by reason of him who hath subjected the same in hope, / . . . [and] the whole creation groaneth and travaileth in pain together until now. /

And not only they, but ourselves also, which have the firstfruits of the Spirit, even we ourselves groan within ourselves, waiting for the adoption, to wit, the redemption of our body. (Romans 8:20, 22–23)

In order, therefore, to understand the sacramental message that nature can give, it would seem that one already needs to know, outside nature's own limited context, something about both the pure creational splendor of the original Eden and the prophesied "redemption" of earthly "bod[ies]" in the New Eden of Heaven.

Yet few theologically astute readers would claim that Hopkins's "Spring" does not complexly affirm a rather orthodox view that Christian sacrament calls its participants to recall, and to embrace through sacrificial life, the whole of heilsgeschichte (Scotus's and Hopkins's departure from tradition comes in their fervor to extend the sacramentally recalled holy history back as far as the Edenic Creation). I would read the multileveled semantics of the last four lines in "Spring" as richly extending their lexicon so as simultaneously to recall Eden and to predict Apocalypse in imperative words of Eucharistic invitation:

[Know that you partly innately] have, [know that you must] [re-]get [in all fullness, through redeeming penance], Christ, [the] lord [of Genesis creation] before it cloy[ed, or proved excessively rich in spirituality for temptable human beings to handle], before it cloud[ed over with postlapsarian deficiencies], and sour[ed] with sinning [;] [this Edenic creaturehood was then the] innocent mind and [Mary's] day [of Christic incarnation] in [now too-often lusty] Mayday['s] girl and boy[;] [this Christic creaturehood-innocence is] most, O maid's child [Christ *and* girl and boy], thy choice, and worthy the winning [through your divine-human partnership in imitatio Christi].

or

[Do make certain to] have, get, before it cloy [prove excessively sin-tainted], before it cloud [over at the eschaton, the Judgment Day], and sour with [human] sinning, [the Christic] innocent mind and [Mary's] day that remains] in girl and boy [who are now young, as Mary's incarnate God-son once also was] [;] [the redeemed creaturehood of the eschatological Resurrection is] most, O maid's child [Christ *and* girl and boy], thy choice, and worthy the winning [through your divine-human partnership in imitatio Christi].

"Spring" can guide prepared readers to Christ-imitative self-sacrifice, for it suggests to them how spiritually rich the Creation of the Logos once was, how it has become tainted by the Fall, how its redemption was begun through the earthly ministry and passional atonement of Christ, and how that redemption will only be seen fully at the Judgment seat of the same Christ.

Few of the Wales sonnets strive to realize such a completed picture of Christian sacramentalism as this. In "God's Grandeur," however, we can almost, but not easily, see Christ, the victor hero of *incarnation's* Palm Sunday and *eschaton's* day of Judgment, in the "shining from shook foil" of the second line; and his *Crucifixion*, too, is suggested (as the Mount of Olives turned to the hill of Golgotha) when the passional "charge" of atoning pain in a post-Edenic world ("God's Grandeur," 1) "gathers to a greatness, like the ooze of [olive] oil / Crushed" (God's Grandeur," 3–4). Yet Christic presence in *creaturehood* is what is most obvious: "never spent" nature, with "dearest [Edenic] freshness deep down," is "bent" (both in prayer and in post-Edenic shame for imperfection) while the Holy Ghost "broods" over it (9–14). As Harris tells us, the poem also reminds us of an earlier, more reverent human creaturehood: Moses's foot was not "shod" as he met God's theophany in the "flame" of the Burning Bush ("God's Grandeur," 2, 8). [64] And the references to both "flame" and "Holy Ghost," at opening and close of poem, place us, as Harris hints,[65] within a post-Pentecost context prior to Judgment where it is appropriate to request our sacramentally reverent response, as Hopkins does already in the fourth line: "Why do men *then now* not reck [God's] rod?"[66]

Hopkins does not, however, place hints of the full Great Sacrifice into the imagery of all the Wales sonnets. They do not all fully mimic both the inner spiritual and the outer visible contours of a complete Christian sacramental vessel. Neither "The Sea and the Skylark" nor "In the Valley of the Elwy," for instance, offers strong images of Christ's earthly Incarnation or Crucifixion.[67] These two works also do not directly ask readers to become sacramental respondents to their pictured nature scenes. In these poems creaturehood puts human beings to shame by reminding them of how Adamic sin imposed on creation Noah's "flood" as a punitive consequence of Edenic "fall" ("The Sea and the Skylark," 3) and of how a "lark" essentially stones its sinful hearers with "pelt music" (5–8) that in its beauty so much contrasts with Darwinian overemphasis upon our human origins in "slime" ("The Sea and the Skylark," 14). Meanwhile, "Only the [human] inmate does not correspond" to the loveliness innate in rural Wales ("In the Valley of the Elwy," 9–11). The exclamation of Hopkins's volta line (9) in the first poem—"How these two [sea and lark] shame this shallow and frail town!"—might be inscribed in order to prick feelings of guilt in its percipient. Yet the line does not imperatively ask him or her to participate in sacrament through acts of contrite confession and sacrifice. The structure of the poem is more strictly limited to Hopkins's originating structure of Ignatian meditation,[68] or at least limited to its first two stages (*composition of place* in the octave, *moral analysis* in the sestet).

"In the Valley of the Elwy" even more completely focuses the Ignatian meditative pattern, moving from *composition of place* in the octave to *moral analysis* in the first tercet, and on to *colloquy* with God in the final tercet: "God, lover of souls, swaying considerate scales, / Complete thy creature dear O where it fails, / Being mighty a master, being a father and fond" ("Elwy," 12–14). These two Hopkinsian nature sonnets are primarily didactic in function, not imitative of sacramental ritual. In liturgical terms, they might be called homilies.

"Hurrahing in Harvest," in its particular use of Ignatian meditative structure, does exemplify how at least one Christian responds to the sacramental experience of Christic nature. In the opening *composition of place*, prayerfully peaked "stooks" of piled harvested grain ("Hurrahing in Harvest," 1) capture the speaker's attention so that he, "walk[ing], lift[s] up [his shoulders] . . . lift[s] up heart, eyes" ("Hurrahing in Harvest," 5) to see, during his *moral analysis*, the Real Presence of both Christ's Incarnation and his crucifixional Bread of Life. This Real Presence seems actually prepared for all who might view the scene; it is a "meal-drift moulded ever and melted across [in the] skies" (4; interpolation and emphasis mine). But we know through this poem only about how one person's physical vision and emotively stirred "heart" (5)—once they are made attentive to the scene—can perceive Christ even more intensely in the Christic creaturehood of "windwalks!" (2), which suggest the presence in "wind" of the Holy Spirit, and "silk-sack clouds!" (3), which suggest Christ's richly garbed ascended presence beyond them. This sky scene, however, does capture for that one speaker a memory of Christ, present to his disciples before the Ascension occurred, and reveals even the eschatological love of a Christ who is eternity's "round[ing]" Alpha and Omega:

I walk, I lift up, I lift up heart, eyes
Down all that glory in the heavens to glean our Saviour;
And, éyes, heárt, what looks, what lips yet gave you a
Rapturous love's greeting of realer, of rounder replies?

(5–8)

Thus the persona, who needed to lift his own shoulders in order to see this sky panorama, notices further signs of Christic creaturehood in the "azurous hung hills [that] are his world-wielding shoulder / Majestic—as a stallion stalwart, very-violet-sweet!" (9–10). He now realizes that the sequence of events depicted has proved that "These things, these things were here and but the beholder / Wanting" (11–12). He, the beholder, is now not "wanting" of a self-sacrificial spirit, without which he would never be a proper sacramental "beholder." He worships, in sacramental *colloquy* with Christ, and in doing so he rises as if to the sky with wings, like a bird that is offspring of the inspiring Paraclete. He feels enabled even to imitate the Atlas-like power of Christ, because the ingesting of the sacramental food of nature has refreshed him with Christ's nourishment. Thus "The heart rears wings bold and bolder / And hurls for him, O [Omega] half hurls earth for him off under his feet" (13–14).

"Hurrahing in Harvest," therefore, does demonstrate one speaker's sacramental response to "barbarous" autumnal "beauty" (1). This beauty is so spectacular that it seems, and is declared by the poem to be, "barbarous[ly]" otherworldly, or foreign to the earth as we usually know it (OED). The speaker himself recognizes how the "barbarous" natural wonders suggest his need to aspire beyond earth, the some-times-barbaric imperfection of which still is demonstrated by the ser-pentine sinuousness of the "wilful-wavier" clouds (3). Those clouds reveal a "drift" toward a Fall[69]—even in natural symbols that partly symbolize Christ's Eucharistic "Meal" (4).

This speaker *presents*, then, his own example of sacramental rever-ence, but he *does not command* the reader to follow his sacramental example, as in "Spring," or *question* why the reader does not follow that example, in the stern querying style of the speaker for "God's Grandeur." The general originating Ignatian meditative pattern serves several different functions in Hopkins's 1877 sonnets. Four poems are ultimately mere didactic homilies ("In the Valley of the Elwy," "The Sea and the Skylark," "The Caged Skylark," and "The Lantern out of Doors"). Three may attempt full-bodied imitations of Eucharistic cere-mony ("God's Grandeur," "Spring," and "The Starlight Night"). Three poems are hymnic psalms ("Pied Beauty," "The Windhover," and "Hur-rahing in Harvest"). Just as the origin of all the poems in meditation does not make them all mere meditation, so, also the creation of would-be rituals of baptism in the most sizable Wales poem, The Wreck of the Deutschland, does not mean that all Hopkins's poems of that era operate at such an elevated sacramental intensity.

Yet "The Starlight Night" does seek to operate with such intensity. Because it is, however, on the surface so argumentatively aggressive, and yet underneath so argumentatively subtle, it is no wonder that it greatly perplexes some critics. More than "Spring" and "God's Gran-deur," this poem seems to test average readers' patience; its lengthy exclamatory presentation of a beautiful external scene may not imme-diately and forthrightly enough convince them of any need to respond to it with the self-sacrifice Hopkins commands of them.

The poem's originating seven-line Ignatian *composition of place* is, after all, not very precisely Christic in symbolism, and not all readers are aware of Dante's starlight saints in Paradiso:

Look at the stars! look, look up at the skies!
O look at all the fire-folk sitting in the air!
The bright boroughs, the circle-citadels there!
Down in dim woods the diamond delves! the elves'-eyes!
The grey lawns cold where gold, where quickgold lies!
Wind-beat whitebeam! airy abeles set on a flare!
Flake-doves sent floating forth at a farmyard scare!

It might well seem to an average neophyte reader as if Hopkins wanted to produce confusion through what Robinson observes here as "fancifulness"[70]—to enact the playful role of a Rimbaudian esoteric symbolist, encoding a secret message and defiantly announcing "J'ai seul la clef de cette parade sauvage" (Rimbaud, "Parade," final paragraph). Then, in the brief two-line Ignatian *moral analysis*, he would shock them out of their first confused queryings and into new ones: "Ah well! it is all a purchase, all is a prize. / Buy then! bid then!—What?—Prayer, patience, alms, vows" ("The Starlight Night," 8–9). Finally, he would return to clear Christic imagery and explain that all the excitement of the opening, indeed, resulted from its having been a sacramental experience deserving "alms" and "vows" in response.

It is true that in the poem's last segment the exclamations cannot be mistaken as mere aesthetic exuberance; indeed, they appear to result from actual theophanies. "Look look: a May-mess, like on orchard-boughs!" (10) exudes enthusiasms for nature perceptions of *incarnation* (an event bred within "May" or Mary"), of the *Crucifixion* (an event celebrated with thanksgiving in the "mess" or mass of Christ), and of Christic *creaturehood* (a quality once possessed even more fully in the original Edenic "orchard boughs"). "Look! March-bloom, like on mealed-with-yellow sallows!" recalls the *Crucifixion* again—with its reference to March, the month of Lent that prepares us for Christ's Bread of Life oblation.[71] And the same poetic line also attests to the Christic *creaturehood* by which Christ's Eucharistic nutriment seems reflected in the bread-grain color of a willow, a tree often associated with sorrow such as that Christ knew.

Now an ultimate tercet concludes with another rapt theophanic experience of Ignatian meditative *colloquy*, as the speaker fully encounters the Christic panorama before him:

These are indeed the barn; withindoors house
The shocks. This piece-bright paling shuts the spouse
    Christ home, Christ and his mother and all his hallows.

(12–14)

Here we cannot mistake what we intuited earlier, that "the fire-folk" (2) are Pentecostal (and Dantesque) saints, fortressed in the "circle-citadels" (3) of divinely rounded eschatology. They have been sanctified by the dovelike spirit of the Paraclete, becoming his "Flake-doves" (7). Surpassing fallen Eden's "farmyard scare" (7), they now themselves embody Really Present altarbread, in Heaven's New Edenic sacristy.

Imagery in "The Starlight Night" thus does call forth Hopkin's typical vision of the quadrupled Great Sacrifice of Christ, memorably visible in earth's phenomena. Once we comprehend that the poet seeks to draw us slowly into a full understanding of the scene's meaning—that he does not fiercely force it upon us from the first upward-looking outburst, nor even exclaim like a naïf out of "an excited urgency of desire that others perceive the spiritual emblems he loves"[72]—we, even if non-Christian ourselves, need not complain, as does Robinson, that the poem's speaker asks too insistingly of us this "exchange of prayers for beauty."[73]

Unfortunately, the poem as would-be assertive sacrament still does not have the same level of argumentative tension as its model, identified by Edward Proffitt as George Herbert's "The Church Porch."[74] Herbert uses six lines to turn his readers from their false judgment that all important earthly purchasing is materialistic; the Anglican Metaphysical writer prepares fairly carefully for announcing humanity's contrasted spiritual need to purchase the stars of God. Hopkin's volta—his first moral analysis, which proposes to convince the reader of his or her spiritual need—only briefly endures during the eighth and ninth lines. Hence, even if Hopkins has created a far more beautiful artifact than has Herbert, as a would-be nineteenth-century sacramental poet he shows much less concern than did his seventeenth-century predecessor to communicate clear reasons requiring readers to participate in sacramental action. And yet the poem does command its audience to such action. If they (like Robinson) are not of a religious cast of mind, they may consider this scene "free" to everyone.[75]

Thus, at the very least, "The Starlight Night" is audacious, aesthetically daring, not so simple as it initially looks.[76] It is a "fusion" of its author's "words" and his "self"—as Hopkins "knew all his art to be," says Downes:[77] "He understood," at least in his later years, "how easy it was to succumb to admiring the design of the [aesthetic] creator rather than the mark of the [cosmic] Creator."[78] And, indeed, in the case of Hopkin's "The Starlight Night," the "design of the [aesthetic] creator," Hopkins, may have inscribed a text that requires so much sympathy with the author and his message that it may always—at least in those first puzzling exclamations in their lengthy litanic listing—offend at least those nonbelievers, like Robinson, who have a more somber vision of life. Downes attacks Robinson for not "trying to see objectively the phenomenology of [Hopkins's] religious experience in his poetry,"[79] but he might also question Hopkins himself for "confus[ing] the artist of God" with the sacramentally officiant "priest of God."[80] This poem's would-be priest has not carefully motivated the self-sacrifice he wishes to evoke in readers. He has forgotten Origen's own warning[81] that most persons are not gifted, as is Hopkins, with an anagogical imagination and its mystical perceptions of theophanous sacrament in all natural things. He has not, therefore, done as he did in "Spring" and "God's Grandeur": he has not spoken to his would-be sacramental congregation in terms they can understand; he has not made the natural vista remind them clearly of their need to repent from sin.[82]

Downes elsewhere reminds readers that a "predisposition" to serve God "does not preclude literary talent [,] as parts of the Bible make abundantly clear."[83] One assumes that Downes is referring, at least partly, to the Psalms. Hopkins as religious poet did perhaps learn from their example, but not in "The Starlight Night." In "God's Grandeur," Peter Milward says that he sees Hopkins simply imitating the psalmists in his vision of God's glory "ring[ing a] . . . symphony of creation."[84] Yet Milward does not note how even that poem, quite unlike the Psalms of Scripture, asks percipients of a natural scene to perceive it not only as a "symphony," but also as a sacrament calling them to self-sacrifice.

Once we examine their writings as sources, we see that the psalmists of the Scriptures consider the physical world as God's reflection, but that they rarely treat the world as a sacrament which by infusing grace into humankind initiates sacrificial response. Only twelve out of 150 psalms can be classified even as primarily hymns of praise to God as universal architect.[85] In only a few of these, besides, does the hymnist suggest that one should become God's sacrificial servant out of sacramental reverence for the beauty of the universe. And all but one of the references to sacrificial action are quite vague.

Psalm 19 (Psalm 18 in the Douay version) perhaps argues by implication (although surely not overtly) that, because "The heavens are telling the glory of God," we should learn to follow the holy ways of that God, whose "commandment" is "enlightening the eyes" of humankind, even perhaps as we regard nature (vv. 1, 8). Psalm 24 (Psalm 23—Douay) states that "the earth is the Lord's" (v. 1) and then—by a possible, but only implicit, linkage of thought—that one should respond with "clean hands and a pure heart" (vv. 3–4). The writer of Psalm 145 (Psalm 144–Douay), like the writer of Psalm 104 (Psalm 103–Douay), pledges meditation, although not sacramental sacrifice specifically, as his response to divinity in nature: "On the glorious splendour of thy majesty, and on thy wondrous works, I will meditate" (Psalm 145:5).

Only in Psalm 95 (Psalm 94 in the Douay version), beginning with the statement that "in [God's] hand are the depths of the earth; the heights of the mountains are his also" (v. 4), does the psalmist extend his message naturally to a liturgically sacramental invitation: "O come let us worship and bow down, let us kneel before the Lord, our Maker!" (v. 6). Then he grows even more desperately insistent: "O that today you would hearken to his voice! / Harden not your hearts, as at Meribah . . ." (vv. 7–8).

Only in this one psalm does the writer's approach to nature and sacrifice resemble that of Hopkins in "The Starlight Night." To the Psalm writers, God's natural handiwork usually is not an "outward and visible sign of an inward and spiritual grace." They do not usually see its manifestations of power and beauty as sufficient evidence that divine "grace" is active therein to prompt human sacrifice. Indeed, even the writer of Psalm 95 seems far less assured than the Hopkins of "The Starlight Night" that persons will respond sacrificially to natural evidence of God.

It is even true that the Psalm writers mostly rely not on the visible signs of outer nature as sacramental testimony to God, but rather on their memories of God's mercy to them as individuals, or on his mercy to the Hebrew nation in its times of trial. Their attention is not primarily directed to God's beautiful natural creation—a visible sign—but to the "grace" of God himself. Hopkins, too, wrote in his journal on 18 August 1874, "As we drove home the stars came out thick: I leant back to look at them and my heart opening more than usual praised our Lord to and in whom all that beauty comes home."[86] The major emphasis here is plainly on an intuition of Christ and on a contemplative aspiration after union with him, and not on any lengthy examination of the original beauty itself. In "The Starlight Night" the emphasis, at least at first, seems to be primarily on the beauty. Perhaps—if the poem wants to do more than to present merely (as it does in the octave) the creational symphony perceived by Scotus, Hopkins, and Milward; if it wants to motivate (in the sestet) a repentant response to sacramental perceptions—it somewhat exceeds, at least for unprepared audiences, its attentiveness to the sky's apparently merely natural signs.

Another of the nature lyrics that Hopkins composed while in Wales is "Pied Beauty," which was composed four to six months after "The Starlight Night." This sonnet appears to correct the other's overextended apparent mimicking of sacrament:

> Glory be to God for dappled things—
>   For skies of couple-colour as a brinded cow;
>   For rose-moles all in stipple upon trout that swim;
>   Fresh-firecoal chestnut-falls; finches' wings;
> Landscape plotted and pieced—fold, fallow, and plough;
>   And áll trádes, their gear and tackle and trim.

All things counter, original, spare, strange;
  Whatever is fickle, freckled (who knows how?)
    With swift, slow; sweet, sour; adazzle, dim;
He fathers-forth whose beauty is past change:
                    Praise Him.

Surely there do exist analogous texts to this one in the biblical Psalms, notably the verse with which those Psalms conclude: "Let everything that breathes praise the Lord! Praise the Lord!" (Psalms 150:6). And for Hopkins the mixture of light and dark tones in nature— "dappled things" ("Pied Beauty," 1)—usually has not led to such cheer. I have already cited his journal entry of the Oxford years[87] in which the phrase series "Distance / Dappled with diminish'd trees / Spann'd with shadow every one" seems, at least symbolically, to define as ominous the mortality tinging nature.

"Pied Beauty" seems, by contrast, not afraid of "dapple . . .," even of the mixed moral light and dark that seems suggested in words like "counter" and "fickle" ("Pied Beauty," 1, 7, 8). Hopkins, seeming temporarily an antinomian, rejoices here even in such beauty, and he is willing for the moment to avoid answering any questions about how moral motley may have come into life. As if to tell the religious skeptics of his own day that even he cannot explain the amorality of Darwinian brute nature with some theory of Original Sin, he proclaims that nature is "fickle, freckled," but "who knows how?" (8).

Yet this question has an answer, which Hopkins offers in this poem. He does not necessarily discount Original Sin, but he points us to God, "who knows how" earth came to be what it is. God is more wondrous than these creatures in their dappled variety—"[his] beauty is past change" (10). Here Hopkins clearly does not want us to judge nature to be innocent and fully able, simply by itself, to motivate sacramental experience. As he announces, "Glory be to God for dappled things" (1), he makes it clear that it is the reflected divine *light* in these creatures, not the companion *darkness*, which allows them to reflect a God whose "glory" is by etymology his "aureole" or "splendor" (*OED*). Yet, at the same time, he asserts that God spreads his light abroad in glimmerings only, because darkness is clouding it on earth, which is, in all sorts of phenomena, both "adazzle" and "dim" simultaneously ("Pied Beauty," 9).

"Pied Beauty" deals fairly and carefully with the meaning of a motley light-and-dark nature. It says that "praise" and "glory" go to God rather than to the things of the world, even while the things of the world are loved (despite whatever flaws they have) because they are his. "Pied Beauty" does not attempt very forcefully to be a sacramental poem.

Content to be a mere "hymn of creation,"[88] like most of the biblical psalms about nature, it also admits earth's partial moral darkness.[89]

Yet Hopkins could not be satisfied with the nature poetry of simple psalmlike praise. He did, I believe, want to write poems that would at least suggest that his readers should not simply praise God, but also, like Hopkins himself, serve him. In "The Windhover," written significantly at a date close to that of "Pied Beauty" and considerably after that of "The Starlight Night," he achieved a psalmlike work which still suggests, although not shouting out, the human need for such sacrificial servanthood. Clearly resembling "Hurrahing in Harvest," another nature sonnet in which psalmic praise results from the speaker's own intense personal willingness to live a sacramental life, "The Windhover" nonetheless diverges from "Hurrahing" by more strongly suggesting that natural objects, like birds of prey, kestrel hawks, can potentially be praised too exuberantly in themselves. If nature is to become a sacramental signal for most of humankind, Hopkins herein hints, natural darkness and imperfection may first need to be foregrounded. Only then may at least some human beings beckon the divine mercy that is the most radiant sacramental light of all.[90]

*   *   *

The Hopkins term *instress* first appears in 1868, already referring to a continuum of related but hierarchically different experiences—some merely sensuous, some suggesting religious or contemplatively spiritual devotion. After visiting the National Gallery on 27 June of that year, Hopkins commented in his notebooks, "Query has not Giotto the instress of loveliness?"[91] He believed the artist had infused a sensuous stress of loveliness into his canvas. Yet in his 1868 essay on Parmenides, Hopkins had already also spoken, metaphysically, about "depth of an instress or how fast the inscape holds a thing," so that "nothing is so pregnant and straightforward to the truth as simple *yes* and *is*."[92] In this essay, Hopkins talks of the profound inbreathing into the world of Being (not yet claimed as Christ's Being). "The depth of [that] instress" (the *yes*) permeates his own being. He has, in other words, "felt the depth" of Being's original instress, as well as his own instressing of the stress left behind. His experience seems spiritual, not a mere meeting of human subject with natural object, but a meeting, through the object, of two subjects: a man and the Being (or God) who created the object. One is reminded of Tintern Abbey's Wordsworth, who, according to Hopkins, had, along with Plato, "seen *something*" in nature.[93]

More precisely than Wordsworth, however, the young Hopkins also states that he had "felt," besides "instress" of subjective spiritual communication, "how fast the inscape holds a thing." He had perceived, he declared, objective Being, the *is*: the inner *scape* or *shape* of all Creation, which belongs to each part of Creation as "inscape."

Etymology suggests two basic meanings for *inscape*, if we study *OED* definitions for *scape*. One definition, the most recent, is a "back-formation from *landscape*," referring to a "view of scenery of any kind." Hence, the discreteness of any individual scene or phenomenon, its innate individuality, seems to be inscape of architectonic *particularity*.

Beyond individuality, however, phenomena contain architectonic *structure* within them, as suggested by the archaic definition of *scape* as "the shaft of a column," or the obsolete definition of *scape* as "the tongue of a balance." These definitions both derive from the Latin and Greek forms *scapus* and σκαπος. The controlling structure of a phenomenon seems its inscape in this sense. As such, says Alan Heuser,[94] an "inscape [emerges as] typical form, the form of the naturalistic ideal . . . a fixed type." Miller[95] indeed believes that for Hopkins this is the usual definition: "that which a number of particulars have in common."

Because of its etymological roots, this latter definition seems related to another suggested etymological source for the term *inscape*, the Latin/Greek *scopus*/σκόπος. Hopkins made note of the etymology "*scopus* / *mark, aim*" in a letter written to Baillie on 10 March 1887.[96] As Cotter notes, Hopkins seems to have believed the essential scope or scopus of things to be that term's old meaning in English, "the person pursued, sought for, and overtaken"—to him "Christ the Alpha and Omega."[97] Thus Hopkins seems to have believed that *structure* and *particularity* of things both bore traces of the ultimate telos, Christ, and that the spiritual, not only physical, purpose of things was inscaped in them.

At the period from 1866 to 1868 when Hopkins was first developing in his journals these concepts of instress and inscape, the most dominant influence upon him, at least as a journal writer, was John Ruskin. Ruskin also seems a likely early influence upon the terms that Hopkins developed, for Ruskin surely found architectonic shaping of both individual and generic sorts in phenomena which were members of a created species. To him "perfection of the creature invariably involve[d] the utmost possible degree of all those properties of beauty, both typical [generic?] and vital [individualized?], which it [was] appointed to possess."[98]

Ruskin's aesthetic philosophy, like Plato's long before him,[99] surely had in itself some affinity with the Scotist idea, later championed by Hopkins, of "being as a common element" in both God and "finite creatures."[100] Ruskin, after all, finds a "necessity of [God's] inherence in all things that be, without which no creature of any kind could hold existence for a moment."[101] To him "there is not any matter, nor any spirit, nor any creature, but it is capable of an unity of some kind with other creatures."[102] He additionally writes that "the unity of matter is, in its noblest form, the organization of it which builds it up into temples for the spirit, and in its lower form, the sweet and strange affinity, which gives to it the glory of its orderly elements. . . ."[103]

Ruskin also often describes natural phenomena with what appear to be delicately subtle religious metaphors implying nature's unity with the Trinitarian Creator. Examples from his prose speak of "sunlight like so many tongues of fire" from the Pentecostal Paraclete;[104] of Christic "resurrection in spirit of . . . new-fallen rain";[105] and perhaps of God the Father's "river-of-paradise blue" in the tinting of the Rhone River.[106] Nevertheless, even if Ruskin indeed intends to link these descriptions to a principle of divine unity in the created world, he is not fully a monist. He writes elsewhere that "every being in a perfect state exhibits certain appearances, or evidences, of happiness,"[107] and yet he certainly does not appear to propose that all creatures on earth dwell in that "perfect state." On the contrary, even if "those [are] most lovely" to him "which are most happy,"[108] he seems to say that none is fully happy in a postlapsarian world. Natural creatures to him have "orders of worthiness and beauty according to the rank and nature of that [moral] lesson [they provide], whether it be of warning or example, of those that wallow [like his example of the "fiend-hunted" Gadarene swine] or of those that soar [like his example of "the dove returning to its ark of rest"]."[109] To John Ruskin, therefore, a partially dualist nature can reflect the moral lessons necessary for a dualist humankind, which also is imperfect and needs "to restore to the body the grace and the power which inherited disease has destroyed, to return to the spirit the purity, and to the intellect the grasp that they had in Paradise."[110] In humankind, especially, Ruskin clearly senses the "immediate and present operation of the Adamite curse."[111]

Hopkin's early notebooks, as if adopting such a dualist theology, often seem to contemplate the moral lessons in spiritually blank or morally somber faces of nature. He remarks, while still at Oxford in 1864, plants called "Snakes'-heads" that appear like "drops of blood."[112] Two years later, he notices "Fields *pinned with daisies*" and "Buds of apple blossoms . . . like *nails of blood*" (emphases mine in both quotations, from journals dated 4 May 1866).[113] Miller judges such details only to describe structural shapings of environmental phenomena.[114] But these passages seem, like the similar passages from Ruskin's prose, inevitably metaphoric—and (given the context from which their metaphors derive) inevitably theological. The same is true of the crow "croaking dolefully" that Hopkins in 1864 sees ominously *"on my left"* (his emphasis).[115] Hopkin's images are strikingly harsh; he seems to suggest, at least in these passages, that the temptation-tinged "Snakes'-heads" or "apple blossoms" of a post-Edenic natural world evoke the "blood" by which Christ ever suffers a repeated Crucifixion. The Hopkins of this early Ruskin-influenced period seems to believe (somewhat like the Calvinist-reared art critic who inspired him) that Christ can still suffer pains in a "dappled" nature which the Devil, crow-imaged, partly owns. The very images of Christ provided by some of these nature scenes do of course at least hint at his sacramental, oblationary presence in "nails of blood" nature, and Hopkins would later be able to utter a more fully positive sacramental response to nature through the 1870s influence of Duns Scotus. Yet there is also evidence that Ruskin, Augustine, Ignatius, and even Scotus gave Hopkins a sense of dualism within his natural theology and that his own sermonic expressions of dualism during the 1880s are not, therefore, sudden returns of a completely extinguished attitude.

For instance, in a diary entry of 31 July 1868, Hopkins writes of traveling to Paris by train and seeing along the train routes "a country of pale grey rocky hills of a strong and simple outscape covered with fields of wormy green vines."[116] The term *outscape* suggests not only the obvious "outer shape," but also the idea that a part of nature (only "pale grey," "rocky," "strong and simple") lacks the spiritual richness held by nature's inscape. By etymology, *outscape* could define that merely physical shaping of nature which, by contrast with inscape, can escape from God's hand (the prefix *es* or *ex-* [*OED*] means "out"). Such outer shaping without blessed inner spirituality may be as if an "inadvertent mistake" in Genesis Creation (based on a definition of *scape* that the *OED* traces to a substantive form of *escape*). Hopkins does speak, in a sermon of 18 January 1880 to which I shall again refer, about that part of Genesis earth which is located outside the bounds of spiritually rich Eden as the "outside earth."[117] Such a scape is "counter," "fickle," perhaps the spiritless dark of dappled creatures as opposed to their spiritual light. Sometimes serpentine (found in "wormy green vines"), it seems to be nature's merely physical outline, while inscape is nature's inner spiritual hint of Christ its Creator—its seeming soul.

It remains true, as Bump has noted,[118] that Hopkins at this time seems also to respond with those more completely positive sacramentalist attitudes toward nature that had been evangelized to their Victorian peers by religious theorists of poetry like John Keble. Keble, for instance, according to G. B. Tennyson, believed "Nature . . . the hand-maiden of theology and at times the vehicle of a sacramental grace that brought man into contact with the divine."[119] Hopkins, who was gradually led by such Tractarian medievalist forerunners to his own greatly superior understanding of authentic medievalist poetics,[120] may none-

theless first have grasped "sacramental symbolism" through them[121]—
although he had been awestruck even earlier by the words of Origen,
that church father who most influentially argued for a "world pervaded
by multivalent types and symbols of the invisible world."[122] Thus,
when in 1872 Hopkins discovered Duns Scotus's "doctrine of the univocity of Being,"[123] the Englishman may gladly have focused upon the
commonality Scotus found between God and creatures who shared in
the category of Being—even though his poems show us that Hopkins
still saw, as did Scotus too, that creatures and their Maker nonetheless
remained vastly different.

Hopkins could early on have gained from Ruskin the admonition that
"Man's use and function . . . [are] to be the witness of the glory of God,
and to advance that glory by his reasonable obedience and resultant
happiness."[124] The reverential Jesuit student, however, was still more
strongly guided toward the goal of "praise, reverence, and serv[ice]" to
God by his commitment to the Loyolan order and its emphasis on these
same spiritual values. And that order's emphasis on its members' forming of vivid pictures when engaged in contemplative meditations[125] is
no doubt the strongest force behind Hopkin's vividly pictorial sacramentalist verse.

Meanwhile, Duns Scotus seems especially to have spurred Hopkins
to write poetry that expresses Scotus's sense of "common" being in
nature and God. In his 1879 poem "Duns Scotus's Oxford" (P, 272),
Hopkins honors Scotus as "of realty the rarest-veinèd unraveller"
("Duns Scotus's Oxford," 12). Scotus, he says, saw divine teleological
control displayed everywhere in creation along with spiritually shaped
physical uniqueness. All unique "real property or estate" (OED definition of realty) was part of ultimate teleological "reality" (another OED
definition of realty) and, most important, as "royal state, dignity, or
power," part of God's kingdom (OED: réalté, réauté). To Scotus, Hopkins
argues, although without his actually using such terms, nature was
surely inscaped (even if outscaped as well).

Hopkin's own search in nature for God's moral wholeness or scopus
had already animated some now-famed journal comments of mid-1870,
in which he had described a particular natural example of inscape. He
surely saw it as "common" with Christ's Being, even though he had not
yet read Duns Scotus: "I do not think I have ever seen anything more
beautiful than the bluebell I have been looking at. I know the beauty of
our Lord by it. It[s inscape] is [mixed of] strength and grace, like an ash
[tree]."[126] In this striking journal entry, Hopkins describes the bluebell's physical peculiarity in detail, even drawing its bell shape. He
does so, however, because he is seeking to define more accurately its
spiritual essence, its structural and moral forces, its "strength and
grace"—physical grace here suggesting spiritual grace. The entire

flower does not only illustrate God's creative power or "strength," but it also displays a "grace" that is like "the beauty of our Lord" and like "an ash [tree]." Hence it perhaps is, if the verbal conjunction of these various terms may suggest something more than what is directly said, a grace known most of all in the love of Christ upon a tree, the love of the Cross.

Most important of all, says Cotter, Hopkins sensed that "Only the pure of heart attain to inscape."[127] Cotter quotes sections from Hopkins's unpublished Campion Hall, Oxford, manuscripts summarizing Aristotle's *Nicomachean Ethics*: "There is an end or object of every course of action," "happiness of all ends."[128] Moral action, rather than mental contemplation, seems the surest route by which human beings can find themselves teleologically in full contact with Creation's scopus: "There must be one end (and only one) to which all the others are subordinate. The knowledge of it will give life an aim, a σκοπόν." Hence, despite the possibility that aesthetic contemplation of inscape can turn into spiritual contemplation of inscape, spiritually purposeful action seems to approach ultimate scape more directly.

Because he wanted to promote in many different potential readers an appropriate sacramental response of such spiritually purposeful action, Hopkins in his Wales sonnet "The Windhover" created an artifact that gauges its lexicon and semantics not only by those readers who, like him, are attuned to an Origenian-Scotist sense of natural sacramentalism—those who see nature as "actually shar[ing] in the presence, the Being of God."[129] At least wishing, I believe, like Saint Paul to be "all things to all men, that [he] might in the end save some" (1 Corinthians 9:22), and probably agreeing with Origen that "only those who were endowed wlith a special 'grace' could achieve the highest spiritual level, the anagogical,"[130] Hopkins created in "The Windhover" a powerful work that could speak sacramental messages both to nearly-monist Origenians and also to stringent dualists. Indeed, this sonnet may seem a work provoking "so many different interpretations . . . that readers are tempted to quit trying to sort them out and simply retreat into pure subjectivism and relativism."[131] Yet "The Windhover" deconstructs rigid interpreting only because it is written in order to cause similar sacramental attitudes of penitent sacrifice in readers of originally different theologies, not because it is a test case for deconstructionist nihilism. No reader is properly greeting it who is not seeing its urgent sacramentalist guiding impulse.[132]

* * *

In "The Windhover," a daring kestrel hawk becomes a striking image, at least, of the architectonically *inscaped* might set at work in God's world. Yet the windhover is also a creature that could be said to have notably *outscaped* spiritual limitations—for it is, after all, a violent bird of prey. The ambivalence between these two attitudes toward the bird provides some of the poem's highly pitched tension. As a univocalist Scotist expression, "The Windhover" seems a testament to the way in which even the bird's preying (but flame-chested) swoop downward reveals in nature transubstantiating Christic Presence. And yet, ambiguous and thus also potentially dualistic language points to the bird's forceful actions in the air as symbols of unredeemed pride. In either interpretation, however, the lyric seems at least to prompt its speaker's receptionist recognition of his personal flaws, so that he responsively renews his dedication to the sacramentally dutiful life.

As this poem opens, the bird, steadying itself in the wind, instresses divine flame upon the landscape and before the speaker's gaze: "I caught this morning morning's minion, king- / dom of daylight's dauphin" ("The Windhover," 1–2). Described partially in the chivalric metaphors emphasized by William Empson, the bird seems to give out flashing light and catch the speaker's eye in order to make that speaker ask "Brute beauty and valour and act" to "here / Buckle!" ("The Windhover," 9–10). The speaker seemingly wants to share the animal's power, gaining it as if by a knightly belt-buckling ceremony.[133]

The great Jesuit Hopkinsian Boyle, in a recently published article, explains this attention to belt-buckling ceremonies much more cogently than did Empson, judging Hopkins's affirmations in this poem to be "deeply in the mood" of "The Kingdom of Christ" meditation from Ignatius Loyola's *Spiritual Exercises*. Boyle writes that "In the Kingdom meditation, or exercise of decision . . . Christ our Lord, in the Jesuit imagination, leads his troops into knightly repulse of the powers of evil. Ignatius thinks of him, somewhat in terms of St. Paul's Letter to the Ephesians, armed and masterful, an invincible leader. Thus the flashing bird, under the oriflamme of the rising sun, mastering the wind, could merge readily in Hopkins' imagination with the Christ the Lord in a vivid and lusty metaphor."[134] Boyle judges that Hopkins "saw himself as the reluctant knight of whom Ignatius speaks in the Exercise: 'if anyone would refuse the invitation of such a king, how justly he would deserve to be condemned by the whole world, and looked upon as an ignoble knight.' " Thus, says Boyle, "when the knightly heart emerges from hiding in 'The Windhover' to do its own desire, to be like the hawk and Christ, its fading fire breaks out into the spreading flames of a dappled dawn, under an oriflamme a billion times told lovelier than the negative cowardly fear which kept him from stirring toward achieve and mastery."[135]

Bump also sees the vision of the windhover causing Hopkins as the poem's speaker to "buckl[e] together all his considerable talents," to "renew . . . his commitment to the *imitatio Christi*," to become a would-be "great knight of faith, one of those who imitate not only the constraint but also the 'achieve of, the mastery of' this great chevalier."[136] And Bump surely captures for us a quite powerful sense of how this bird's very physical movement could reveal to Hopkins that the "Christ of [kenosis] could have remained above the earth, but he chose to swoop down, not to destroy but to save his prey, the hearts of men, to restore them to the kingdom of heaven."[137] One also can interpret the windhover's descent as a revelation of warning that Christ will one day descend to harrow hell, but it is probably more centrally suggested in the sonnet that he comes in the way Bump describes, invading human souls while they are living on earth.[138]

In a reading of this lyric that mixes univocal and dualist perspectives, Warner strongly argues for the bird's necessary alliance with creative Deity, noting how "the particular combination of freedom and bondage that is shown by [its] hovering upon the wind . . . attracts the speaker rather than the kestrel's 'lordly aspect.'"[139] Warner catalogs the many terms of the poem's lexicon that submit the bird to the control of a higher power; these include "minion" ("The Windhover," 1), "dauphin" (2), "rung upon the rein" (4), and "on swing" (5), with its description of a "prescribed pattern" of "pendulum-like movement." He also mentions "the achieve of, the mastery of the thing" (8), which ambivalently refers as much to "being mastered" as to "mastering" with seeming self-assertiveness. Yet Warner also makes clear that the phrase "of the thing" (8) emphasizes the animal's "createdness"; he is thus at least paying attention to Scotist notions of creatures' "intrinsic limitation," or "*carentia entitatis*" of the universal within the individual.[140] Thus, basically, Warner throughout strives to keep the univocal and dualist interpretations in balance. He contends that the sonnet's culminating line, "Fall, gall themselves, and gash gold-vermilion" ("The Windhover," 14), suggests that "the [Satanic?] quest for a false freedom has led to the 'fall,' but . . . through acceptance of his sin and submission to the will of God, man can transform his sin into a joyous affirmation [felix culpa] just as the embers by galling themselves can 'gash gold[-] vermilion.'"[141] Surely the medieval idea of felix culpa does help Scotus,and Hopkins as his follower, to accept sin-tinged nature as still revelatory of divine goodness—still partially reflecting univocity with divine being.

Sulloway and Emily Yoder provide most of the manifest lexical support for a Ruskinian dualist interpretation of "The Windhover." One cannot, I think, fault their provisions of scriptural evidence which suggests that a "king- / dom of daylight's dauphin" ("The Windhover," 1–2) at least partly symbolizes Lucifer—"perfect in beauty" (Ezekiel

28:12);[142] "the prince of the power of the air" (Ephesians 2:2);[143] a spiritually fallen "son of the morning" (Isaiah 14:12–15).[144] After all, the poem ends with a "striding" bird ("The Windhover," 3) forgotten, as Hopkins's speaker attends to "blue-bleak embers" (13), symbols of a Christ who triumphs by self-sacrificial (although inwardly powerful) Passion, rather than by lofty Luciferian self-vaunting.

For Hopkins there was surely Scotist-Origenian relevance in a meditative experience by which he saw the Really Present soldier-Christ transubstantially revealed even in a kestrel hawk; Hopkins could then urge Christ to "Buckle!" his power onto the heart of his human follower (10). Yet there was also relevance for Hopkins, one surmises, in a revelatory sacramental discovery that would be more in keeping with the perceptual limitations of readers who had not "reached the anagogical level" of insight available to him.[145] Readers less mystical than he could still join him in moving through and past the physical vision of the bird's powerful beauty—eventually commanding that beauty to "Buckle!" or to collapse and cease from being their chief focus of attention. They would thus reject "hiding" *from* God—as perhaps excessively rapt admirers of nature's tremulous physical sensations—and accept another sort of "hiding" *with* the lowly (although surely eventually triumphant) Christ—he who self-sacrificially serves others. Indeed, Hopkins was to be ordained to the priesthood only shortly after the time when he wrote this key sonnet;[146] it was perhaps because he wanted meaningfully to serve parishioners in his charge that he later wrote sermons for his congregations which spoke in terms more understandable to them than those of Origenian-Scotist anagogy. Hopkins's parish sermons are full of imagery that treats nature as dualist, fallen.[147]

In a dualist reading of "The Windhover," the bird may at first be seen to reflect as its archetypal "pride" ("The Windhover," 9) the Christ who is to the nun in *The Wreck of the Deutschland* "her pride" (st. 28, 8). But the bird may also prove to symbolize that "pride" which is chief of the postlapsarian world's seven deadly sins, and the verb to "plume" (9) may mean "to . . . pride oneself" *(OED)*.[148] The windhover is described as submissive, to be sure, but it is also described as "striding" (3), a pose often associated with "pomposity" *(OED)*. It cannot by itself claim its full "achieve" ("The Windhover," 8),[149] for it is only a "dauphin" (2) or "provisional heir to the kingdom" *(OED)*. It is also only "morning's minion" (1), or a "favorite" *(OED)*—favored in a potentially pejorative sense, if we think of minions sometimes as foppish or foolish lackeys and sometimes also as courtesans.[150] Thus, if Christ as the Logos or creative Word extended God's Heavenly Kingdom to immanent earth, God, according to this poem's syntax, still seems transcendent in that "king- / dom," his own emphatically stressed dominium.[151] Only if we

instinctively attach the suffix "dom," which Hopkins strongly sepa-
rates, to "minion" as a prefix, can we place the bird even in full
linguistic contact with its divine source. As Warner notes, Hopkins has
always made us see the bird as needing a divine source, the "underneath him steady air" ("The Windhover," 3), to control his "rolling"
with its "level" (3).[152]

Warner thus maintains that the poem does seem to argue for at least
one dualistic contention: "in asserting his freedom, Satan condemned
himself to eternal servitude; in being willing to submit to the will of
God, Christ found 'perfect freedom.' "[153] Yvor Winters once long ago
derided the kestrel hawk as unfit to call forth religious exuberance;
because such birds prey on and devour other animals, he deemed them
less moral than his own prize Airedales.[154] Winters's commentary is
surely glib and probably a bit distant from the issues of the sonnet, yet it
states a salient point about what for most persons would seem the
limited apparent Christlikeness of the poem's strutting kestrel. As Joris-
Karl Huysmans, in 1898 France, noted not many years after Hopkins
wrote this 1877 sonnet, research in medieval bestiaries shows birds
sometimes assigned symbolic identities as "les justes," but also, as in
Boethius, sometimes treated as symbols of "inconstance."[155] Hopkins's
windhover can be read as both "juste" and "inconstan[t]."

Hopkins perhaps expects at least some readers, like Winters, to imagine the bird's acting out actual moral limitations when it plunges down,
at the poem's climax, to devour a victim animal. In its descent, it would
"buckle" its wings.[156] In any case, the poem ends with the speaker's
withdrawing attention from the bird and paying attention to Christ,
who as Herbert's "my dear" ("The Windhover," 13) can be sensed
lustrously ("a billion / Times told lovelier"—10–11) within the
speaker's "heart" (7), as well as in other natural objects humbly located
on the ground.[157]

Hopkins assuredly now has more in mind than simply to see inscape
in everything. He has chosen humbler objects for this tercet than the
kestrel, objects that can inscape, better than the bird can, that humbly
accepted suffering labor through which human beings can share the
Passion of Christ. Yet, through the "gash" of such self-sacrifice, the
"vermilion" blood of the Cross does become beautifully mixed with the
"gold" of God's royal honor;[158] "No wonder of it: shéer plód makes
plough down sillion / Shine, and blue-bleak embers, ah my dear, / Fall,
gall themselves, and gash gold-vermilion" ("The Windhover," 12–14).

In the self-crucifying collapse of "blue-bleak embers," as in "the ooze
of oil / Crushed" ("God's Grandeur," 3–4), the "grandeur of God"
("God's Grandeur," 1) most fully "gathers to a [transubstantial sacrament's] greatness" ("God's Grandeur," 3). Indeed, in the "Windhover"

image of the breaking embers we sense rather obvious sacramental symbolism, as the outer hull of the ember (i.e., the sacramental *species*) breaks apart to reveal the burning coal of the sacramental *substance*, of Christic Real Presence. And, since the speaker's "heart" ("The Windhover," 7), located "here" (9), is associated with "fire" that flashes at the point of the bird's "Buckl[ing]!" (10), perhaps Hopkins is suggesting that the speaker's receptive heart is one more—perhaps even the poem's central—sacramental vessel: one that gains sacramentality as "fire" . . . breaks from [Christ]" (10). If so, then "The Windhover" clearly foreshadows Hopkins's sonnets of the late 1880s depicting transubstantiation from inside Christian souls. Both types of Hopkins poem share some sense of apparent dualism even as they believe in ultimate possibilities for earthlings to become radiant with indwelling transubstantial power.[159]

To Hopkins nature both reveals God-given universal beauty and suggests the dualistic human being's need to seek God's even greater redemptive gifts. A man or woman can only properly seek these greater gifts by rejecting all proud sense of self-sufficiency. Unduly confident creaturehood renders one defiled like a dualist bird of prey; all pompous "air, pride, plume" must "buckle," collapsing in humble obedience before the so-much-greater "achieve" of Christ.

*   *   *

It is startlingly intriguing to examine Mariani's charting of Hopkin's 1877 nature sonnets according to their dates of composition. Some were identified by Hopkins with the very date of their origin, while others he noted only by the season of the year; Mariani uses stylistic features in order to muster the most accurate chronology of composition possible.[160] Mariani's charting clarifies that the three sonnets of an apparently mimicked liturgical Eucharist pattern came first—imitating the Eucharist either by trenchantly questioning (as in "God's Grandeur") why human beings do not *acknowledge* the sacrament everywhere revealed, or (as in "The Starlight Night" and "Spring") by placing within the lyric a direct imperative upon readers to receive the sacrament. By May 1877, however, Hopkins had begun also to write a different kind of nature sonnet—a type that did not mimic the Eucharistic liturgy so much as it recalled the homily—a part of worship functioning only as a preparation step leading to the later Eucharistic rite. Two of Hopkin's 1877 homily sonnets ("In the Valley of the Elwy" and "The Sea and the Skylark") the poet identified clearly as products of that May; Mariani, probably rightly, calls two others (which are dated simply "St. Beuno's 1877") likely near-contemporaries of the other pair. Among three even later sonnets, "The Windhover" seems to recall its own speaker's participation in sacrament as revealed in nature, but it does not, at least directly, urge others, through any dramatization of the Eucharistic invitation pattern, to follow his personal example. This poem precedes, on 30 May, the two Wales sonnets that in liturgical type it seems most to resemble: the hymnic psalms "Pied Beauty" (dated "Summer") and "Hurrahing in Harvest" (dated 1 September).

When in these Wales sonnets he seems most completely to mimic the Eucharistic rite, Hopkins experiments with two different means of presenting the Eucharistic invitation on two successive days, in "God's Grandeur" (23 February) and "The Starlight Night" (24 February). But he finally arrives at an ideal method of presenting the invitation, as well as the most orderly progression of the mimicked sacramental rite up to the point of the invitation, only in the May sonnet "Spring." This sonnet clearly seems the most likely of the three poems of this type to cause potential readers to see the Eucharistic visible sacrament in nature and to respond to it with what its author deems an appropriate Christian attitude of self-sacrifice.

The homily group chronologically divides into two perhaps-weaker pieces (the probable earlier pair) followed by two clearly excellent efforts. Both of the first two sonnets might be called weak because ambiguous as to their lessons; Hopkins appears a theological universalist at the end of "The Lantern out of Doors" and sounds Darwinian in "The Sea and the Skylark" (although he no doubt recalled that even the Bible itself says that humanity arose from "slime" [Genesis 2:7]). "In the Valley of the Elwy" and "The Caged Skylark," in any case, are truly meditations made resonantly tender homiletic expressions of how Hopkins sensed in humankind both real spiritual limits ("In the Valley . . .") and real spiritual possibilities ("The Caged Skylark").

"Pied Beauty," although chronologically central and the most definitively hymnic among the psalm grouping, actually has less final richness than the two psalms grouped with it. "Hurrahing in Harvest," while expressing a generalized hymnic fervor toward nature, also shares such personalized contemplativeness as to make vivid the author's life in sacrament, although it does not specifically call for others' emulation. The same revelation of authorial involvement in sacrament strikes us in "The Windhover." And that poem's rich linguistic matrix produces an artifact that particularly challenges forth, even in the mere act of careful exegesis, a reader's participatory immersion in its sacramental experience.

Whatever the potential fallacies of biographical criticism may be, there remains a strong undertone in "The Windhover" suggesting that the man Hopkins—who was accepting the "shéer plód" ("The Windhover," 12) of daily priestly vocation—was in the poem primarily revoicing a commitment to the sacrament of Holy Orders: that was Hopkins's official sphere for saying *yea* to personal, rather than only to public, sacrament. "The Windhover" is a personal poem, launched with an "I," not an imperative encounter with an imagined public audience ("The Starlight Night" and "Spring"). If those poems' sacramental analogue is the Eucharist, this poem's sacramental analogue could be called Holy Orders.

But, even more ultimately (given that Hopkins had not yet actually taken on priestly parish duties and, also, that the work demonstrates so well the personal sacramental gift of his writing itself), the sacrament most fully revealed here seems to be confirmation. The hard working preparer of this sacramental vessel is "confirming" that throughout all his life he will refuse to be as self-serving as the kestrel in its flight might be, but that instead he will clearly give life as a reverent, self-sacrificial offering "TO CHRIST OUR LORD" (The Windhover," dedication).

Hopkins was soon to depart Saint Beuno's for the churches of Bedford Leigh and Liverpool. Not through poetry but through priestly deeds, he would there be in charge of guiding not imaginary, but real, elective wills "TO CHRIST OUR LORD." In a more muted personal voice, he would also emphasize personal commitment to Christ through further poetic verbalization. But he would rarely strive in these later poems chiefly to prove Christ a worthy Savior because of his visible creative presence in nature. Such a turn from poetic emphasis on the affective will to poetic emphasis on the elective will may not mean at all that nature ever became to Hopkins any less a revelation of Christic Real Presence.[161] Yet a change in poetic focus surely did result both from Hopkins's own personal spiritual struggles and from his daily "confirmed" ministry to sacramentally *real*, not only *imaginary*, human congregations.

C. The Compleat Cleric: A Man For Others

Hopkins's priesthood poems are important, not as evidence for the Jesuit defense in a debate over his vocational conflicts, but as revelations of that spiritual growth which any self-sacrifice might breed. And these poems do often become rather successful sacraments, not because the priest is bestowing "outward and visible sign[s]" of Christ's favor upon us (as he tried to do in "The Starlight Night"), but because the man Hopkins is using the poems as obvious sacramental acts of confirmation for himself. He is poignantly recognizing his own constant need to subordinate himself to Christ's "inward . . . grace."

The poems of Hopkins's parish years find him seeking to develop further the activity of this "inward . . . grace" within himself, while they also show him working to develop such activity within his parishioners. Most of these poems treat both him and these other persons as figures of concern. For example, a letter to Bridges of 8 October 1879 mentions a beloved soldier-parishioner sent to the Afghanistani battlefield of "Mootlan [Mooltan] in the Punjaub [Punjab] . . . Sept. 30."[162] This soldier who is bound for Afghanistan—according to Hopkins's note as he encloses the poem for Bridges[163]—is the hero of "The Bugler's First Communion."

Hopkins, as a character in this poem, does become the priestly "bestowing" celebrant ("Bugler's," 7) of a sacramental "outward . . . sign": a Eucharistic thanksgiving. Yet he tries clearly to suppress his pride in that role. He at first tells us that the boy "Came, *I say,* this day to it—to a First Communion" (8; emphasis mine). Yet the Eucharist and the boy's well-being through it eventually prove more important to Hopkins than his own achievements.

The emphasis the poem places upon the unity of these two human characters under Christ is vitally important. Both the bugler and the priest, although good persons, know the personal deficiencies that coexist with their virtues, deficiencies which Christ must conquer with the spiritual fullness he alone possesses. The young soldier, for instance, seems to Hopkins gifted in his genetic inheritance; as becomes obvious later in the poem, he is physically attractive, and perhaps he seems intellectually and emotionally rich, too. At least Hopkins assesses that he is ". . . born, he tells me, of Irish / Mother to an English sire (he / Shares their best gifts surely, fall how things will)" ("Bugler's," 2–4). Nonetheless, such gifts still seemed imperfect (*"fall* how things will"—emphasis mine), and so the boy came to Hopkins in order to receive a gift he did not have naturally. The "boon . . . / . . . begged" of the priest (5–6) was the Eucharist.

Hopkins describes the boy bowed before the altar as himself a potential sacramental being of given physical beauty ("outward . . . sign") and emerging spiritual loveliness ("inward . . . grace"). He seems "Christ's [own] darling" (14), a unique descendant of troubadors' idealized loved ones. But Hopkins distrusts that his own poetic envisioning of the boy's spiritual potential can securely define that potential. A guardian angel (17–20), he says, must respond to the poet's request for aid if the boy would reach fully that spiritual beauty which Hopkins wishes for him. And the Eucharist, that "sealing sacred ointment" (33), must also provide the boy with protection.

As a poetic prophet, the priestly artist *can* summon forth the evidence he has seen of the boy's spiritual maturation. His "Breathing bloom of a chastity in mansex fine" (16) seems almost ready to ripen as a "pushed peach" (23) of spirituality, in which the "self-will" has been made "self-wise" (24). But the vates cannot be assured of this prophecy. For the boy to reach his finest spiritual beauty, the sacramental protection of Christ's sacred rites will need to provide magical "charms" (34), and join the "arms" of angels with the armor of an emerging sanctity. That is, the boy must receive the sacrament and himself continue to become a sacrament; Christ, it appears, must transubstantiate the boy's outer species, "lock . . . love ever in a lad" (35).

Therefore, the priest-poet, in evident cowardice but partly in humility and wisdom, declares, concerning his relationship with this bugler, "Let mé though see no more of him" (36).[164] He knows himself to be full of fretting, not dispassionate enough; part of his response surely is excessive fear of "see[ing] . . . disappointment" (36). Yet he also responds with proper self-abasement. Because overly sensitive to visible signs of beauty or sadness, he should not "see" the boy's future if seeing it causes his wrongheaded challenge of God's will. If the lad is killed in battle, or has his face marred, such seemingly disastrous results may still be among the wishes of the Eucharist's Lord. Hopkin's withdrawal from further sight of this boy thus partly indicates a worthy submission to a mysterious hiddenness in Providence, and this poem thus almost reverses the 1865 plea for visible presence in the lament "Where art thou, friend . . .?"

The very danger of excessive personal involvement, which Hopkins suspects will occur if he does not respect Christ's sovereignty by becoming willing to live in darkness concerning the boy's future, may be highlighted in the poem's closing lines:

> Recorded only, I have put my lips on pleas
> Would brandle adamantine heaven with ride and jar, did
>   Prayer go disregarded:
> Forward-like, but however, and like favourable heaven heard these.
>   ("Bugler's," 45–48)

Here is a poet who knows that even in praying he would force all his artistic energy, impolitely "forward-like," into cajoling God to grant his own wishes for a boy—assuming the role of Gabriel as he "put[s] . . . lips on pleas." He has felt similarly about his religious activity as the sacramental priest:

> Then though I should tread tufts of consolation
> Dáys áfter, só I in a sort deserve to
>   And do serve God to serve to
> Just such slips of soldiery Christ's royal ration.
>   (25–28)

Despite a patina of apparent pride that glistens on the surface of such utterances, their frank honesty seems, paradoxically, to betoken humility. Hopkins admits that he is simply doing his best, "however" weakly self-centered it sometimes is (48). He leaves, in his prayer and poem, a verbal sign of his spiritual goodwill—his constant (although sometimes troubled) faith. The prayer and poem show him aware of his vanity, which has made him, both as poet and priest, too anxious to see visible signs of success and beatitude. The sacrificial believer, however, can accept darkened visions and knows that he must.[165]

Significantly, then, Hopkins in an apparently sermonic poem from this era treats not the elfin "quickgold" lawns of which we read in "The Starlight Night" (5) of 1877, nor even the mixed hints of natural glory and Christ's sacrifice that we saw in the "gold-vermilion" at the end of "The Windhover" (14), but rather "Goldengrove unleaving"—a darkened nature which also reveals clearly its "fall," even for a child in the "spring" of her years. Hopkins's goal of a sacramental art now operates once again, as in the poems of the 1860s, in voicing direct human confrontations with a world that tokens forth darkness and death:

Spring and Fall:
to a young child

Márgarét, áre you gríeving
Over Goldengrove unleaving?
Léaves, líke the things of man, you
With your fresh thoughts care for, can you?
Áh! ás the heart grows older
It will come to such sights colder
By and by, nor spare a sigh
Though worlds of wanwood leafmeal lie;
And yet you *will* weep and know why.
Now no matter, child, the name:
Sórrow's spríngs áre the same.
Nor mouth had, no nor mind, expressed
What heart heard of, ghost guessed:
It ís the blight man was born for,
It is Margaret you mourn for.

Portraying Hopkins now as a preacher-catechist in the sacrament of Holy Orders, "Spring and Fall" may also portray a young parishioner archetype who does not actually represent any one specific person from Hopkins's biographical experience. Sigurd Burkhardt reminds us, in a long-known essay, that "Margaret . . . is Greek for 'pearl' "; he indeed senses a link with Robert Herrick's "To Daffodils," which treats "the pearls of Morning's dew / Ne'er to be found again."[166] Mariani also has called attention to the poem's stylized accents that make the girl a child ("Márgarét") at the poem's opening and an adult ("Margaret") at the close.[167] The childlike epithet may even allude to Goethe's too-innocent heroine Gretchen (Margarethe) in *Faust One;* of all Continental writers of his century, Goethe is the only one who receives repeated discussion in Hopkins's letters.[168]

Despite stylization, however, this lyric voices a powerful and surely sincere message. Through deliberate accentuation, Hopkins not only awakens readers to transformations within his female character, but also to the essential moral of the sermonette. "Léaves" *are* "líke the things of man," especially "ás the heart grows older" and dies. Other potentially accented words focus the poem's thematic message: "Sórrow's spríngs áre"; "What heart heard . . . ghost guessed / . . . ís."[169] When parishioners cry over nature's death, as this stylized child parishioner seems to be doing, they might not know that they are sobbing because they innately sense Original Sin as the cause of their own future deaths. Yet Hopkins as priest-persona is responsible for making them know consciously (and much more directly than he did in his priestly guise as narrator of "The Starlight Night") what they only sense on their nerve endings.

Several other lyrics of this period reveal Hopkins as an unstinting parish sacramentalist. He wants always, we find, to see in his parishioners the "tríumph and immortal years" that the bridal couple are wished by his blessing upon their 1879 sacrament of marriage ("At the Wedding March," 12; *P*, 86, 278). In the blacksmith whom he names Felix Randal (although Mariani once again does not think that the character is based, any more than Margaret, on a specific acquaintance),[170] Hopkins does see such "tríumph and immortal[ity]." The blacksmith, however, has gained such immortal victory only by facing with stalwartness the moral imperatives raised by his encounter with terminal illness:

Felix Randal the farrier, O is he dead then? my duty all ended,
Who have watched his mould of man, big-boned and hardy-
    handsome
Pining, pining, till time when reason rambled in it and some
Fatal four disorders, fleshed there, all contended?

Sickness broke him. Impatient, he cursed at first, but mended
Being anointed and all; though a heavenlier heart began some
Months earlier, since I had our sweet reprieve and ransom
Tendered to him. Ah well, God rest him all road ever he offended!

This seeing the sick endears them to us, us too it endears.
My tongue had taught thee comfort, touch had quenched thy tears,
Thy tears that touched my heart, child, Felix, poor Felix Randal;

How far from then forethought of, all thy more boisterous years,
When thou at the random grim forge, powerful amidst peers,
Didst fettle for the great gray drayhorse his bright and battering
    sandal!

Although he knows that priestly service with Felix has enriched his own life,[171] Hopkins again portrays himself accepting his role in the sacraments (this time in Extreme Unction) as subordinate to Christ's: "Felix Randal the farrier, O is he dead then? my duty all ended" (1). Yet, despite the emphasis upon teleologically *ended* duty—as a priest helps Christ to unsheathe a transubstantial "heavenlier heart" within this externally crude blacksmith (6)—we see in this poem, even more than in its predecessor about the bugler's Eucharist, the tender outpouring of love by the personally concerned priest: "My tongue had taught thee comfort, *touch* had quenched thy tears, / Thy tears that *touched* my heart, child, Felix, poor Felix Randal" (10–11; emphases mine).

Through his priestly encouragement of those in his charge to "take up [their] cross[es], and follow [Christ]" (Matthew 16:24), Hopkins sought to instill within them sacramental completeness, through passional rebirth of that Edenic potential in all created things which he recalled in an 1881 spiritual note:

All things therefore are charged with love, are charged with God and *if we know how to touch them* give off sparks and take fire, yield drops and flow, ring and tell of him.[172]

It was Hopkins's responsibility as priest to "touch" persons, so that they saw their need of imitating Christ's Passion of spiritual love and thus eventually becoming transubstantial with Christic power. Hopkins had surely "touched" Felix, or real persons like him, so that they gained that Christic power.

These priestly poems therefore clearly do demonstrate how, for Hopkins, his work as an officiant over liturgical sacraments of all types became "the means and expression of community."[173] About such communal sacramental expression Saint Augustine long ago spoke in *Contra Faustum* 9.2: "Men cannot be united in any profession of religion, whether true or false, unless they are connected by some communion of visible signs or sacraments."[174]

Yet the poems of this period not only illustrate Hopkins's sense of sacramental union with others; they also depict forcefully his own continued will to answer sacramental calls to personal self-examination and penitence. We later will see reflected in the imagery of the 1885 "Terrible Sonnets" his Beaumont meditation of 8 September 1883 on Christ's Baptism (and Temptation by Satan), and his own response to that meditation—his wishing to become "freer from sin."[175] And on 20

August 1880, in his meditation on the *Principium sive Fundamentum* of the Ignatian *Spiritual Exercises*, he will seem to be announcing why, in poems of the 1880s, he will devote his attention to the inner elective will. Whereas natural splendor did, in the 1870s nature sonnets, seem to reveal the presence of Christ as nature's Creator, Hopkins now surely believes that persons can most potently encounter their Creator's commanding authority through elective activity within their own souls. Ignatius had declared, in the *Principium sive Fundamentum*, "Man was created to praise, reverence, and serve God Our Lord, and by so doing to save his soul. And the other things on the face of the earth were created for man's sake and to help him in the carrying out of the end for which he was created."[176] Hopkins is thus a thoroughly orthodox Ignatian as he interprets that ". . . We may learn that all things are created by consideration of the world without or of ourselves the world within. The former [the world without] is the consideration commonly dwelt on, but the latter [the world within] takes on the mind more hold."[177]

It is in this meditation that Hopkins utters his vivid description of the "taste of myself" as "more distinctive than the taste of ale or alum, more distinctive than the smell of walnutleaf or camphor"—more distinctive, indeed, than anything in that nature to which he had devoted his attention in the 1870s poems of the affective will: "searching nature I taste *self* but at one tankard, that of my own being."[178] And "myself," he declares, includes "my pleasures and pains, my powers and my experiences, my deserts and guilt, my shame and sense of beauty, my dangers, hopes, fears, and all my fate."[179]

It is especially striking how he calls attention to his elective moral self, with its need to reduce personal "guilt" and "shame," in "The Candle Indoors," a poem of 1879 (*P*, 274) that differs notably in emphasis from its seeming 1877 companion—the affective paean to human Christic beauty, "The Lantern out of Doors":[180]

> Some candle clear burns somewhere I come by.
> I muse at how its being puts blissful back
> With yellowy moisture mild night's blear-all black,
> Or to-fro tender trambeams truckle at the eye.
>
> By that window what task what fingers ply,
> I plod wondering, a-wanting, just for lack
> Of answer the eagerer a-wanting Jessy or Jack
> There / God to aggrándise, God to glorify.—
>
> Come you indoors, come home; your fading fire
> Mend first and vital candle in close heart's vault:
> You there are master, do your own desire;

What hinders? Are you beam-blind, yet to a fault
In a neighbour deft-handed? are you that liar
And, cast by conscience out, spendsavour salt?

As Mariani succinctly states this poem's ultimate theme, Hopkins is
here recognizing that even his own sincere "concern" with "Jack's or
Jessy's spiritual light" could become "a tactic to divert attention from
his own 'fading fire.' "[181] Reminding himself of Christ's command to
correct one's own sizable "beam" of faultiness before standing in judgment of others' faulty "mote[s]" (Matthew 7:3–5), Hopkins knows that
even a priest—whose very vocation demands that he urge others sacramentally "to aggrándise" and "glorify" God ("The Candle Indoors,"
8)—is also duty bound to keep the sacramental "fire" of his own inner
soul from "fading" (9). His "desire" to elicit others' sacramental loyalty
to God must also be a personally "do[ne] . . . desire" within his own
elective "close heart's vault" (10–11). Otherwise, he will not as his own
personal "master" be attuned with the cosmic Master Christ (11); his
"vital candle" (10) of ínner sacramental flame will be, it seems, extinguished, and "conscience" will then "cast" him "out," as he seems
to feel himself to be in this poem, within a lonely outer world (14). That
world has a potential to provide for his affective will a sacramental
illumination whenever that affective will perceives another person's
spiritual inscape: his or her "candle clear" (1). Yet unless one's own
elective will is sacramentally prepared to greet others with a genial
dispassionateness, one may cause the others to react defensively, to
"cower" rather than to "submit" willingly, as the "to-fro tender tram-
beams" from their eyes encounter the eyes of the importunate invader
("The Candle Indoors," 3–4; *OED* for "truckle"). As the Matthean Jesus
was reported to declare, the wrong sort of eye is bound to bring ill
feelings into the world it meets improperly: "The light of the body is the
eye: if therefore thine eye be single [reverent, sacramentally prepared?],
thy whole body shall be full of light. / But if thine eye be evil [irreverent,
unprepared to treat the world sacramentally?], thy whole body shall be
full of darkness. If therefore the light that is in thee be darkness, how
great is that darkness?" (Matthew 6:22–23).[182]

If Hopkins had now felt it appropriate to write such a poem (and even
this sonnet's second quatrain implies that he might have liked to be
writing such a poem, although he judged such a work inappropriate to
his current situation), he could have shouted to "Jessy or Jack" (7),
much as he had shouted to an imaginary audience in "Spring" and
"The Starlight Night" two years before, that they should stalwartly
demonstrate their sacramentalist servanthood by visible acts of Christian devotion in the external world. The Matthean Christ is reported to

have asked his followers for just such visibly flaming acts of devotion in public settings: "Ye are the light of the world. A city that is set on a hill cannot be hid. / Neither do men light a candle, and put it under a bushel, but on a candlestick; and it giveth light unto all that are in the house. / Let your light so shine before men, that they may see your good works, and glorify your Father which is in heaven" (Matthew 5:14–16).

Yet Hopkins recognizes in this 1879 poem what he may not so completely have recognized in 1877—that a soul's inner sacramental beacon must be nourished by the human elective will before that luminescence can grow to any outer actions of properly blazing sacramental devotion. He does not speak of flames "set on a hill" in this poem; both he and "Jessy or Jack" are, in different senses, "indoors" ("The Candle Indoors," 5, 9). Thus he seems to sense that no human spiritual flame can burn with sacramental force in the outer world (as sacrament's *outer and visible sign*) until its inner embers are first empowered with *inward and spiritual grace*.

Indeed, the Matthean Jesus seems to have had the same sense of priorities. Before he ever spoke of a disciple's "light of the world" that "shine[s] before men," Matthew's Christ also emphasized, like Hopkins, the primally necessary sacramental energy within the soul. He spoke of a disciple's need for a permeating inner zest of sacramental flavorfulness and thus used the same gustatory image to define the proper human self's required inner life as that which Hopkins (aware of his full allusive Matthean context) carefully paired (14) with his description of the sacramental soul's required "vital candle" (10): "You are the salt of the earth; but if salt has lost its taste, how shall its saltness be restored? It is no longer good for anything except to be thrown out and trodden under foot by men" (Matthew 5:13).

As a proper exegete of scripturally revealed priorities, then, the Hopkins of 1879 knows that—no more than he can be the proper "salt of the earth" without inner "saltness"—he cannot be "light of the [external] world" until his inner elective will chooses devoutly to develop, within his soul, the Light of the World. That Light, it appears, has been divinely sent through the Holy Spirit to dwell as a sacramental radiance within his soul. To that particular inner sacramental "beam" (the imitatio of Christ's crossbeam) he surely dares not be "blind" ("The Candle Indoors," 12). He does not wish to find himself "cast by conscience out" to morose alienation ("trodden under foot by men"—Matthew 5:13) in a lightless, seemingly godless world.

Despite the fears he sometimes powerfully expressed in later years, Hopkins truly seems never to have been "cast . . . out" according to the poems of these parish years. Sacramentalist lyrics of this period may show us too many of the mundane activities of a priest for us always to feel ecstatic about the subject matter. yet we should not allow ourselves to believe that the poems, or the years of service they commemorate, do not represent an important time in Hopkins's own spiritual growth. After all, we know from the evidence of "The Candle Indoors" that he wrote the following 1879 admonition (P, 276) to himself as much as to any parishioner:

> The dappled die-away
> Cheek and the wimpled lip,
> The gold-wisp, the airy-grey
> Eye, all in fellowship—
> This, all this beauty blooming,
> This, all this freshness fuming,
> Give God while worth consuming.
>   ("Morning, Midday and Evening Sacrifice," 1–7)[183]

4

Hopkins's Final Decade: The Taming of Tempests

I wake and feel the fell of dark, not day
> —Hopkins, Poem 67 (1885)

mould / Those limbs like ours . . . / . . . our daystar
> —Hopkins, "The Blessed Virgin compared to the Air we Breathe" (1883)

ALTHOUGH WE HAVE seen how Hopkins's priestly poems are very often affirmations of a necessary death to self, Jean-Georges Ritz, when reading Hopkins's letters of the period, finds emphasized instead the *pain* of that death to self. Hopkins, Ritz says, "payait ainsi chèrement sa passion pour la beauté. Il eût voulu retrouver dans sa vie paroissiale la beauté des corps et des âmes qu'il avait appris à découvrir chez les poètes grecs, et dans la Bible, et que ses années d'étudiant à Oxford, auprès de Walter Pater et de Henry Liddon [,] lui avaient 'rendue si chère [paid dearly enough for his passionate love of beauty. He had wanted to rediscover in his parish life the beauty of bodies and souls that he had learned to discover in the Greek poets, and in the Bible, and that his years as an Oxford student, under the tutelage of Walter Pater and Henry Liddon, had rendered so dear to him]."[1]

As Robinson, however, notes along with me,[2] it is not only sensory deprivation of beauty that perplexes Hopkins, although he does indeed complain about ugly industrialized landscapes.[3] More steadily troubling him are the frustrations of his parish work, with its lack of many kinds of physical rewards. Thus he does not only vilify ugly city landscapes but also sets poetry writing—which might, at least potentially, provide him visible achievements—against the religious vocation that seems to produce rather slight success: ". . . The parish work of Liverpool is very wearying to mind and body and leaves me nothing but odds and ends of time. There is merit in it but little Muse, and indeed 26 lines is the whole I have writ in more than half a year, since I left Oxford."[4]

Yet if Hopkins's continued desire for consolatory visible signs, both as poet and priest, remains astir throughout the 1880s, it is also true that this is the decade in which any conflicting tensions in subject matter diminish. Even his nature poems become less a description of the external world than a clear delineation of a saint's inner life. And most of this decade's lyrics transfer his incarnational theology into a study of a passional human process within the soul undergoing *imitatio Christi* (and, as a result, rebirth and spiritual maturation). Paradoxically, Hopkins forged some of his most aesthetically brilliant (although also most extraordinarily devout) verse during this same period. In that verse he delineated the way his elective will, or soul, or *arbitrium*, could spiritually revivify his sometimes-tainted human "self" and affective will, by guiding him through the painful process which might gain him union with the Sacred Heart of Christ. Hopkins thus proceeded toward that point at the decade's end when he was prepared to move past poetry altogether—awaiting, in near silence, the experience of the eschaton. In the transcendent illumination of that experience's "flash, at a trumpet crash" ("Heraclitean Fire," 21), Hopkins believed he would see finally overwhelmed the darkening dimness of earth's "winter world" ("To R. B.," 13).

A. From Celebration to Prayer: The Remaking and the Death of Art

If Hopkins the priest still had "reserves" about his decision to sacrifice a poetic career, these "reserves" may be briefly glimpsed (although not ultimately with very great intensity) in "Henry Purcell." This sonnet was written by 26 May 1879 but discussed with Bridges also, and in great detail, on 22 June 1879 and as late as 4 January 1883.[5] In this tortuously wrought poem, first of all, Purcell exemplifies the power of art to give voice to human essence. And Hopkins loves this "dear" composer, whose music "throngs the ear" ("Henry Purcell," 1, 8). The poem does not state that art either deifies its maker or redeems one from sin. But it does hint that art with a proper *structure* (something more than mere emotions like "love or pity" or aesthetic "sweet notes"—6) may seem to evidence how (at least in Purgatory) its artistic creator will eventually elect divine inscapes of saintly rectitude.

In prose, Hopkins wrote the following epigraph:

The poet wishes well to the divine genius of Purcell and praises him that, whereas other musicians have given utterance to the moods of man's mind, he has, beyond that, uttered in notes the very make and species of man as created both in him and in all men generally.

Then Hopkins launched the poem:

Have fair fallen, O fair, fair have fallen, so dear
To me, so arch-especial a spirit as heaves in Henry Purcell,
An age is now since passed, since parted; with the reversal
Of the outward sentence low lays him, listed to a heresy, here.

                                                                          (1–4)

Hopkins, because he himself finds Purcell's "spirit" "so dear," hopes, despite his own fervent Roman Catholicism, that the purgatorial "age" which has passed since Purcell's 1695 death should have led to the "reversal" of the artist's condemnation as a Protestant heretic, "the outward sentence [that some would say] low lays him" (4) in Purgatory still.

In order to justify his wishes for Purcell's soul, Hopkins de-emphasizes the composer's mere aesthetic effects, instead writing in both epigraph and sonnet with emphasis upon the man's mind, an "arch-especial . . . spirit" (one that Hopkins apparently might desire to have "fall" to him in his own art of two centuries later). That spirit, as Purcell's music seems to prove, contacts the world-arching scopus of God (2) and expresses that scopus first through the inscaping of individuality—"an abrúpt sélf" (8)—and also through the inscaping of a structure or "forgèd feature" (7). It thus demonstrates what Ruskin, in The Two Paths of 1859, called two major characteristics of "good art": "observation of fact" and "manifestation of human design and authority in the way that fact is told."[6] In Purcell's music, it is

Not mood in him nor meaning, proud fire or sacred fear,
Or love or pity or all that sweet notes not his might nursle:
It is the forgèd feature finds me; it is the rehearsal
Of own, of abrúpt sélf there so thrusts on, so throngs the ear.

                                                                          (5–8)

Purcell's particular "sélf" breaks suddenly, "abrúpt[ly]," from the music (8). Hopkins also suggests that Christ, in a sense Purcell's "divine genius" (epigraph) or "sheer" self (OED definition of "abrúpt"), may have inspired Purcell's art, which, through Purcell's affective will, partook in Christ's "creative strain."[7]

But Hopkins also hopes that Purcell's music, in its especial vibrancy of intellectually tough affective will, may foreshadow how Christ's "redemptive strain"[8] has ultimately responded to Purcell's elective willing of saintly inscape. A "rehearsal," or "recital in a legal document" (OED), has now perhaps become, in Purgatory, a successful defense of Purcell's soul before its Master-Judge ("Henry Purcell," 7–8). Before the tribunal now, it seems, Purcell may have capably defended his own "abrúpt sélf"—in death "broken off," and "suddenly" so (OED).[9]

On the surface, Hopkins now ends his poem simply by comparing Purcell in his music to a bird with uniquely attractive, "quaint," "moonmarks" ("Henry Purcell," 10); they identify its structural "make and species" (epigraph). The bird's "motion" of wings, shaping a curve like a "smile" (13), reveals, simply in its natural activity, the wonder of architectonic inscape. Miller chooses to read the poem, therefore, as simply referring to this level of inscape. To him, Hopkin's affective will, affirming architectonic inscape, responds positively to Purcell's similarly inscape-affirming affectivity. Miller[10] does not read Hopkins to be at all considering here Purcell's *elective* will, in which he is potentially fallible and turned away from God.[11] Surely it is true that Hopkins, in this transitional and perhaps too zealously optimistic poem from the late 1870s, does not appear very clearly to differentiate between the elective and the affective. This vagueness results from his perhaps wanting so fervently to believe that Purcell, whose music affectively reveals considerable architectonic divine order, *must* in Purgatory have elected fuller saintly obedience to God. Notwithstanding the exuberance of his admiration for Purcell, however, Hopkins does allow in his poem's lexicon—through the ambiguity of words such as "rehearsal" and "abrúpt"—for a belief that there could be no nonelective moral salvation, for any person or musician.

After all, the two tercets' sensuous envisioning of a bird battling off beachfront storms itself carries overtones not only of captivating sense impressions, but also a religious "underthought":[12]

Let him oh! with his air of angels then lift me, lay me! only I'll
Have an eye to the sakes of him, quaint moonmarks, to his pelted
    plumage under
Wings: so some great stormfowl, whenever he has walked his while

The thunder-purple seabeach plumèd purple-of-thunder,
If a wuthering of his palmy snow pinions scatter a colossal smile
Off him, but meaning motion fans fresh our wits with wonder.
                                                        (9–14)

In the final tercet Hopkins mixes, in both the beach and bird images, "thunder," the sign of God's wrath both to the Greeks and the Hebrews, with the "purple" liturgical color of penitential Christian Lent. Wrath and the penitence that absolves wrath are reconciled in a "smile." The passage may suggest Origenian theological universalism, for, if Hopkins does here discuss Purcell's religious redemption, he appears to make such redemption occur as naturally as any bird's upward flight.

Yet Hopkins also makes statements reflecting nonuniversalist theology. Within his music Purcell displayed, Hopkins told Bridges, two
sorts of "sakes," defined by Hopkins as "the being a thing has outside
itself, as a voice by its echo, a face by its reflection, a body by its shadow,
a man by his name, fame, or memory, *and also* that in the thing by
virtue of which . . . it has this being abroad. . . ."[13] A sake therefore
seems to be, in one of its senses, a creature's inscape, that "in the thing
by virtue of which . . . it has this being abroad," but, in another sense,
also its outscape, or "being . . . outside itself." Inscape may always link
humankind and nature to Christ the Creator. But if morally fallen
creatures also remain somewhat spiritually separate from Christ the
Redeemer, Hopkins would seem to define this separation as their outscape.

Purcell did reveal, according to Hopkin's epigraph, the "very make
and species of man as created in him and in all men generally"—
human innate worth, the human inscaping of Christ's "smile" of creational "wonder." But the bird that images Purcell here is dappled—both
"purple" and snow[y]" ("Henry Purcell," 12–13). Because it is partly
illumined as a creature of God, it can "praise Him" as all the dappled
creatures of earth seemed to do in "Pied Beauty." Yet Hopkins also
seems to suggest that full praise of God, the praise of the redeemed soul,
demands that each *morally* dappled individual must seek, through the
elective will, redemptive ascent past penitential "thunder" (12). Purcell, like Statius in Dante's *Purgatorio* (canto 21, 58–60, 67–72), apparently had to purge his outscape before being freed from sin by
thundertremors. Because of his burdens as a sin-tainted man, he could
not be portrayed as a bird of redeemed status just because his music had
a quality of physically "wuthering" (13) storminess. He needed that
experience of Purgatory about which Hopkins also had written in 1878,
at the climax of *The Loss of the Eurydice* (109–20); Purcell needed
redemptive "weathering" (*Scottish National Dictionary* definition of
"wuthering").

"Henry Purcell" is a significant Hopkins poem. Partly this is so
because it hints at a not-quite-timid wish that Origenian universalism
could be realized beyond a doubt. If that were so, all artists, with their
rich affective wills, would prove innately redeemed. And yet this poem
is most significant because its final purgatorial images point ahead to
later Hopkins poems about the *elective* will. In those poems, many of
which feature Hopkins's own self as one of the potential personae,
Purgatory occurs on this earth, in the individual's battle for personal
spiritual redemption. Henry Purcell's melody, with its "forgèd feature,"
may have suggested aesthetic-intellectual intuitions of divine order and
purpose. Yet Hopkins's 1880s poems will not find aesthetic-intellectual

intuitions of any order and purpose to be adequate proofs of one's full unity with the Orderer and Purposer. In later years Hopkins will identify his own outscaped "self" as potentially the singer of its own Luciferian "self-praise"—on the "age-old anvil" of sin ("No worst, there is none," 6).[14]

* * *

During the very season (the spring of 1879) when Hopkins was writing "Henry Purcell," he was also inscribing the first of a number of poems in which he argued the supremacy, over against mere physical beauty, of spiritual beauty in the self-sacrificial soul. This new Hopkinsian theme (but also a Ruskinian one, as Sulloway notes)[15] proves corollary to the emerging dominant Hopkinsian argument for the supremacy of elective versus affective will.

To be sure, of this stage in Hopkins's life one cannot say what one could say of his life ten years later: that he has the same stern devotion to self-sacrificing spiritual beauty as the Frenchman Huysmans was to utter in a markedly moving passage:

. . . Personellement, j'ai b[e]aucoup trouvé dans les églises pauvres, au crépuscule, alors qu'il n'y a plus que de très humble gens qui prient. Il y a là des expressions de simplesses et de si vive foi qu'elles transportent et vous aident vraiment. Au fond, ce qu'on appelle la beauté n'existe pas au sens où nous avons si longuement entendu. Je l'ai vue une fois dans ma vie la beauté radieuse, la beauté divine, la seule. C'était une assez laide femme qui vint un soir chez moi. Je la vis dix minutes et ne la reverrai jamais plus, puisqu'elle est entrée le lendemain dans un cloître à grilles de la dure observance.

J'avais été mêlé par un prêtre, une minute, à la vie de cette étonnante créature. Mon cher, chez moi, elle me parla de la joie de souffrir—et cette femme si laide s'illumina. Les yeux devinrent inouïs, comment rendre cela! La vraie beauté n'est pas dans les formes, dans les traits, puisqu'une poussée d'âme les change; la religion anoblit tout.

[Personally, I have found out much in poor churches, at twilight, when one finds only very humble people praying. There one sees expressions of simplicities and such living faith; they transport and truly aid you. At heart, what one calls beauty does not exist in the sense of which we have so long heard. I have seen it one time in my life: radiant beauty, divine beauty, the only kind. It came with a rather ugly woman who visited me one evening. I saw her ten minutes and will never see her again, because she entered the next day into a barred cloister of very harsh practices.

I had been introduced by a priest for one minute into the life of this astonishing creature. My dear friend, in my home, she spoke of the joy of suffering—and this woman, so ugly, became illuminated. Her eyes became something of which one has never heard, but how do I describe it? True beauty is not in forms, in traits, because a glimmer of soul changes those; religion ennobles everything.][16]

Hopkins's young boy character in "The Handsome Heart" (1879; *P*, 275) is not spiritually beautiful and physically ugly like Huysmans's depicted mystical woman. Like the boy in "The Bugler's First Communion," he does receive Hopkins's notice partially because of his "more than handsome face" ("The Handsome Heart," 9). And yet Hopkins, although clearly also admiring both the boy's outer physical and intellectual gifts ("Beauty's bearing or muse of mounting vein"—10), does simultaneously remark that the lad's inner "mannerly-hearted!" behavior (9) was worth "more than handsome face"—as he graciously accepted whatever gift the priest wished to offer as a reward for volunteer sacristy work. Two lines afterward Hopkins will not so strongly enshrine spiritual beauty above physical or intellectual radiance; he will simply with gladness recognize how "All, in this case, [is] bathed in high hallowing grace" (11). Still, as the poem concludes, he urges that his young friend, in imitation of Saint Paul's spiritual olympiad (Philippians 3:14), continue to increase his own elective will's fervor in choosing self-sacrificial action:

> Of heaven what boon to buy you, boy, or gain
> Not granted!—Only . . . O on that path you pace
> Run all your race, O brace sterner that strain!
>
> (12–14)

A year later, in August 1880, Hopkins's own reverence for spiritual beauty has already increased in intensity. In "Brothers," he praises human love, even when it makes one sibling seem rather silly to be fretting in the audience over his brother's actually quite self-confident performance on a drama hall stage. Hopkins obviously judges even silly philia love a relative of the Christian agape lauded by Saint Paul, for the artistic brother is "bráss-bóld" onstage (25), and—even while Hopkins does not actively depreciate his "Dog, he did give tongue!" onstage antics (34)—the poem seems designed as an allegorical illustration of 1 Corinthians 13:1: "Though I speak with the tongue of men and of angels and have not charity, I am a sounding brass or a tinkling cymbal." It seems possible to read here a subtly gradual transformation in Hopkins's attitude toward art and artists. Purcell's music he assumed, without much true explanation of his rationale for the assumption, to be an "air of angels" ("Henry Purcell," 9). Yet this boy actor, although not deemed fully vile, is proclaimed a "Dog" (a reversely acronymed false god?). The moderately harsh-minded allegorization with which

Hopkins treats an actual biographical event from his priestly teaching career[17] seems to reveal that he was creating the poem not especially in order to commemorate the originating biographical event, but rather in order to proclaim a theologically oriented hierarchy of human values. Henry, the silly but loving brother, is focusing his elective will toward values of at least mild self-sacrifice (deep love of a brother, which makes him look like a fool himself). But John/Jack, the actor brother, is merely enjoying the pleasures—and evidently the incipiently dangerous tendency to pride—of his affective selfhood.

In general terms, "The Leaden Echo and the Golden Echo" of 1882 (P, 282) sets once again lasting spiritual beauty at odds with fleeting physical splendor. Spirituality is clearly declared victor in the contest:

THE LEADEN ECHO

How to kéep—is there ány any, is there none such, nowhere known
    some, bow or brooch or braid or brace, láce, latch or catch or key
    to keep
Back beauty, keep it beauty, beauty, beauty, . . . from vanishing
    away?
. . . .
No there's none, there's none, O no there's none . . .
. . . .
                                                         (1–2, 5)

THE GOLDEN ECHO

There ís one, yes, I have one (Hush there!),
Only not within seeing of the sun.
. . . .
. . . O it is an all youth!
. . . .
. . . beauty-in-the-ghost, deliver it, early now, long before death
Give beauty back, beauty, beauty, beauty, back to God, beauty's self
    and beauty's giver.
                                                (2–3, 13, 18–19)

Because written as choruses for Hopkins's incomplete play *St. Winefred's Well*, these echoes may rely too much on musical effects to convey with full conviction their sober message.[18] That message, nevertheless, is the same uttered in the more militantly stern rhythms of "To what serves Mortal Beauty?" from 1885 (P, 285)— a poem that also still enshrines some physical splendor even as it bears affinity with the "Terrible Sonnets" and their rigorous considerations of the personal cost of spiritual self-sacrifice.

Hopkins primarily exemplifies physical splendor here by the "lovely lads" (6) who inspired the punster Saint Gregory's forecasting of a mission to the English, when he declared their youths "Not Angles but Angels" (P, 286). Later, too, Hopkins calls "men's selves" the "World's loveliest" (11). He even praises mortal beauty itself as an affective cue to "what good means" and thus as an aid to the electively self-sacrificial person, who will deem a quick spiritualized "glance" at beauty "more" ultimately valuable than a "gaze" too sensuously ardent (3–5). But the poet does reject the human tendency to enshrine mortal beauty too high in one's temple of values, to "worship block or barren stone" (9). Although "Self flashes off frame and face" (11), *self* is not the proper goal of spiritual devotion; "Home at heart" (13), in the soul (Hopkins's "Natural heart" [Patience," 6]) is "heaven's sweet[est] gift" ("To what serves Mortal Beauty?" 13). Like all that belongs to mortal beauty, even its "gift" to the soul must be only acknowledged ("Merely meet it; own [it]"—12), and then it must be "wish[ed] . . . God's better beauty, grace" (14).

Spiritual beauty thus becomes ever more strongly Hopkins's most lauded subject, and he does not treat it as innate in every human being, except in potential. One cannot say that spiritual beauty is ever with full comfort his sole subject, even in his very last poems, and it seems patent that he recognized—now just as much as during the novitiate when he gave up versing—that artists would always be tempted to place the physical before the spiritual. Art cannot redeem; involving "mortal beauty," it is "dangerous" ("To what serves Mortal Beauty?" 1).

A key statement of his evolving belief that art was potentially amoral is a poem fragment titled by Bridges and later editors "On a Piece of Music." The fragment declares that "What makes the man and what / The man within that makes: / Ask whom he serves or not / Serves and what side he takes"; it adds the corollary thought that "this masterhood, / This piece of perfect song, / This fault-not-found with good / Is neither right nor wrong" (21–24, 29–32; P, 184–85). The elective will's decisions for God are clearly more important to the writer of this fragment than are the affective self's feelings for created beauty.

Miller, with support from Christopher Devlin's sermon commentary, quite correctly analyzes "On a Piece of Music" and Hopkins's attitudes expressed in it:

> If art is a part of nature's "growth in every thing" [P, 81] then art is indeed trivial, and Hopkins is right to have a sense of guilt about his penchant for poetry. If poetry is a hymn to beauty which must die and the expression of the mortal inscape of the poet, it is perfectly reasonable that Hopkins, as Devlin says, should treat his muse "as a Victorian husband might . . . a wife of whom he had cause to be

ashamed" [S, 119]. The writing of poetry seems to Hopkins neither right nor wrong; it is insignificant, like a talent for billiards or cricket.

This view of poetry explains why Hopkins burned his poems after his conversion, repudiated the writing of poetry as something which would "interfere with [his] state and vocation" [L 1:24], and wrote poetry only after he could persuade himself that he had been ordered to do so by his superiors. He also tended to emphasize the undeliberate quality of poetic composition, as when he said, of those late poems, the "terrible" sonnets, that they "came like inspirations unbidden and against [his] will" [L 1:221]. The poems were not his responsibility, but were written spontaneously by his nature, or by some force moving his nature. . . . A letter to Dixon expresses unequivocally Hopkins' remorse for his poetry and the reasons for it: "The question then for me is not whether I am willing . . . to make a sacrifice of hopes of fame . . . but whether I am not to undergo a severe judgment from God for the lothness I have shewn in making it, for the reserves I may have in my heart made, for the backward glances I have given with my hand upon the plough, for the waste of time the very compositions you admire may have caused and their preoccupation of the mind which belonged to more sacred or more binding duties, for the disquiet and the thoughts of vainglory they have given rise to" [L 2:88].[19]

Miller does overemphasize Hopkins's disparagement of his art. He exaggerates, for instance, in the words that I have deleted from the long quotation above ("Though writing poetry is what comes most easily and naturally to him, it must be rejected, and for that very reason, for the natural man will never get to heaven"). Hopkins certainly judged, despite a few moments of quibbling doubt, that, despite being a natural poet, he as Pauline "spiritual man" (1 Corinthians 2:15) *would* get to heaven. It surely makes Hopkins appear overly lugubrious if he is said to find poetry "not trivial or neutral, but, like other positive ways of affirming selfhood, a means to damnation."[20]

Hopkins to the end of life finds his art potentially of worthy service to God, for he surely finds that it is possible to affirm selfhood without denying God, if one affirms it in subordination to God's will. Harris, in contrast here to Miller—who is in many ways his critical antecedent— does not forget that Hopkins wrote Bridges, as late as 1886, that even if "Art and its fame do not really matter, spiritually they are nothing, virtue is the only good," one might still "Let . . . light shine before men that they may see your good works (say, of art) and glorify yr. Father in heaven (that is, acknowledge that they have an absolute excellence in them and are steps in a scale of infinite and inexhaustible excellence)."[21] I agree with Harris that Hopkins always hoped to have his poems reach publication, although not before his death without Jesuit permission.[22]

Hopkins's poems become, during the 1880s, ever-more-painstaking meditative exercises. They remain beautiful, often dazzling, intellectual structures of great density and tautness; they are challenges to penetrating, controlled examination by any reader's mind. Yet they also seem rather humble attempts to utter in human words hidden and complex mysteries about the Divine Word, and Hopkins thus sometimes shows himself perplexed (or apparently so) by dim human sight and insight, as well as by potentially arbitrary language. Aesthetic and etymological richness—with considerable ambiguity of persona, image, and syntax—still do characterize the poems. Yet they are works firmly committed to gnostic revelations about the imitatio Christi, and they thus demand of their readers an attention (difficult to give, and therefore not always given) to Hopkins's own theological writing, to the history of mystical and biblical literature, to Roman Catholic creeds. After etymological magicianship has ceased, for example, simple statements from the Nicene Creed rule over even two key poems of this era: "Heraclitean Fire," with its exclaiming of "Enough! the Resurrection!" (16), and "Thou art indeed just, Lord," with its final prayer (14) to the Comforter "lord [and giver] of life."[23]

By the end of the decade, Hopkins in his last poem ("To R. B.") has become rather like Socrates in the *Cratylus*—rebuffing any further attention to the ambiguity of language, almost retiring to contemplate the eternal forms. This near-Socratic voice is almost his, too, in the penultimate work of his pen, "The shepherd's brow":

> The shepherd's brow, fronting forked lightning, owns
> The horror and the havoc and the glory
> Of it. Angels fall, they are towers, from heaven—a story
> Of just, majestical, and giant groans.
> But man—we, scaffold of score brittle bones;
> Who breathe, from groundlong babyhood to hoary
> Age gasp; whose breath is our *memento mori*—
> What bass is our viol for tragic tones?
> He! Hand to mouth he lives, and voids with shame;
> And, blazoned in however bold the name,
> Man Jack the man is, just; his mate a hussy.
> And I that die these deaths, that feed this flame,
> That . . . in smooth spoons spy life's masque mirrored: tame
> My tempests there, my fire and fever fussy.

Coupled with the barbed portrait of human folly in this sonnet is a poet's statement of human art's frailty. Here he seems to voice some of the staunch disparagement of his writing that Miller so emphasizes. When contrasted with Hebraic-Christian revelations of Fall and Redemption, involving the "shepherd's brow" of Moses, David, or Jesus (1) and the "towers" of falling Satanic archangels (3), how "tame," he says (13), are any human "tempests." And "tame" is the comic "fever fussy" uttered in the middle of this sonnet, where the persona apparently wishes merely to vituperate, in self-pity, over being a member of a lowly human species. But the poem never does fully deny this assertion of human lowness. Its last line at least suggests, as Thomas Beyette seems to hint,[24] Prospero's epilogue in *The Tempest*, arguing that all artistic "charms" must be "o'er-thrown" as we prove to be feeble, "most faint" creatures (1–3). Our tendency to want vengeful rage against our fellows must extinguish itself, as Prospero's indeed does; we must realize that we are not in our own final power, that we too—Prospero's "stuff / As dreams are made on" (4. 1. 156–57)—will be extinguished. Without "art to enchant," says Prospero in his epilogue of act 5 (14, 16–18), we must "be relieved by prayer, / Which pierces so that it assaults / Mercy itself and frees all faults."

Hopkins's seeming antipoet thus suggests that all human histrionics have a tendency to accompany themselves by a vile "viol" and a base "bass" ("The shepherd's brow," 8). The proper response following recognition of their folly seems not even a Miltonic epic, but the quiet final prayer of these fourteen lines—Hopkins's imitation of Prospero's epilogue penitence. He seems to recall George Eliot's declaration, in *Middlemarch*, that "Even Milton, looking for his portrait in a spoon, must submit to have the facial angle of a bumpkin."[25] Meanwhile, he admits with rue that he (to the degree that the persona actually is in part Hopkins) only infrequently writes "tame / . . . tempests" ("The shepherd's brow," 13–14)—tiny foolish sonnets, "smooth spoons" mirroring his sad face (13). Yet he also asks God to "tame / My tempests there" (13–14), to "tame" them where the primal fire of divine love strikes the "shepherd's brow" head of God's own Son (1)—for the sake of "Jack" Adam, "hussy" Eve (11) and all their subsequent progeny.[26] In essence, he asks cosmic sacramental fire to extend its radiance down to his own fiery, "fever[ish]," self (14), which is limited by the dimness of its current Platonic cave home.

Hopkins's sonnets, like Milton's epics, are to him always virtuous focuses of contemplation. Through them he shows—even if in a warping, diminishing spoonlike image—a mirrored reflection of near-Platonic forms: the cosmic events that were to him of most importance—the Fall of Lucifer, and Redemption through the Savior Shepherd Christ. Nevertheless, he asserts here that a whispered prayer of humility ("tame / My tempests") is the most spiritually eloquent of all human statements.

And such seems to be the message of his one poem written after "The shepherd's brow," a poem specifically crafted for a fellow poet less traditionally religious than he—Robert Bridges:

To R. B.

The fine delight that fathers thought; the strong
Spur, live and lancing like the blowpipe flame,
Breathes once and, quenchèd faster than it came,
Leaves yet the mind a mother of immortal song.

Nine months she then, nay years, nine years she long
Within her wears, bears, cares and combs the same:
The widow of an insight lost she lives, with aim
Now known and hand at work now never wrong.

Sweet fire the sire of muse, my soul needs this;
I want the one rapture of an inspiration.
O then if in my lagging lines you miss

The roll, the rise, the carol, the creation,
My winter world, that scarcely breathes that bliss
Now, yields you, with some sighs, our explanation.

This poem actually gives more direct attention to the positive values of aesthetic work than had "The shepherd's brow." Cotter, Mariani, and Boyle have all demonstrated[27] how Hopkins images inspirational fiery wind emerging from a phallic blowpipe, thus fathering human thought and song. The impregnating wind leaves its seed within the "mind" (4); in Hopkinsian terms it instresses divine scopus (aim, telos) within that mind. This eternal "aim," first made "insight" within the artist, becomes, in the realized poem, an "aim / Now known" (7–8). In part, then, this poem supports Hopkins's Aristotelian-Scotist credos that divine intellectual gifts operate teleologically in human art.

It is noticeable, however, that Hopkins is making the Holy Spirit, not Christ, the "sire" (9) of these intellectual gifts.[28] The combination of "wind" and "fire" together, from Acts 2:2–3, makes the post-Pentecost Spirit the obvious giver of the rich "insight" offered (7), and it is thus not directly transferred from Christ, as it seems to be in the poems of the 1870s. Hopkins seems clearly to argue with humility that he and all poets of his age are post-Pentecost creatures, who need the Spirit's help before they can perceive Christic inscape.

It is a spiritually humble Hopkins who is writing here, then—a man with admitted spiritual needs, a Prospero of the penitent epilogue in act 5, not the magician of act 1. And readers must not fail to note that the metaphor of intellectual impregnation, hidden gestation, and eventual birth in this sonnet's octave later translates itself into a companion metaphor. In the sestet Hopkins emphasizes spiritual awakening, hidden germination of the spiritual insight awakened, and eventual birth of a higher state: deep—but quiet—spiritual understanding.

In the noun of direct address beginning the sestet (9), Hopkins seems still to address the Holy Spirit as intellectual and poetic inspirer ("Sweet fire the sire of muse"). Yet the remaining language of the sestet does not focus upon the intellect of the poetic craftsman. It focuses, instead, upon a human being's spiritual life in the "soul" (9), even though that sober spiritual life may be reflected in poems with sober "lagging lines" (11).

By analogy with the poet's ultimate mental situation after "nine years" (5) of intellectual gestation, this speaker "want[s]" his original "rapture" of "inspiration" in the "soul" (9–10). Like the intellectually fructifying poet, he is "widow of an insight lost" (7). But he knows that the original "rapture" has remained within him and has developed itself into something new. Thus, when the poem repeats, at its close (14), the "Now" of line 7, it translates the confidence of the refined poet, nine years after his poetic insight began, to the current spiritual man. The spiritual being has evidently gained sanctifying power just as the writer gained poetic power. Hopkins's speaker, who in continuing the analogy seems to sense his spiritual "aim" becoming "known" (7–8), thus "yields . . . some sighs" (14) even while he "scarcely breathes [the poet's] bliss" (13). The "sighs" he shares with us through a poem, but in "our explanation" (14; emphasis mine) he shares them with someone else—most likely the Holy Ghost, now ministering in the "winter world" (13) of the "soul" (9).

Hopkins surely knew the biblical text declaring all human words inadequate for voicing humanity's deepest need: "The Spirit helps us . . . for we do not know how to pray as we ought" (Romans 8:26; Revised Standard Version). Hopkins's "winter world" was a realm where he learned to echo Saint Paul's disclaimer of human syllables, his awe (Romans 8:26) before the Spirit's "sighs too deep for words."

Certainly, Hopkins in his Dublin years after 1885 often regretted his lack of poetic productivity. Letters to his correspondents do belabor, frequently, that "if I could get on, if I could but produce work I should not mind its being buried, silenced, and going no further; but it kills me to be time's eunuch and never to beget."[29] It is therefore no wonder that readers of "To R. B." so invariably believe it to be a poem merely versifying such laments. It is, however, a rhetorically structured poem, and it clearly formulates a turn in its argument at the point of an Italian sonnet's volta line, just like any standard Hopkins sonnet. Besides, its ultimate theme is hardly revolutionary, at least in the history of Christian literature. It is in the tradition of Geoffrey Chaucer, who could conclude a very energetic poetic life with a retraction of any "enditynges of worldly vanitees"[30] that "rise," "roll," or "carol" (Hopkins, "To R. B.," 12) our mere creation. And perhaps one can see it as Hopkins's warning to Bridges—who still sailed at this historical point in the "piccioletta barca" of agnosticism—that what Hopkins was preparing to see was too distant from his school friend's as-yet-limited ken. Awaiting his spiritual translation into the undimmed realm of God, Hopkins admonishes, like Dante, "O ye who in a little bark, eager to listen, have followed behind my ship that singing makes her way, turn back to see your shores again; do not put forth on the deep, for, perhaps, losing me, you would be left bewildered" (*Paradiso* 2:1–6). Poetry, which Hopkins and Bridges had sometimes intensely debated and enjoyed during a brief lifetime, could not ultimately, the Jesuit believed, provide any more than a roadway toward—surely not a bridge over—the gulf between humanity and God.

B. The Death of Earth: The Rent in the Veil of Creaturehood Symbols

Like Miller[31] in their recognition of a truth that many critics have failed to perceive, Harris[32] and Bump[33] observe that in the 1880s the bounties of a nature poetry which had dominated Hopkins's work in the previous ten years are now all but disappeared, replaced by fervently moralistic work that often makes nature only a symbol for decisive human limitations. Nature's daily signs of devastation prefigure Hopkins's own approaching death and devastation. This shared fragility of all earthly things testified, the priest believed, that he needed more than ever to seek Christian sacrament's apex in heavenly eschatology.

Although Hopkins does during this decade present some images from nature of Christlike inscape, he now often presents nature as if it truly were a mere Heraclitean cycle of life and death in meaningless successions, not a firm structure of Aristotelian-Scotist teleology. As a pattern of flux, unable to give visible assurance of God's kind favor toward human beings, or even steady displays of Christ's suffering within it for humanity's redemption, nature often seems rather to suggest God's disfavor. His threat of eternal punishment for the indecisive elective will seems to loom within the cosmos that the affective will perceives. Those who want visible divine signs of ascertainable beneficence, it seems, will only receive a blank stare in response. In the few "nature poems" he wrote during the 1880s, Hopkins suggests such dreary possibilities, although the dreariness is not his final tone.

In speaking about "Divine Providence and the Guardian Angels," on 25 October 1880, Hopkins already asserted,

> . . . [P]rovidence is imperfect, plainly imperfect. The sun shines too long and withers the harvest, the rain is too heavy and rots it or in floods spreading washes it away; the air and water carry in their currents the poison of disease; there are poison plants, venomous snakes and scorpions; the beasts our subjects rebel, not only the bloodthirsty tiger that slaughters yearly its thousands, but even the bull will gore and the stallion bite or strike; at night the moon sometimes has no light to give, at others the clouds darken her; she measures time most strangely and gives us reckonings most difficult to make and never exact enough; the coalpits and oil wells are full of explosions, fires, and outbreaks of sudden death, the sea of storms and wrecks [;] the snow has avalanches, the earth landslips; we contend with cold, want, weakness, hunger, disease, death, and often we fight a losing battle, never a triumphant one; everything is full of fault, flaw, imperfection, shortcoming. . . .[34]

Elsewhere, Hopkins wrote, about the natural creatures in Eden, that they could be used by either a "black" or a "white" spirit, by Satan or God, for either disastrous temptings to sin (as with Adam and Eve) or for divine praises.[35] Suddenly sounding Calvinist once again, Hopkins asserts that Adam's Edenic duty "was to keep Paradise, no doubt, against the Devil, for what other creature could have harmed it? . . . But alas! he did *not* keep it and so far from turning the waste wilderness of the outside earth into a Paradise he was cast from paradise out into the waste wilderness."[36]

As Hopkins declares forthrightly in the 1880s, humankind can only leave the outscaped "waste wilderness," and return in the Resurrection to an inscaped Paradise that Adam lost, by making a decision with the elective will to imitate God's holiness and attain saintly inscape. Nature, now seeming spiritually neutral, can seemingly teach human beings little about their essential spiritual needs, however awesome its physical beauty. Hopkins penned "Spelt from Sibyl's Leaves," in late 1884 or early 1885 (P, 284) as one "wáre of a wórld where bút these | twó tell" (13), "twó flocks, twó folds—black, white" (12).

The first couplet of this outstretched sonnet—

Earnest, earthless, equal attuneable, | vaulty, voluminous, . . .
    stupendous
Evening strains to be tíme's vást, | womb-of-all, home-of-all, hearse-
    of-all night—

recalls the vision of Genesis 1:2, when "the earth was void and empty, and darkness was upon the face of the deep."[37] And, to be sure, this primal dark Being of Genesis, existing before light, seems to reassert itself in Hopkins's poem about earth's final evening. Nature here remains "attuneable" (1)—at one, unified and harmonious within the cosmic scheme. Thus it still has its telos, but it hardly seems the lustrous telos attributed to spiritually purposeful nature in Hopkins's Wales poems. Rather, Hopkins's speaker finds threatening the equanimity with which affective nature acepts unity with what has become to his elective self (much as in "*Nondum*") a primeval chaos. Because of his fearful reaction, he tries to force the surroundings to reassure him about his own potential for knowing a similar harmony, to provide him sibylline sortilege predicting good fortune. But nature refuses to cooperate with his request.

"Her fond yellow hornlight wound to the west" (3), evening in "Spelt from Sibyl's Leaves" seems "fond" of folk, but meanwhile "her wild hollow hoarlight [is] hung to the height / Waste" (3–4). A "fond yellow hornlight," seeming charitable to an author who long ago had seen the ultimate etymology of "horn" as "horn of salvation," only briefly counteracts the dire atmosphere of the "wild hollow hoarlight." Indeed, trust in the "hornlight" itself could be emotionally "fond," or "foolish" (*OED*).

The persona sees here "self ín self steepèd and páshed" (6)—although in this "equal, attuneable" setting (1) there appear to be no conscious selves but the speaker's own. To the troubled human elective will, an equable affective disintegration of nature toward primal Being renders lonely human death more horrible. Persons have spiritual consciousness that "equal, attuneable" nature lacks.

Answering his spiritual consciousness, the Hopkins speaker commands his inmost soul to remember the moral imperative: "Heart, you round me right / With" (7–8). Not only does he ask his emotionally supportive heart to stay close to him ("right / With"), but he also asks his heart as *soul* to "round" him with "right" righteousness. Now, when the "round" circularity of divine architectonic inscape seems to have become alien, instead of reassuring, in nature, he knows that the only place he can meet "round" divinity is within his spiritual center, the "heart" as right-"round[ing]," right-"whisper[ing]" (*OED*) soul.

Firmly, Hopkins continues to address himself:

> . . . Óur tale, O óur oracle! | Lét life, wáned, ah lét life wind
> Off hér once skéined stained véined varíety | upon, áll on twó
>   spools; párt, pen, páck
> Now her áll in twó flocks, twó folds—black, white; | right, wrong;
>   reckon but, reck but, mind

But thése two; wáre of a wórld where bút these | twó tell, each off
  the óther; of a rack
Where, selfwrung, selfstrung, sheathe-and shelterless, | thóughts
  agáinst thoughts ín groans grínd.

(10–14)

He does not speak about earth at all now, but only about hs own "life"
(10)—an elective spiritual entity. It has coexisted affectively with earth
but has made all its spiritual decisions on its elective own, as a fully
exposed inner sacramental substance, "sheathe-and shelterless" (14).
Like earth, it is in the end allowed no dapple, no "véined varíety" (11).
While the dapple denied earth principally is outer diversity, the dapple
denied humanity, during this evening that foreshadows the eve of
Judgment Day, is spiritual indecisiveness—human refusal staunchly to
serve God, the "white," rather than also serving "black" Satan (12).

The major lesson offered by "Spelt from Sibyl's Leaves" is that God is
known only intermittently through spiritual glimmerings set within an
apparently fickle physical nature. God is known most reliably through
spiritual sanctification: the inner elective development in human
beings of saintly inscape.[38]

In one seeming "*summa*" of his life as priest-poet,[39] the poem of 1888
(*P*, 293) "That Nature is a Heraclitean Fire and of the comfort of the
Resurrection," Hopkins again is able to seize upon a few visions from
nature that can give him trust in a kind divine providence. Yet "Heraclitean Fire" also, like "Spelt from Sibyl's Leaves," carries a key theme of
nature's spiritual fickleness.

However "Delightfully" nature may behave, says this poem (5), however striking it may be to the human eye alert to sensation, it seems only
a showplace for creatures who are in truth fragile as clouds. Whether
these clouds are cumulus, cirrus, or stratus (described in successive
order), they carry their own destruction within them: "Cloud-puffball,
torn tufts, tossed pillows" (1). These clouds, apparently like all of
nature, are illusionists, ready to deceive anyone who has trust in them;
and the very sky is "dazzling whitewash" that hides the "roughcast" of
its underlying molding (3). "Million-fuelèd, | nature's bonfire burns on"
(9)—perhaps a divinely ordained or good (*OED*—by French etymology,
bon) fire, serving a teleological purpose, but still hardly of spiritual
reassurance to the person who watches it. After all, it is surely also,
according to Anglo-Saxon etymology, a "fire of bones" (*OED*). Thus
bone-fire it proves for humankind:

But quench her bonniest, dearest | to her, her clearest-selvèd spark
Man, how fast his firedint, | his mark on mind, is gone!
Both are in an unfathomable, all is in an enormous dark

> Drowned. O pity and indig | nation! Manshape, that shone
> Sheer off, disseveral, a star, | death blots black out; nor mark
>   Is any of him at all so stark
> But vastness blurs and time | beats level. . . .

$$(10–16)$$

We readers, who in Hopkins's Wales nature sonnets seemed to gain such positive proof of our own divine inscape from his affective observations of nature's inscape, here have lost our sense of our scopus or "mark" through the affective indifference of that very same nature. It buries us as an "indig | nation" (13).

Yet, evidently according to some hidden tenets of faith, Hopkins has been able to declare that we remain nature's "bonniest," or "bright[est]," "comeli[est]" creatures (OED). As an etymologist, too, Hopkins perhaps knew that a "bonny" was a separate "bed of ore, not forming a vein, nor communicating with any other vein" (OED). Perhaps, then, our sources of richest elective inscape, our souls, can be compared with the richest affectively discovered inscape of nature: the light of nature's richest gem, the diamond. Crudely dark when first mined, the diamond iridescently shines when polished as a separated ore. Perhaps we have not necessarily, any more than the diamond, lost our potential "firedint" (11) just because death has buried us within the "black[ing-] out" earth (14). And, indeed, so says the penultimate line of this caudated sonnet, when its persona calls us "This Jack, joke, poor potsherd, | patch, matchwood, immortal diamond" (23).[40]

On the other hand, this powerful poem by no means focuses only on slim natural tokenings of God's providence. The main lesson of nature here is death—somber and filled with miseries. "[W]orld's wildfire, leave but ash," Hopkins writes (20), and the best hope that can evidently be derived from nature in such an observation comes from a pun—one that makes the ash formed by nature's conflagration, like the burning of the coals at the end of "The Windhover," a symbol of the Passion. Nature still knows its passional inscape of the Cross: an "ash," as a tree, could provide such a cross's wood.

But the Hopkins of this poem now refuses to concentrate further on any visible inscape given him in nature. He is more concerned with the invisible; the "not yet" of "Nondum" has become the Resurrection that is only promised by faith in biblical revelation, not by natural evidence except in a few hints like diamonds and greening ash trees. It is the Resurrection, too, that makes a person a truly "immortal diamond":

>   Enough! the Resurrection,
> A heart's clarion! Away grief's gasping, | joyless days, dejection.

> Across my foundering deck shone
> A beacon, an eternal beam. | Flesh fade, and mortal trash
> Fall to the residuary worm; | world's wildfire, leave but ash:
> In a flash, at a trumpet crash,
> I am all at once what Christ is, | since he was what I am, and
> This Jack, joke, poor potsherd, | patch, matchwood, immortal
> diamond,
> Is immortal diamond.
>
> (16–24)

Through the philosophy of inscape and its affective imaging in his exuberant poems, the theology student Hopkins of 1877 in Wales wrote nature sonnets seeking to prove that Christ *is*, at least to Christian eyes, transubstantial from within "what I am" and from within what exists around me—windhovers, trout, "stooks" in harvest, starlight. Christ as "creator and end of all things" still reveals himself to Hopkins in this poem of nature in "Heraclitean Fire"—if only because of the marvels of lexical etymology and natural observation that see humankind as nature's "bonniest," and thus united with sacramental substance of "immortal diamond." Nevertheless, in a world that for all its boisterous fire seems destined for inevitable darkness, a world where lovely "Cloud-puffball" is also a simultaneously self-destructive "Cloud-puffball" (1), a man of even such firm Christian faith as Hopkins's needs more trustworthy bonds with Christic substance on which to rely than visions from the landscape.

Such a man needs to put his elective will's trust very firmly, as he has throughout his years of writing poetry, upon the verbal revelation that Christ "*was* what I am" (22; emphasis mine). The documents of Scripture, telling Hopkins that Jesus the man was also Christ the Son of God, must now for him more than ever sacramentally become "a lamp shining in a dark place, until the day dawns and the morning-star rises in [his] heart . . ." (2 Peter 1:19). Hopkins has been told by Peter's second epistle (1:19) that the Gospels' accounts of Jesus are not only past history, but also "the prophetic word made [ever] more sure."

For that reason he can be jubilant, despite his morose response as he looks out on the panorama of Heraclitean destruction and sees humankind to be apparently only pyre for a conflagrant disaster-heap. In the Resurrection he expects to be what Christ is now, a *supernatural* "diamond." Only in the Resurrection, still, can the long-ago writer of "*Nondum*" plan fully to know the glowing sacramental revelation of Christ the Son, God the Father, and—as the title of this poem makes clear—the Comforter of sublimest "comfort."

C. Joseph and Mary: The Eucharists of Hopkins's Self and Soul

In examining both Hopkins's poems about art during the 1880s and his poems during that era about nature, we have seen him become ever more insistent that one must de-emphasize the search for affective sacramental visions of God in the outer physical world. One must seek, instead, and despite external visionary darkness, to develop electively willed saintly inscape within apparently dark caverns of one's soul. When we encounter the poetry and prose through which Hopkins portrayed during the 1880s such a development of inner saintly inscape, we recognize clearly that saintly inscape—like the term *inscape* in general—is synonymous with sacramental *substance*. As Hopkins uses in many of his last decade's poems the trope of a Christian soul's biography in imitatio Christi, he gives renewed poetic life to the Pauline concept of the Mystical Body of Christ. He images spiritual growth of an individual saint within the Mystical Body of the Church as making that person both an offspring of God and a sacrament (a human "mystical body," akin to a consecrated Eucharistic wafer). This person comes to share Christ's body and blood through the parenting union of the personal Marian soul and the seminally invading Holy Spirit.

The principal poems to be discussed at length in this section of my study have been called "Dark Sonnets."[41] These compositions truly do portray, in their surface arguments, speakers who seem to reside in a sacramentally dark outer world from which all visible signs of God's comforting presence have disappeared. But through the use of poetic "underthought"—a Hopkinsian poetic term that now proves apt for describing an art sacramentally transubstantial at its obscured inner core of revelation—Hopkins reveals to us the inner sacramental light and the inner sacramental gestation of Christliness in poetic narrators who otherwise appear merely "natural," spiritually darkened, creatures (1 Corinthians 2:14). These narrators are shown as tormented by darkness and yet spiritually receptive to God's purpose despite that darkness; their reward for such *receptiveness* (or perhaps, Hopkins would no doubt say, the guiding force behind it) is *transubstantiation:* they are inwardly being made divine Eucharists of sacramental power themselves. Thus they can eventually participate in the climactic event predicted by all Christian sacrament: apocalyptic eschatological victory.

* * *

Two recent studies of autobiography focus conflicting approaches to Hopkins's 1885 "Terrible Sonnets." Avrom Fleishman observes a strong Victorian "impulse toward self-writing" in this "sequence."[42] On the other hand, Jerome Hamilton Buckley finds Hopkins able to perceive, at least, "the tyranny of self-awareness," and, at most, "a higher religious purpose," as he locates in his personal struggles the "general plight of mankind."[43]

Hopkins's own comments about these sonnets have long led critics to treat them largely as autobiography of a period in spring and summer of 1885. Hopkins then claimed that "madness" seemed imminent for him.[44] He also reported his production of "five or more" sonnets, "four" of which "came like inspirations unbidden and against [his] will." Three and a half months earlier he had spoken of two other sonnets, one "written in blood."[45]

Buckley, by perceiving these sonnets as a conscious "sequence" with a "turn" toward "a higher religious purpose" than mere "self-analysis," proves a sensible critic, like Boyle many years ago. By contrast, Harris, in his controversial recent study, greatly exaggerates Hopkins's autobiographical depression, even judging Hopkins to be sincerely blasphemous. The "Terrible Sonnets" surely arose, at least in part, from Hopkins's personal turmoil. Yet they still fit into his attempt throughout nearly a decade ("nine months . . . nay [nine] years" ("To R. B." [1889], 5) to distance himself from self-torment, creating in verse an archetypal Christian sacramental biography. According to Hopkins's November 1881 meditation on the Incarnation, such a biography belonged to every Christian, for all Christians were born, like Jesus, of Mary. The Christian bios, he said, emerged "with great birthpangs," but blessedly, "in the spirit."[46]

This decade-long Hopkinsian cycle, sometimes "written in blood" simply because painstakingly composed, begins with the poem "Andromeda" of August 1879. There the first Paraclete, Perseus-Christ, instantaneously translates himself into the second Paraclete, the Holy Spirit, and comes on "Pillowy air" (10) to be united with the Marian Andromeda-soul of the individual Christian or the corporal Christian Church, who would otherwise be Satan's "doomed dragon food" (4). Mary/Andromeda thus becomes in this poem the Holy Spirit's bride, able to mother Christ in all Christians' souls.

In "Peace," a poem of October 1879, Hopkins's persona asks for encounter with the Holy Spirit: "When will you ever, Peace, wild wooddove, shy wings shut, / Your round me roaming end, and under be my boughs?" (1–2) He asks the Spirit to descend with baptismal blessing on his head, while his Hopkinsian arms stretch out as the boughs of a Christ-imitative cross (cf. Matthew 3:16–17). He also suggests that the Holy Spirit will come to a nest in the Hopkinsian boughs; in the eggs lying upon that nest the Christ-imitative Christian soul may grow toward its birth.[47]

But not until four years later did Hopkins compose the most central poem in this metaphoric series. In "The Blessed Virgin Compared to the Air we Breathe" (1883), Hopkins most precisely tells us that the Holy Spirit can be breathed with Mary into every human being; within their Marian Andromeda-souls she will create "New Nazareths" (60), birthplaces for human Christliness.

Amplified still more by later Hopkins poems, this metaphor of divine sacrament's impregnation in the human soul flourishes throughout the "Terrible Sonnets," and controls their central argument. Thus, while these poems may partly voice Hopkins's autobiographical doubts of faith, they far more dominantly voice his will to participate in an archetypal process of Christian sacramental biography.

In the opening "Terrible Sonnet," "Carrion Comfort," a conceptive act occurs, in the soul, through a fierce, Donnesque, ravishing by the Holy Spirit. This act seems, however, to have been repeated throughout "That night, that year / Of now done darkness [when] I wretch lay wrestling with (my God!) my God" (13–14). The allusion to Jacob involved in this line recalls Donne's Holy Sonnet 11, where Jacob is a symbol of that "vile mans flesh" which in Holy Sonnet 14 requests of God a "ravish[ing]."[48]

Hopkins's parenthetical exclamation "my God!" is usually treated by readers of "Carrion Comfort" as a curse or the apologetic memory of a curse (and he certainly wants to suggest that an agonized soul, on one level of reading, is near to the point of cursing). Yet the exclamation also functions to introduce the spiritual impregnation of that agonized soul, which after all features as the persona of this sonnet cycle with its trope of Christian sacramental bios. In that poetic context, the soul's outcry "my God!" is a potential orgasmic shout of the soul being ravished by deity.

In the first quatrain of the next manuscript poem, the spiritually fraught anima already suffers labor pains (probably *hysterical* labor pains). She demands the physical manifestation of her spiritually germinating offspring:

> No worst, there is none. Pitched past pitch of grief,
> More pangs will, schooled at forepangs, wilder wring.
> Comforter, where, where is your comforting?
> Mary, mother of us, where is your relief?
>
> (1–4)[49]

The now-absented ravisher (the Comforter) and Mary, the model for the soul's virginal impregnation by that Comforter, receive attack for not stilling the soul's anguish. While Mary knew "relief" for nine months of fetal husbandry when Jesus was born, the soul's birthing throes seem only to know a constantly higher "pitch"; earlier incomplete pangs have "schooled" the later ones.

To be sure, there are other symbolic clusters in the "Terrible Sonnets" besides this one of inner gestation. For instance, Michael Moore strongly emphasizes the influence of Hopkins's Loyolan meditation on Hell.[50] Hopkins's characterized anima seems to deserve hellish punishment for such near-blasphemies against the Holy Ghost as "Comforter, where, where is your comforting?" She thus *almost* commits the sin (blasphemy against the Holy Ghost) "not . . . forgiven, either in this age or the age to come" (Matthew 12:32). Yet she does *not* commit that sin, evidently trusting the Holy Ghost as one who did not fully leave the archetypal model Mary a comfortless victim of rape. As was declared in the opening poem of Hopkins's sonnet cycle, where the ghostly engendering of Christ occurred, the persona will not "feast" on "carrion comfort, Despair," will not "blaspheme against the Holy Spirit" by turning unduly "anxious" (Luke 12:10–11). The soul and Hopkins are not in hell, although they may seem to be, for they have not committed the one sin, blasphemy against the Spirit, that could surely confine them there.

These two also will not blaspheme against Christ, the original Paraclete. They will, despite much tension, remain stalwart, as Christ himself did when tempted by Satan to prideful suicide. When, according to the sonnet "No worst,"

> Fury had shrieked 'No ling-
> ering! Let me be fell: force I must be brief,'
>
> (7–8)

Hopkins and his soul inclined to yield to suicidal temptation (becoming their own "fell"-like mountains of false Godhead):

> . . . the mind, mind has mountains; cliffs of fall
> Frightful, sheer, no-man-fathomed. Hold them cheap
> May who ne'er hung there. Nor does long our small
> Durance deal with that steep or deep.
>
> (9–12)

Yet they did not, any more than Jesus (Matthew 4:7) leap from "the pinnacle of the temple" (Matthew 4:5) and become, by default, disciples of the tempter Satan. Instead the Hopkins personae, each inclined to deem him or herself a "wretch" (13), "creep, / . . . under a *comfort* serves in a whirlwind: all / *Life* death does end and each day dies with sleep" (12–14; emphases mine). They are like Job, who, even before encountering God in the whirlwind (Job 38), was able to assert "I know that my Redeemer *lives*" (Job 19:25; emphasis mine). Hopkins and his soul trust, like Job, that "Life" "ends" all "death." Thus they are able to judge that they behave like demon-possessed Gadarene swine whenever they lament, like their contemporaries, about *Weltschmerz* or world-sorrow; they know that this ailment is essentially despair, the "chief-/ woe" ("No worst," 5–6) or chief sin.[51]

At the end of "No worst," therefore, Hopkins's persona-soul, along with a persona-self, gains "comfort" in rest (the rest, indeed, may be a gift from the Comforter himself). And at the beginning of the next lyric in Hopkins's folio manuscripts, both soul and Hopkinsian self awaken to accept "life / Among strangers" as their "lot" ("To seem the stranger," 1–2). Within this poem, the twinned personae seem conscious, if not cheerily conscious, that the spiritual "life" in which they believe (along with Job) denies them easeful life with their peers.

Hopkins's own parents, whom he had indeed visited in summer 1885, surely are models for the "Father and mother dear, / . . . in Christ not near" (2–3) of this poem. Yet such parents also befit Christian archetypes: "Do not think that I have come to bring peace on earth; I have not come to bring peace, but a sword. For I have come to set a man against his father, and a daughter against her mother . . . and a man's foes will be those of his own household" (Matthew 10:34–36). Many Hopkins critics have noticed this allusion, but they have not always seen how it serves to distance Hopkins's material from mere autobiography.

The same distancing occurs in the reference to

> England, whose honour O all my heart woos, wife
> To my creating thought, would neither hear
> Me, were I pleading, plead nor do I: I wear-
> y of idle a being but by where wars are rife.
>
> (5–8)

To be sure, Hopkins had been rebuffed by England, perhaps even by English Jesuits in their reluctance to channel his gifts as theologian or poet to a large audience.[52] And yet, whatever his bitterness, Hopkin's metaphors again generalize his treatment of personal data. In a world of "wars and rumors of wars" (Matthew 24:6), Hopkins's English persona captured inspiration from the Holy Spirit for "creating thought." Voicing that "creating thought," he tried to "woo" England as his "wife." But any poet, Hopkins later says in the 1889 poem "To R. B." (9), shares the "sweet fire" of the Holy Ghost that is the "sire of muse." The later poem, unlike "To seem the stranger," argues that a poet must primarily mother his thoughts personally. We can see that in Hopkins's judgment his experience as one who wished to speak meaningfully to an unmotherly England resembles the experience of any lonely would-be communicator.

In "To seem the stranger," still another inhospitable place where "wars are rife" is Ireland. Although a hard life as professor in Ireland is part of Hopkins's autobiography also, an allusion to Herbert's "Jordan" (1), discovered by Harris,[53] again generalizes Hopkins's persona, making him one with Herbert, who could sense that overly ornate poetry merely "Catch[es] the sense at two removes" ("Jordan" [1], 10). Hopkins portrays his persona in Ireland, "at a third / Remove," as one who wants to say simply, together with Herbert, *My God, My King*" ("Jordan" [1], 15). Yet circumstances make him capable only of expressing fraternal union with fellow human beings ("Not but in all removes I can / Kind love both give and get"—"To seem the stranger," 10–11; my emphasis). He wants, however, to have a more fulfilling union with his fellows— not that of mere friendship (philia) but that of divine love (caritas). Thus we hear his persona-soul expressing how

> . . . Only what word
> Wisest my heart breeds dark heaven's baffling ban
> Bars or hell's spell thwarts. This to hoard unheard,
> Heard unheeded, leaves me a lonely began.
>
> (11–14)

In notes on Loyola's *Spiritual Exercises*, "On the contemplating Persons, Words, and Actions," Hopkins defined gnosis, a key term in his thought, as "the sense of the presence of God," which can be gained progressively by "Imagination" and then by an even more intensely prayerful "heed."[54] And his personified anima feels that she "hoard[s]" without being "heard," then speaks without being" . . . heeded." Developing in the soul is the "presence" of God—part of which is divine agape or caritas, a love far richer than a fraternal "kind love" one can easily "give and get." Having grown responsive to, and even partly transformed by, divine charity, Hopkins's soul and self both feel alienated from uncharitable neighbors.

Therefore, as "To seem the stranger" ends, Hopkins's anima asks why "the word / Wisest" that her "heart breeds"—Christ the Word—cannot yet be born into full vitality. Where are the "New Nazareths" that were to produce "More Christ [to] baffle death" ("The Blessed Virgin," 60, 67)? The marriage of God and human soul in "To seem the stranger" seems a personal "ban[ishment]," no marriage "ban[n]" that clearly "baffle[s]" spiritual enemies (12). Yet the poem is not desperate autobiography on Hopkins's part—his "all but parthenogenetic effort to give rebirth to himself as a Christian."[55] It is, on the contrary, a generalized Christian biographical portrait of a soul whose husband has retreated according to the logic of his name: Holy *Ghost*. And its heroine persona, the portrayed Hopkinsian soul, is a "lonely began," not a desolate completion; the poem is not about "hideous despair."[56]

In the next sonnet, the persona is not even fully "lonely." She and someone else ("we") have spent a "wak[ing]" night together. Her "heart," the someone else, has seen shocking "sights" as it "went" shocking ways. And it must continue to do so for "yet longer light's delay." This "heart" appears to be a fetus, stumbling through its confusing adjustment to life in the dark womb where it is trapped until "longer light's delay" ends in birth ("I wake and feel," 1–4).

Thus "I wake and feel," a poem whose first verb proclaims not only gloomy insomnia but also "wak[ing]" *life*, reaffirms "life" in the midst of the loudest lament yet by the deserted bride-soul. Her babe is her "witness" (5–8) for "cries countless, cries like dead letters sent / To dearest him that lives alas! away." Hopkins's inner soul seems to speak for all who "in thy sight, O Lord," are "like as a woman with child that . . . crieth out," lonely for her husband, "in her pangs" (Isaiah 26:17). Still, the "Hours" and "years" of gestating torture ("I wake and feel," 7), like the "night" or "year" of the original spiritual ravishing by the Holy Spirit ("Carrion Comfort," 13), remain all involved in the soul's spiritual "life."

Even if in the flesh of Hopkins that is that womb's residence he feels ("I wake and feel," 9–12) that he is "gall . . . heartburn," that "God's most deep decree / Bitter would have [him] taste . . . ," that "Bones built . . . flesh filled, blood brimmed the curse," that "Selfyeast of spirit a dull dough sours," he seems to remember other words of Jesus during his temptation by Satan ("Man shall not live by [sourdough?] bread alone, but by every word that proceeds from the mouth of God" [Matthew 4:4]).[57] Hence he and his soul do not forget that they are God's spiritual lieges, a pledged Christian man and his spiritually impregnated soul, made to form out of a curse's "blood" the "new wine" of Christ in "new wineskins" (Matthew 9:17). The "lost," they believe, may be "like" them (12–13). Yet, because the lost are not "like" them in becoming transubstantial human Eucharists of Christic Real Presence, the "lost" are surely "worse" (14).

In the next sonnet, the Holy Spirit, along with the portrayed anima, bears the special name "Patience." The Spirit seems to have withdrawn from the anima, but only in order to test her trust in his indwelling power. The soul must develop spiritual fruitfulness by doing battle, like Milton's Samson, with sanctifying Patience. According to the providence of the "day-spring" Spirit, says Milton (*Samson Agonistes*, 11; Luke 1:78), "patience is . . . oft the exercise of Saints" (*Samson Agonistes*, 1287–88). Thus Hopkins indeed declares:

Patience, hard thing! the hard thing but to pray,
But bid for, Patience is! Patience who asks
Wants war, wants wounds; weary his times, his tasks;
To do without, take tosses, and obey.

(1–4)

According to Hopkins, "Rare patience roots in these [sorts of toughening experiences], and these away, / Nowhere" (5–6). The anima character, as the "Patience who asks" for patience, finds that her spiritual husband remains "root[ed]" within a gestating spirituality. Thus, although "weary," she is an expectant mother, no longer the "idle a being" of "To seem the stranger."

Her child is assuredly present. We see (6–8) the blood-swathed "Purple eyes" of a fetus emerging through "seas of liquid leaves," the soul's embryonic fluid. As Patience "basks" the "Purple eyes" of the child within her ivied womb, she ("Natural heart") forgets ("masks") her memories of "wrecked past purpose." Christ, the Sacred Heart, is being born within this soul's "Natural heart," and Christ himself, as Hopkins elsewhere so eloquently states, knew what it was to suffer from "wrecked past purpose."[58] Remembering such a fact, the Christ-imitative anima of Hopkins will cease lamenting the toughening process of birthing, as will both Hopkins himself and the child being born—the Sacred Heart of Jesus now dwelling in the human soul:

We hear our hearts grate on themselves: it kills
To bruise them dearer. Yet the rebellious wills
Of us we do bid God bend to him even so.

("Patience," 9–11)

If Hopkins is to become like Christ, to have Christ born within him, then he and his soul must follow the historical Jesus of Gethsemane and Golgotha; they must reverently "bend" "rebellious wills" toward God.

The Holy Ghost, to be sure, still seems absent: "And where is he who more and more distills / Delicious kindness?" (12–13). The answer to this question is that if he is absent, he is so quite properly, like drones from a hive where female worker bees bring honey to fruition: "He is patient. Patience fills / His crisp combs [with the honey of the spiritual child Christ], and that comes those ways [of the metaphoric beehive filling] we [as armchair natural scientists] know" (13–14).[59]

The motherly soul will now turn to quieter mothering, in the final sonnet of this series ("My own heart"); she will care for her babe, an "own heart" of a "sad self" (1–2), with a "Charitable" agape love (3) that he as Christ can give her—and "not live this tormented mind / With this tormented mind tormenting yet" (3–4). To locate her missing husband simply by complaining about his absence is a futile ambition.

A pregnant woman does not find it easy to be comfortable, as she "grop[es]" around her world, but this pregnant soul identifies her discomfort with that lack of ease known to her "groping" child in the "dark" and "wet" womb:

> I cast for comfort I can no more get
> By groping round my comfortless, than blind
> Eyes in their dark can day or thirst can find
> Thirst's all-in-all in all a world of wet.
>
> (5–8)

The soul speaks these words along with Hopkins, who might, as in "To seem the stranger," "cast for comfort," seek to be a "fisher . . . of men" (Luke 5:10) in the external world, while not seeking needed inner strength from his apparently "comfortless" soul. Yet the first tercet of "My own heart" shows Hopkins's nonspiritual "Jackself," "jaded," remembering (9–10) to unite with his "soul." They together must "leave comfort root-room; let [the] joy [of their spiritual progeny] size / At God knows when to God knows what" (11–12).

God's "smile," after all, " 's not wrung" (13) by enforced, even by false or premature, labor pain. "[U]nforeseen times rather—as skies / Betweenpie mountains," the returned Holy Ghost, the "comfort" who was always in the baby finding "root-room," now clearly appears—as the Lord and Giver of Life, who, in the life of nature and in the future birth of now-gestating infants, "lights a lovely mile" (11–14).

These "Terrible Sonnets," ultimately, do not report "the disappearance of God," as Miller would have us believe, nor do they show a humanist autobiographical psyche "in extremity", as Robinson's book about Hopkins asserts. Hopkins wants us to see in these poems a basic Christian biography's extremity: the tormenting pangs of rebirth. As sexual imagery becomes transubstantial sacramental imagery, his Christian biographical persona is portrayed (in nine out of sixteen poems after 1883) as a virginal soul, penetrated by the potent Holy Spirit, striving to nurture, against all foes, the Spirit's inner Eucharistic "fruits" (Galatians 5:22–23). The spiritual fruits are not described, in the poetry, as blossoming with outsized corollas, huge stalks, vast outspread leafage; there are few obvious visible signs here of blessing, holy plenitude, repleteness of joy. The "war within" still is fought with a divine spiritual fecundator—the same God whose enormous organic power has "hew[ed] mountain and continent, / Earth, all, out . . . with trickling increment, / Vein[ed] violets and tall trees ma[de] more and more" ("In honour of St. Alphonsus Rodriguez," 6, 9–11). Yet the human soul, unlike nature, seems to produce its fruits of divine gestation in a physically stark atmosphere. The humble Jesuit doorkeeper

Alphonsus Rodriguez, says Hopkins, saw his "career" "crowd[ed] . . . with conquest while there went / . . . years and years by of world without event" (12–13).

Believing that the Spirit, with "sighs too deep for words," "intercedes" for human beings who "do not know how to pray as [they] ought" (Romans 8:26), Hopkins could write—in his very last poem, to which we once again return—of a notably non-hysterical labor pain. In the "winter world" of the "To R. B." persona, "some sighs" "yield . . . our explanation" ("To R. B.," 13–14; emphasis mine). To Bridges, ever uncomprehending of his friend the Jesuit's spirituality, Hopkins now sends the word that Christian prayer within the soul has nursed the Spirit's child. That child's long-delayed birth will soon provide an "explanation" for what until now may have looked like illegitimate pregnancy. This spiritual offspring of the Holy Ghost and Hopkins's mothering soul offers no earthly infant's squawled acknowledgment of life: no "roll . . . rise . . . carol . . . creation" (12). But the "winter world" reference recalls another likely medieval topos as allusion: while "Winter wakeneth . . . care" for "this worldes joye" that "geth all to noght,"[60] Hopkins in his ultimate lines announces an Afterbirth for his Christly spiritual child.[61] The emerging youngster, Hopkins's sanctified soul, is readied for its ultimate dwelling place: Heaven.

From the writing of "Andromeda" through the writing of "To R. B.," the "nine months" and the likely nine "years" noted in "To R. B." (5) as a poet's mothering time of composition passed, quite literally and nearly exactly (in nine years, eight months, and twelve days). What resulted is an extended array of poetry (interspersed, granted, with poems on different themes) about the common notion of the Christian soul as a mother of sanctification through imitatio Christi. The "Terrible Sonnets," a major grouping of poems within the larger collection of work, share this central theme; they do not so much chronicle autobiographical lamentings as they delineate a general pattern of Christian experience. Boyle, who glimpsed this truth long ago, also correctly identified the "thread" that holds all Hopkins's poems together. That "thread" is their focus upon "life,"[62] but a special kind of life: "supernatural life," a sacramental gift, to "one degree" of which many "thousand degrees of natural life could never add up."[63] Hopkins, by accident, was to die not long after he wrote this poem. But he expected to die into Via Aeterna.

The Hopkinsian soul pictured in his late poems undergoes that process which, as Wolfgang Riehle reminds us, the medieval mystics, following the church father Irenaeus, called the "*deificatio.*"[64] Although that doctrine certainly could hint at heresy, and did produce heretics among some German mystics in late medieval Bavaria, it has affinity with such biblical passages as "His divine power has granted to us all things that pertain to life and godliness . . . promises . . . by [which we] might be partakers of the divine nature" (2 Peter 1:3–4).

Meister Eckhart is one late medieval mystic whose imagery of spiritual rebirth in the soul undergoing deificatio is especially striking. He is fervently certain that in prepared human beings "this birth is going to happen and the Son will be born in [them]."[65] Within this special "work of ingress," Eckhart preaches, "God must act and pour in as soon as he finds that you are ready," just as "when the matter of which a child is made is ready in the mother's body, God at once pours in the living Spirit which is the soul—the body's form."[66] To be sure, we find that Eckhart as a mystic, unlike Hopkins as an active Ignatian meditator and poet, basically denigrates all "sense perception" and "imagination," as well as "ideas of God" that are "creatures of the [mere] reason," although "divine."[67] Eckhart trenchantly insists that "if you are to experience this noble birth, you must depart from all crowds and go back to the starting point, the core [of the soul] out of which you came."[68] Surely Hopkins, who never quite completely rejected the "crowds" of sense experience in the world, did not create the rich imagery of the "Terrible Sonnets" while enduring any radical mystical experience; he was not, as Eckhart recommends, "alone in the darkness of unselfconsciousness," "himself a wilderness, alienated from self and all multiplicity."[69] Yet one might well speculate that Hopkins in these sonnets' richly imaged portrait of the interior soul tries to *depict* Eckhart's recommended state of spiritual isolation. "I wake and feel the fell the dark" would seem to portray such a beneficent mystical experience of self-emptying during "longer light's delay." Similarly "My own heart"—with its rich desiring for a child's awestruck emergence into a world of dazzling sky and mountainscapes—may call to mind Eckhart's dictum that "when this birth really happens, no creature in all the world will stand in your way and what is more, they will all point you to God and this birth."[70]

Affinities between Hopkins and Eckhart thus do exist, as do affinities between the nineteenth-century Jesuit and the twelfth-century Cistercians, who developed radical "homey" images of the soul's mothering process.[71] Hopkins had available the work of the Cistercian Bernard of Clairvaux during his years of Jesuit education,[72] although the poet never seems to have made references either to Bernard or to Eckhart in his letters or journals. We know, however, that, while he was an Oxford student, Hopkins had encountered the church father Origen's writing with "real feeling,"[73] and we have also observed how in the 1870s he was strongly influenced by Origen's tendency toward theological universalism.[74] Now, when Hopkins in his 1880s poetry describes the birth of Christly sanctity in the human Marian soul, it seems clear that he is adapting one more Origenian theological pattern.

> The soul becomes sterile when God abandons it; but becomes a mother when he is at work in it. . . . Just as the seed is formed and shaped in those with child, so is it in the soul which accepts the WORD: the conception of the WORD is gradually formed and shaped in it. . . . In his Epistle to Timothy Paul says that "woman will be saved through bearing children, with modesty" (I Tim. 2:15). But who is this woman, if not the soul which conceives the divine Word of truth and brings forth good works which are like Christ? . . . . Not just in Mary did this birth begin with an "overshadowing" (cf. Lk. 1:35); but in you too, if you are worthy, is the WORD of God born.[75]

> . . . If then the Savior is continually . . . generated by the Father, so with you also; if you have the spirit of sonship (cf. Rom. 8:15), God will continually generate you in the spirit with each good work and each disposition. And thus born, you will be continually born a son of God in Christ Jesus.[76]

In August 1885 Hopkins had visited Coventry Patmore at Hastings, England, and there had read Patmore's prose manuscript *Sponsa Dei*, later described by Edmund Gosse as "not more or less than an interpretation of the love between the soul and God by an analogy of the love between a woman and a man."[77] Around Christmas 1887 Patmore destroyed the manuscript,[78] because, as he told Bridges in a letter of 12 August 1889, "The *authority* of [Hopkins's] goodness was so great with me that I threw the manuscript . . . into the fire, simply because, when he had read it, he said with a grave look, 'That's telling secrets.' "[79] Did Patmore misread Hopkins? For it seems that Hopkins—who probably had been working on his "Terrible Sonnets" since the May before,[80] and had even written the "bride of Christ" poem "Andromeda" as far back as 1879—understood Patmore to be "telling secrets" only because he had himself already been telling similar ones.

Hopkins surely seems in the 1880s to have sought to create a verse biography of the archetypal Christian life. He also thus declared himself zealously striving to live out both the tensions and the victories of that archetypal biography. Yet it is not his own *autobiography*; even the Christian faithful do not at this moment *know* that he succeeded in reaching Heaven, just as the skeptical surely do not *know* that his life reveals a "failure of grace."[81]

We do, however, know that Hopkins persistently strove to demonstrate how Christ as inscape-kernel ever transubstantiates the husk of his creation. When read as works that depict the human soul becoming the blood-swathed birthplace of Christ, so that the soul's own interior substance is transfused and transformed by the pulses which energize the veins and arteries of the Sacred Heart, the "Terrible Sonnets" and other late Hopkins poems no longer seem at all to support Miller's (and others') dire analysis of Hopkins's supposed spiritual impoverishment in the 1880s, his loss of that vital sacramental faith which he had presented successfully in the 1870s nature poems. No, these late poems are not intended as testimonies to the "failure of grace." Instead, they are Hopkins's illustration in verse of that exclamatory prose passage which Miller quoted and yet later seemed to find "unsubstantiated" by Hopkins's life:

> [Grace is] an exchange of one whole for another whole, as they say in the mystery of Transubstantiation, a conversion of a whole substance into another whole substance, but here is not a question of substance; it is a lifting from one self to another self, which is a most marvellous display of divine power.[82]

Indeed, given the fact that poetry did serve as a form of spiritual meditation for this Jesuit, and that he therefore expected his writing to aid his own sanctification, his developing of more Christliness, might we reinterpret the letter in which he told Bridges that at least one of the "Terrible Sonnets" was "written in blood"?[83] Should we not judge those words according to the images and themes of the entire sonnet sequence they partly describe? Hopkins may well have been saying that the "blood" which wrote these "inspirations unbidden"[84] was, finally, not only his own, but also his Savior's. And so these works about a transubstantial regeneration of the archetypal Christian's soul surely seem the richest manifestations of sacramental poetry in Hopkins's entire corpus.

*   *   *

One of Bump's many great strengths as a Hopkins critic is his frequent noting of Hopkins's "extraordinarily allusive" method.[85] He records how "allusions to Jesus, Dante, and other followers of the *imitatio Christi* . . . become," for Hopkins, "the deepest, most personal identification with texts and authors possible."[86] And therefore within such allusions, Bump says, the poet places his work "in the resonant context of tradition,"[87] but meanwhile is "revising . . . rewriting . . . these texts," in a marked "attempt to completely and utterly revise and remake himself."[88] Bump appears correct; those who refuse to grant Hopkins's allusiveness are wrongly protesting against obvious truth.

As a student of Victorian medievalism, however, Bump in general, and rather convincingly, downplays any ultimate large-scale influence upon Hopkins from the English Metaphysical poets, even that Metaphysical poet, George Herbert, whose influence—especially during Hopkins's youthful years—one cannot deny. Yet it seems clear to me as much as to critic Mary Ann Rygiel[89] that Hopkins in 1885 turned once again to Herbert (as well as to his own contemporary Newman).[90] Hopkins's complexly wrought poem "Carrion Comfort," the opening "Terrible Sonnet," repeatedly recalls, although with important variations, the language and situations of Herbert's "The Collar," as well as those of Newman's "The Dream of Gerontius." The Herbert persona in "The Collar" shouts "No more" as he rejects the collar of discipline and seeks a return to prodigal roamings; the Hopkins persona pleads that he "can no more" as he fights the "Despair" that such prodigal roamings produce ("The Collar," 1; "Carrion Comfort," 1–3). The Herbert persona wants his "life and lines . . . free" ("The Collar," 4), while the Hopkins persona wishes, according to an only slightly obscured textual pun,[91] to "[k]not" together his already "slack . . . last strands of man" ("Carrion Comfort," 1–2). In the end, however, the Herbert persona, after having been interrupted from his "wild[ness]" of "rav[ing]" (33) by the gentle call *"Child!"* (35), penitently "replie[s], *My Lord"* (36); the Hopkins persona meanwhile also discovers, at his poem's ultimate moment of catharsis, that "I wretch lay wrestling with (my God!) my God" (14).

Hopkin's likely return to Herbert as a source suggests complex speculations as to his purpose. Herbert had influenced him before during his Oxford years, when Hopkins was vacillating between his Protestant family heritage and the Roman Catholicism with which he would eventually ally himself. An allusion to Herbert's "Love" (3) also had in 1877 permeated "The Windhover," when Hopkins's persona addressed Christ as "ah my dear" ("The Windhover," 13). It may be significant that this most famous Hopkins sonnet has at least some Herbertian Protestant coloration, as it suggests on one level of reading a *via media* caution about treating nature as radically sacramental to all its watchers.

Now, in 1885, Hopkins demonstrates recurrent interest in his Protestant forebear Herbert at the same time as he is demonstrating ambiguous responses to his patristic Roman Catholic forebear Origen. In the case of his reaction to that Alexandrian church father, he simultaneously now uses Origen's imagery of the human soul as a mother of sanctification and seems to call into question Origen's doctrine of universally salvific apocatastasis. While he had, as late as 1881, spoken of Mary as "mother of *all* men in the Spirit" (emphasis mine),[92] in these "Dark Sonnets" we sense that Hopkins is only willing to claim that she mothers *Christians* in the Spirit—and that Christians themselves, including Hopkins, have plenteous imperfections which sometimes make them actually feel worthy of God's spiritual banishing. In any case, the "Terrible Sonnets" do not seem to express Hopkins's previous Origenian confidence in universal salvation; here "the lost" do seem to exist, and their state is "worse" than that of even a doubt-plagued Christian ("I wake and feel," 12–14). The most seemingly Protestant feature of Cardinal Newman's theology—his emphasis on "the face of human society" as "the fruit of human nature" that is "evil"[93]—may early in life have dismayed Hopkins.[94] Yet Newman's rigorousness would seem to describe, much more than it had in an earlier era, Hopkins's late attitude toward the human condition.

Hopkins's return to Herbert as well as to Newman may thus have been encouraged by his increased sense around 1885 that he and these predecessors shared a common Christian concern with redeeming themselves from the company of "the lost." Yet it is also true that Hopkins's attention to Herbert's "The Collar" may just as much have sparked (or been sparked by) his sense of how much the two poets still *differed* in belief.

"The Collar," after all, portrays an Anglican priest's fantasied Prodigal Son–like rejection of his sacramental duties. Perhaps after seeing Herbert reconfirm in "The Collar" doctrinal receptionist devotion to the Eucharist, Hopkins chose to begin his own cycle of the "Terrible Sonnets"—a series of poems that was radically to adapt Roman Catholic doctrines of sacramental transubstantiation—by declaring that his persona was not only a transubstantiationist but even more *receptive* to sacrament than Herbert's officially receptionist character.

It is surely intriguing that Hopkins chose two allusive sources for his poem: one the transubstantiationist Roman Catholic Newman, the other the receptionist Anglican Herbert. "Carrion Comfort" itself, because of its many revisions and its presence on a draft sheet of only two "Terrible Sonnets," appears to be the "sonnet" of "two" that was "written in [transubstantiating?] blood."[95] And yet this sonnet is also the poem of a man who knows that the inner sanctification of a Christian soul is an extraordinarily slow and arduous process and that it most likely comes to no one who does not constantly urge his elective will to a receptive sacramental readiness.

We see these complex sacramental truths once more on display in what is perhaps the finest of all Hopkins's allusive poems: "Thou art indeed just, Lord," dated from just months before his death, on "March 17, '89," as Milward reminds us.[96] Here the main allusive source is rather forthrightly proclaimed by the inclusion of an epigraph from Jeremiah 12: "*Justus quidem tu es, Domine, si disputem tecum; verumtamen justa loquar ad te: Quare via impiorum prosperatur? &c.*" In the first three lines of the Hopkins sonnet itself, the first verse of Jeremiah's chapter seems translated: "Thou art indeed just, Lord, if I contend / With thee; but, sir, so what I plead is just. / Why do sinners' ways prosper?" Yet already ironies build into this supposed paraphrase, for Hopkins's persona uses a "so what [if]" that is more timid than Jeremiah's Septuagint "*verumtamen.*" His "contend" also suggests how he moves along with God, not only "disput[ing]" his will. He does "contend" with God, both as a disputant and as a penitent *follower,* although his penitent following is only clear after we have regarded the poem's intricate ironic texture with special care. Then we shall see rather clearly that the Hopkins persona and the Deity he characterizes on the other end of the conversation "contend" or "strive earnestly" together *(OED);* their dealings do not involve a mere *disputation* of mechanical computations,[97] but instead they prove to be the dealings of a beloved God and his ever-receptive devotee:

> *Justus quidem tu es, Domine, si disputem tecum; verumtamen justa loquar ad te: Quare via impiorum prosperatur? &c.*

> Thou art indeed just, Lord, if I contend
> With thee; but, sir, so what I plead is just.
> Why do sinners' ways prosper? and why must
> Disappointment all I endeavour end?

> Wert thou my enemy, O thou my friend,
> How wouldst thou worse, I wonder, than thou dost
> Defeat, thwart me? Oh, the sots and thralls of lust
> Do in spare hours more thrive than I that spend,

> Sir, life upon thy cause. See, banks and brakes
> Now, leavèd how thick! lacèd they are again
> With fretty chervil, look, and fresh wind shakes

> Them; birds build—but not I build; no, but strain,
> Time's eunuch, and not breed one work that wakes.
> Mine, O thou lord of life, send my roots rain.

The first key to seeing the trenchant irony in this poem's presentation of a comic buffoon speaker is the little "*&c.*" abbreviation placed at the end of the epigraph. Hopkins thus directs us past the first Hebrew verse, requiring us to notice that in the biblical chapter Jeremiah whines at God for only a very short while. Pleading for Israel's salvation from enemies who cause the people to fear (vv. 1–4), he presents his credentials in the third verse ("And thou, O Lord, hast known me, thou hast seen me, and proved my heart with thee"), and, even if confused about the "why" of evil men's bounty (vv. 1–2), he rests confident that God will "prepare them for the day of slaughter" (v. 3).

Jeremiah is not pleased to see Israel's enemies "planted" so that they "bring forth fruit" (v. 2). Yet he more strongly queries why the fruits of his own Israel should be shrinking and its "beasts and birds [should be] consumed" (v. 4). In Hopkins's supposed paraphrase, "birds build"; they are not "consumed." So why should his speaker be so petulant?

When the Lord answers Jeremiah's questions, declaiming through his own as well as through Jeremiah's voice, he assures the prophet that the Israelites' enemies "have sown wheat" but, despite their apparent profiting, "reaped thorns." The Hebrews, meanwhile, he proclaims just as reprehensible as their foes: "you shall be ashamed of your fruits" (Jeremiah 12:13).

Hopkins, the sonneteer who modifies his biblical source material, does so in order to play the role of one of these Israelites "ashamed of [their] fruits." He sees no fruits, and so he wails against fruitlessness, forgetting that spiritual fertility is primarily known in the inner being. Yet Hopkins's irony here meanwhile repeats the lesson of "Nondum," the "Terrible Sonnets," even "Soliloquy of One of the Spies left in the Wilderness." He still knows what he has always known: human wailings against the darkness of redemptive Passion are wrong—and wrongheaded.

The irony is reinforced as we see in the sonnet another ironic allusion. Donald McChesney has found echoed in "Thou art indeed just, Lord" the "Miltonic thought and cadence" of the following passage from the proem to Book 3 of *Paradise Lost*: ". . . Thus with the Year / Seasons return, but not to me returns / Day, or the sweet approach of Ev'n or Morn" (40–42).[98] In Milton, however, such self-pity is clearly not tolerated for long. Milton announces his poetic task to be imitation of "the wakeful Bird / [That s]ings darkling, and in shadiest Covert hid / Tunes her nocturnal Note" (38–40). Even earlier, he put his physical blindness in perspective by declaring that "God is light" (3), "unapproached light" (4), "before the Sun, / Before the Heavens" (8–9). Milton knows that such spiritual light is a "sovran vital Lamp" (22) which he can "revisit safe" (21) whenever he so wills. Despite his lack of physical vision, he can still be spiritually receptive, can still "see and tell / Of things invisible to mortal sight" (54–55).

Adopting the critical method of Bertrand F. Richards,[99] who has similarly studied "Carrion Comfort" through testing various syntactical potentialities, I find Hopkins expressing, at least on one level of the poetic text, just such receptive understanding. Traditionally, two key lines of the first tercet of "Thou art indeed just, Lord" have been read, with surface gloominess, as "birds build, but [on the contrary] I [do] not build; no, but strain [agonize], / Time's eunuch, and [do] not breed [even] one work that wakes" (12–13). One translates "but" here according to the German original *sondern* or "on the contrary" *(OED)*. If, however, we read the conjunction as the German *aber*, or "nevertheless" *(OED)*, the ambiguous text reveals a rather different message: "birds build, but [nevertheless] not I [a "Nay"?] build; no [not exactly], but [I] strain [toward the goal, to the prize of God's heavenly call in Christ Jesus—Philippians 3:14], / Time's [but not Eternity's] eunuch, and [do] not breed one work that [nevertheless, at the same time] wakes [with liveliness]" ("Thou art indeed," 12–13).

The key phrase here is "Not I," so deliberately chosen a Latinism (in Milton's manner), which is placed in the text so that "not" modifies both the expected verb, "build," in the pessimistic surface reading, and the pronoun "I," in the optimistic reading that becomes foregrounded lexically just because the "not" is so oddly situated. The "not I" is eventually, of course, God, in the person of the Holy Spirit, the "lord of life" addressed in the sonnet's final line.

And here we have the greatest marvel of all in this grand poem. Prayer to the Holy Spirit is uttered by a persona who is both male ("Time's eunuch") and possessed of female characteristics that can "breed." The last line asks seminal "rain" for the "roots" of both—the male's testes, the female's uterus. Hopkins is again praying, as he did in the "Terrible Sonnets," for productivity in his anima, but he is not here forgetting himself, the man who houses that anima. A passage from his January 1888 retreat notes helps, I believe, to explain which person in the Bethlehem story is the most nearly analogous to Hopkins:

It is for this that St Ignatius speaks of the angel *discharging his mission,* it being question of action leading up to, as now my action leads from, the Incarnation. The Incarnation was for my salvation and that of the world: the work goes on in a great system and machinery which even drags me on with the collar round my neck though I could and do neglect my duty in it. But I say to myself that I am only too willing to do God's work and help on the knowledge of the Incarnation. But this is not really true: I am not willing enough for the piece of work assigned me, the only work I am given to do, though I could do others if they were given. This is my work at Stephen's Green. And I thought that the Royal University was to me what Augustus's enrolment was to St. Joseph: *exiit sermo a Caesare Augusto etc.;* so resolution of the senate of the R. U. came to me, inconvenient and painful, but the journey to Bethlehem was inconvenient and painful; and then I am bound in justice, and paid. I hope to bear this in mind[.][100]

With a "collar" like Herbert's "round [his] neck," this great Christian poet of a later era goes forth to Bethlehem and past it to Nazareth. He is a seeming eunuch, like his predecessor Joseph, but still receptively ready even to endure apparent sacramental darkness "for the kingdom of heaven's sake."[101]

He does not, however, go forth with perfect calm. His psychic tension is clear, although he must have recalled Frederick William Faber's commentaries concerning Saint Joseph as a "steward of God's house," making him "parallel" in his tasks to priests.[102] The priest Father Gerard must also have recalled Faber's earlier statement that Joseph was "rather fitted for contemplation than for action, both on account of his exceeding tenderness and also of his remarkable quietness of spirit; yet, out of the bashful timidity of a contemplative he had to draw the bravery of an apostle."[103] These ideas about Joseph do appear reflected in Hopkins's 19 March 1885 Dublin Meditation Points, his first notable prose passage about Jesus's earthly father:

> He was thought the father of Christ our Lord. Therefore there was nothing in him visibly unworthy of what Christ visibly was. Consider how great then his holiness and his humility, for the thought, the mistake made, was itself a burden to him[.]
> He is the patron of the hidden life; of those, I should think, suffering in mind and as I do. Therefore I will ask his help[.][104]

Faber recognized, too, as does Hopkins, that "To Saint Joseph, the Sacred Infancy was his Cross . . . instead of Calvary. The earthly troubles and inconveniences which the Incarnation brought along with it fell in great measure upon him as his peculiar burden."[105] Indeed, it may very well be true that Hopkins derives from Faber his use of the word "burden" as he describes "the mistake made" by Joseph's neighbors (a "mistake" which on one level of interpretation may refer to their suspicion that an overdemanding sex drive in Joseph had caused his fiancée to become "illegitimately" pregnant). Yet Hopkins's words "the mistake made," if applied to neighbors who accused Joseph of sexual wrongs, certainly more precisely define the embarrassment of Joseph's situation than do Faber's words "earthly troubles and inconveniences."

Greater precision marks Hopkins's words even if we interpret the Meditation Points passage differently. He probably intends to convey primarily the meaning suggested by the first two sentences. Joseph, he may indicate there, was not thought by the neighbors during Jesus' later childhood to be spiritually or physically "unworthy" of being spiritual or physical Jesus' father. And yet that complimentary evaluation, Hopkins says, was a "burden" to Joseph. Hopkin's Joseph continues to feel himself very much human, and thus very much inferior to the Jesus who is also the Christ. Thus the saintly father's "hidden life," which remains no less a life of faith in and service to Christ, includes plentiful self-doubts (his peers, however, do not seem to share those doubts).

The personally scrupulous and frequently self-doubting Hopkins obviously seems to identify very strongly with these human problems that he attributes to the biblical character he is analyzing. Thus he manages never to treat Saint Joseph in the cloyingly pious manner that inspires his likely influence Faber, who quite differently exults that Bethlehem was "Joseph's cross," but also his "land of pleasantness, "world of joy."[106] Nor does Hopkins downplay what even the Bible portrays as Joseph's pre-Bethlehem suspicion about Mary's pregnancy (Matthew 1:19). Faber, on the other hand, only emphasizes the later Joseph, whose "conjugal love was actually part of his religion," with "tender mercies" and "worship" to Mary making him "sanctified" as he was "raised . . . nearer to God."[107]

In further marked contrast to such Faberian pieties, Hopkins deliberately associates the "hidden life" and "burden" of Saint Joseph with problems of a real human psyche "suffering in mind"—much like that suffering Hopkins was himself enduring due to migraine headaches, a heavy workload, and isolation from homeland on his Dublin teaching assignment.[108] It is certainly not any wonder, therefore, that Hopkins sees holiness in Saint Joseph emerging from the fully human, for Hopkins hopes that he can also see holiness emerging from his own human strife.

As we see in "Thou art indeed . . . ," Hopkins to the end remains a great dramatic poet. He portrays even the Satanic villainy of Caradoc in his incomplete drama *St. Winefred's Well* with potent "negative capability," like that which helped Milton to create a vitally dramatized Satan in *Paradise Lost*. Observing this Hopkinsian dramatic gift, Mariani recently found, in examining the Caradoc soliloquy, that Hopkins "knows what despair tastes like. . . ."[109] The identification with Saint Joseph is even more pointed, for Hopkins and Joseph both knew what human-but-saintly spiritual doubt "tastes like." Had Hopkins written a poem about Jesus' earthly father, it might have resembled Rilke's portrait of the same historical personage, in *Das Marien-Leben:*

ARGWOHN JOSEPHS	JOSEPH'S SUSPICION
Und der Engel sprach und gab sich Müh an dem Mann, der seine Fäste ballte: Aber siehst du nicht an jeder Falte, dass sie kühl ist wie die Gottesfrüh?	And the angel, striving to explain, told the man who stood shut-fisted, surly: Can't you see that she is pure as early dawn—does not each fold there make it plain?
Doch der andre sah ihn finster an, murmelnd nur: Was hat sie so verwandelt?	But the shadow stayed upon his brow, What, he growled, has changed her? The reply
Doch da schrie der Engel: Zimmermann, merkst du's noch nicht, dass der Herrgott handelt?	then came loudly: Joiner, even now can't you see the hand of the Most High?

Weil du Bretter machst, in deinem Stolze,	You who work with boards, is your pride such
willst du wirklich den zur Rede stelln, der bescheiden aus dem gleichen Holze Blätter treiben macht und Knospen schwelln?	you would argue with the One who urges buds to fullness, at whose quiet touch, and from this same wood, the green emerges?
Er begriff. Und wie er jetzt die Blicke, recht erschrocken, zu dem Engel hob, war der fort. Da schob er seine dicke Mütze langsam ab. Dann sang er lob.	Then at last he saw. And when he lifted his scared look to meet the Angel's gaze, found him gone. At that his slowly-shifted heavy cap came off. Then he sang praise.

Rilke evokes the humanity of Joseph because it is the human as holy that he always wishes to consecrate. Hopkins, who surely could see as much as Rilke the understandable but silly folly of a Joseph who for too long refuses to remove his cap before an angel, understood fully the raw humanity out of which saints are finally made. Yet their "journey needs raw human faith," even though it "is not guaranteed" success: "One needs to give up everything, and yet, one cannot anticipate that the empty spaces are going to be filled."[110] Assuredly, Hopkins's late "dark" sonnet monologues about struggling spiritual human beings do prove, just as much as did his earlier nature sonnets in Wales, his attempts to penetrate the deftly detailed outer hull of at least certain human creatures so as to reveal their continued receptive will to be visited with inner showers of divine "rain"—"rain" by which arrives transubstantiating divine inscape.

Hopkins to the end revealed his own possession of such inscape. He might seem to prove, in his plaintive prose especially, the "querulous, sensitive" sort who left the young Yeats, after they had met, dismayed.[111] In Hopkins's prose writings he often seems in his last years a whimperer much like those personae whom he fittingly chastises in his own ironic late poems. Yet the Jesuit, we must remember, was the same poet who accomplished the ironic chastising of those personae.

Even after one confronts all Hopkins's expressions of doubting and anguish in the letters, in the journals, and on the seemingly nonironic surface of the poems, one senses that those plaintive outcries are only the exterior Hopkinsian husk of doubt, lying superficially unsteady on the outside of a trustingly confident inner utterance. To use Hopkins's own language, the self-pitying external voices are the "blue-bleak" outer species; the surprising sacramentalist substance within is poetic "underthought," which in Hopkins's poetry always testifies to the inner fire of a faith that sustains both the speaker and his creating poet. Inside an embered wafer of words, the affirmations of faith may lie linguistically hidden, but they are discoverable to careful readers, and they declare Hopkins ever a willingly receptive candidate for rebirth into sanctity, for transformation into his own "gold-vermilion" Christly substance.

No, he does not appear very fully glowing with such "gold-vermilion" sanctity as he writes, in the 1888 retreat notes about himself and Saint Joseph, that it surely would have been more decent of God to ask him to assist in "the work . . . of the Incarnation" at some other spot besides the bothersome "Stephen's Green" of the bothersome "Royal University." Why should this be, he asks, the "only work [he] is given to do, though [he] could do others if they were given"? Yet he hardly has finished inscribing this grumbling on the paper before him when we see the sacramentally dedicated Jesuit meditator begin to reveal the inner Christ, the "heart['s] charity's hearth's fire" (*Wreck*, st. 35, 8) of his spirit. Hardly does he need a religious text upon which to meditate briefly *("exit sermo a Caesare Augusto")* before he is speaking on the page as the inner committed Christian instead of as the outer human lamenter: "so resolution of the senate of the R[oyal]. U[niversity]. came to me, inconvenient and painful, but the journey to Bethlehem was inconvenient and painful [for Joseph]; and then I am bound [to Christ] in justice, and paid. I hope to bear this in mind[.]"

This sort of Christian resolve always culminates even the most trenchantly depressing of Hopkins's prose meditations, just as it culminates his poems. The Dublin Meditation Points discussion of Joseph, which is actually rather constantly able to speak of a resolved faithfulness, still concludes with its writer promising himself to "ask" Saint Joseph for "help." A man who so consistently moves past petulance to renewed spiritual commitment is a man who—like Saint Joseph as Hopkins described him in 1888—feels himself spiritually "paid." Hopkins felt "paid" even amid personal depression, because the depression did not matter to him so much as did his receptive wish to see Christ Jesus born in him, making his soul a Eucharist. As he declared, he wanted the "lord of life" to send spiritual "rain"—to conceive in him, as in Saint Joseph, the "fruits of the Spirit" (Galatians 5:22–23).

If Hopkins did not ever quite seem to know, as we would like to see it displayed, a full spiritual fruit of "peace," he surely knew, and learned to bear, "longsuffering" with "patience" (Galatians 5:22). In the "Terrible Sonnets" indeed, he may illustrate various of the Pauline spiritual fruits in the various poems: Pauline "self-control" in "Carrion Comfort"; the quelling of fury toward Pauline "gentleness" in the "sleep" ending "No worst"; the Pauline "kindness" of human love, available even "at all removes" in "To seem the stranger"; Pauline "patience," of course, in "Patience"; and Pauline "charitable[ness]," striving after Pauline "joy," in "My own heart." Even "I wake and feel," despite its evident inattention to any specific spiritual fruit, may attribute Pauline "goodness" to a persona who—despite his "selftaste of spirit [that] a dull dough sours"—is not damned, like "the lost." "Against" those who bear "the fruits of the Spirit," says Saint Paul, there is no lostness, "no [punishing by the] law" (Galatians 5:18).[112]

Saint Paul tells his Galatian readers that "those who belong to Christ Jesus have crucified the flesh with its passions and desires" (Galatians 5:24). However "querulous" he could be, Hopkins was one of the passional persons who had "crucified the flesh," or at least striven to do so. And if the one "fruit . . . of the Spirit" he seemed unable to express fully in his life was "peace," he himself had long known, at least since 1879, how hard peace was to find (and yet, perhaps, how easy, if the receptive soul that electively willed a Eucharistic commitment to sanctification could certainly trust that he would receive all the spiritual fruits he sought). Returning to "Peace," a poem only briefly touched upon earlier in this study, one reads,

When will you ever, Peace, wild wooddove, shy wings shut,
Your round me roaming end, and *under be* my boughs?
When, when, Peace, will you, Peace? I'll not play hypocrite
To own my heart: I yield you do come sometimes; but
That piecemeal peace is poor peace. What pure peace allows
Alarms of wars, the daunting wars, the death of it?

O surely, reaving Peace, my Lord should leave in lieu
Some good! And so he does leave Patience exquisite,
That plumes to Peace thereafter. And when Peace here does house
He comes with work to do, he does not come to coo,
        He comes to brood and sit.
                                                            (Emphasis mine)

Hopkins's "Peace," of course, is the fruitful, but darkly brooding, Holy Spirit himself. And Hopkins could not long "play hypocrite / To [claim he] own[ed his own] heart" ("Peace," 3–4). He was too receptive to the Christ who he believed transubstantiated his soul through the Spirit; he firmly believed his soul to be "own[ed]"—and Eucharistically infiltrated, if only "piecemeal" (5)—by that Spirit. To be sure, in Hopkins's often-frustrated life,[113] the Spirit often may have seemed an absentee. The human being, after all, wanted allurements, wanted comforting "boughs" (2) of feathery spiritual wings, carrying his tired self ever upward. The Holy Spirit's dove, however, proved, as long ago in *The Wreck of the Deutschland*, sometimes to "work" harshly and rarely to "coo" within (10). But that fact of necessary passional pain did not mean that the Spirit had not found a protective nest—its home becoming, indeed, eunuch Joseph's own "boughs." If the Comforter indeed blessed Hopkins's spiritual baptism as he had once blessed the Baptism of Jesus (Matthew 3:16), then that Comforter truly sent him the "rain" for which his depressed poetic narrator might have begged ("Thou art indeed just, Lord," 14). Baptism's sacramental inner rejuvenation allowed him to live Joseph's drudging daily life in this world's Nazareth. And the masculine power of the Spirit was thus given even to Mary's secondary, seemingly emasculated, doorkeeping domestic groom:

Jesu that dost in Mary dwell,
Be in thy servants' hearts as well,
In the spirit of thy holiness,
In the fullness of thy force and stress,
In the very ways that thy life goes
And virtues that thy pattern shows,
In the sharing of thy mysteries;
And every power in us that is
Against thy power put under feet
In the Holy Ghost the Paraclete
  To the glory of the Father. Amen.
      "(*Oratio Patris Condren. O Jesu vivens in Maria*"—P, 212–13;
      emphasis mine)[114]

5

Hymns, Oblations, Sighs to the Lord of Life

Let him easter in us, be a dayspring to the dimness of us, be a crimson-cresseted east[.]
—Hopkins, *The Wreck of the Deutschland*, st. 35, 5

COTTER FIFTEEN years ago valuably undertook "a reappraisal of Hopkins's theology," especially its patristic sources, in order to demonstrate "literature" and "theology" in "realistic encounter with one another."[1] Likewise, I have examined several dimensions of Hopkins's sacramentalism, hoping thus to bring into new and meaningful "encounter" our divergent senses of his biography, his spirituality, and his poetry. Much of my discussion clearly has depended on the large body of already-extant criticism by writers with many different attitudes toward Hopkins. But my special focus on Hopkins in relation to diverse sacramental theologies may here have added new knowledge about his motivations and practices.

We first saw in this book the early receptionist Oxonian Hopkins, a young man who longed to add to his liturgical experience the certainty of visible divine revelation associated with transubstantiationist doctrines. We then saw Hopkins, now a Scotist Jesuit theological student in Wales, turn into exuberant odes and sonnets his newfound sense of confidence about nature as a sacramentarian vessel for Christic Real Presence. Both these phases of Hopkins's biography have been long familiar to scholars of his life and work.

However, this special study has also highlighted less familiar facets of Hopkins's sacramentalist life and poetry. In some of the Wales works he appears to have tried even to mimic major sacramental rites such as baptism or the Eucharist, summoning participants in such mimicked sacraments to responsive self-sacrifice. By the time the last Wales sonnet is written, however, he appears less ardently anxious to call others directly to the practicing of sacramental devotion, for he now is focusing chiefly on his *own* willingness to be a sacramental participant.

In such poems as "The Windhover," therefore, Hopkins effectively portrays his own confirmational sacramental spirit. He later sketches himself, in poems about the years of his active public priesthood, officiating over the sacramental rites of marriage, extreme unction, and a soldier's first communion. Sometimes still represented in these poems as an apparently impatient persona, he nonetheless seems basically to be growing toward deeper humility. He now strives more firmly to emphasize the "inward and spiritual grace" of sacrament, through development of the elective will in himself and in others, rather than to fasten his attention, so much as he had in Wales, upon sacramentalist "outward and visible sign[s]."

Indeed, by the time the Briton Hopkins becomes an alien classics professor serving amid the troubles of 1880s Ireland and its new Roman Catholic university,[2] he is able even to fend off apparent psychic despondency by writing brilliant meditational poems concerning the spiritual biography of an archetypal Christian soul. These poems concerning the spiritual biography are also verbal testaments to inner sacramentalization. Their imagery of a spiritually inseminating Paraclete, a ravished Marian soul, and the substance of a Christ-Child growing within that human soul propose as possible the divine infusion of human body and blood with Christic body and blood.

Thus we have seen that by the time of Hopkins's death and the completion of his canon, for many years his Augustinian-Origenian work has recorded a consistent sacramentalist response to all of life. His "overthought" might be natural vista or narrated catechism lesson or the seemingly hellish fury that besets a tormented human self, but his "underthought" is always the availability of divine Real Presence— sometimes, as in the Wales nature sonnets, its availability to a receptive, sacramentally committed eye, and always, but especially in the writings after 1880, its declared availability to the receptive, sacramentally committed soul.

* * *

To come to these insights about Hopkins's sacramentalist themes and poetic method one should not need to have doctrinal religious faith. It is probably quite obvious that I do have such faith, although mine is not exactly equivalent to Hopkins's. I am not, like him, a Roman Catholic, and I was not even raised in liturgical Protestantism. My thematic balancing of receptionist and transubstantiationist theologies in this treatment of Hopkins's sacramental thinking probably does result from my having come as an adult to belong to the via media Anglican tradition from which he as a young man departed. I can thus sense how later Roman Catholic experience enhanced, and yet fused itself with, his earlier Anglican views of various theologies: receptionist, transubstantiationist, even memorialist. My own experience inevitably colors the way I see Hopkins's life of faith. But the personal experiences by which I most consistently arrive at my judgments about him are objective literary experiences: study of sacramental theology; attention to common Christian Scriptures and creeds; and close perusal of his writing and varied critical assessments of it.

Ultimately, therefore, the faith upon which this examination of Hopkins is most reliant is a faith in reading.[3] I am one with Milroy, who believes for himself that "Language, like nature, has . . . order and purpose,"[4] much as he proclaims that Hopkins "believed . . . language, like nature, conform[ing] to natural laws . . . organized and structured in consistent and systematic ways."[5] For most, it is admittedly hard to share the fullest sacramentalist fervor about language that Hopkins seems sometimes to have maintained, to believe language almost directly perceptive of Platonic forms or divine Real Presence. I know that I am no naïve Cratylus, expecting language to be unchanging and unified in focus, nor is Milroy a Cratylus when he writes that "the relation of word to concept is never static or clear, much as we might wish it to be.[6] And yet Hopkins was not ultimately Cratylus either; in such a passage of stammering word choice as "not I build; no, but strain" ("Thou art indeed just, Lord," 12), he admits that he sometimes has difficulty in locating adequate linguistic signs for expressing certain perceptual-conceptual "moments." By redefining "not I build" to "no, . . . strain," he admits how difficult it is to convey his own particular sense of tenuous bond with a "not I" God who somehow "build[s]" a sacramental home in a human soul.

Such Hopkinsian admissions of linguistic inadequacy do not, however, justify Miller's attempt to prove that Hopkins, because of inevitable linguistic vagaries, could only write inevitably deconstructing poems. Miller asserts that stanzas 22 and 28 of *The Wreck* show Hopkins's "theological thought and its linguistic underthought . . . at cross-purposes."[7] Hopkins in these stanzas truly does demonstrate Miller's contention "that there is no way of speaking of . . . theological mystery except in a cascade of metaphors whose proliferation confesses to the fact that there is no literal word for the Word."[8] And yet, at the same time, the two cited poetic stanzas still show Hopkins actually quite confident that if there is no one "literal word for the Word," there are at least *many approximate* words for that Word. By collecting those approximate sacramental words together in a "cascade of metaphors" that resembles a liturgical incantation, Hopkins in 1876, and indeed even in 1889 (although by then with calmer forms of metaphoric "cascade") still believes what he had believed in 1868—that the consecrated page of religious poetry can reflect at least something of all words' Edenic, Platonically formal "prepossession."[9]

Even if we do not share Hopkins's sense that language can contact Edenic unity, we may still concur with the poetic theory of Richard Gunter, who does judge readers able to reach some interpretive consensus about any poetic text. He says that while poetic interpretation "may be in error," still "decisions of one native speaker" about meanings of "pieces of language" need "not [be] vague and uncertain," but may instead be "rather definite." If "It is true," he says, "that there is always a measure of indefiniteness in content" so that "we must simply be cautious and keep trying," still at least "the grammatical side of [linguistic] value is categorical."[10]

In discussing such poems as Hopkins's "To R. B." and "The shepherd's brow" both in this book and as part of an earlier article,[11] I may sometimes have appeared peevish about others' seemingly oversimplified readings of Hopkins's poems. Yet my plaints against oversimplified reading result from a sense that even good critics have sometimes interpreted entire Hopkins sonnets without giving their semantics careful attention. This attention has been lacking at both the sentence level of grammar and lexicon and on the more expanded ranges of larger constructive rhetorical modes (like patterns of argument versus counterargument and patterns of analogy).

Hopkins the meaningfully complicated stylist has too often been read, and shockingly so, as a simple transcriber into poetry of the more obvious prose statements from his letters and journals. He should rather have been consistently studied as the deft artist he is. Besides, as a firm believer in a deep-hidden but ever-present divine substance, Hopkins may sometimes even deliberately have obscured in his prose letters a clear focus on the inscapes of sacramental faith. One may of course judge that the preponderance of outscaped lament in the prose means that the affirmation of inscape which we find in the poems was in life ultimately defeated by grim reality. Yet one is still required, even when one reaches such decisions about how to interpret Hopkins's total biography, to read the poetry as poetry, not as a versified gloss of his extant autobiographical documents. It is principally in reading the poetry as poetry that I have found ample reason for asserting that grim reality may not have conquered Hopkins at all, but that personal disappointment for him was felt only as life's accidental species. Grim doubt seemed to obscure, but ultimately did not "black out" ("Heraclitean Fire," 14), the substantial and developed faith within.

I began my serious study of Hopkins's poetry in Diane Leonard's Chapel Hill classroom in 1974, as a graduate student of comparative literary criticism. My study of Hopkins's works over the years since has surely included much partial vision that had to be conquered and which is still surely not fully conquered. But error and partial vision have only come to be transcended at all because of continued attention, such as that Dr. Leonard taught me, to Hopkins's artifacts and to as many as possible of the other relevant documents by and about him.[12]

In that graduate school course with Dr. Leonard I wrote a lengthy essay about "That Nature is a Heraclitean Fire and of the comfort of the Resurrection," using the Czech linguistic structuralist methodology of Roman Jakobson and Lawrence Jones, as exemplified in their monograph *Shakespeare's Verbal Art in 'Th' Expence of Spirit.'* In that publication, the authors present their detailed "structural analysis of . . . text and poetic texture in all [their] interrelated facets."[13] Jakobson and Jones would defend their methodological soundness by comparison of their reading of Shakespeare's Sonnet 129 with other readings, which they find either "forced, oversimplified, and diluting"[14] or else too ready to adapt "the surmise of the free and infinite multiplicity of semantic load."[15] To the Jakobson and Jones of this 1970 monograph, poems often become "subliminally adapted by editors and commentators" to their own viewpoints,[16] but the answer to such rigid and yet ultimately subjectivist interpretation is not (as it is today for many equally subjectivist deconstructionists) "free and infinite" interpretive "multiplicity."

Jakobson and Jones here speak from Czech phenomenological structuralist perspectives about poems' having "a cogent and mandatory unity of . . . thematic and compositional framework."[17] All Hopkins critics may not make such extraordinary claims as these, which argue for one "mandatory" interpretation of a particular text. But the best Hopkinsians surely do judge it necessary to examine the artifact completely. As Johnson wrote, when American New Criticism was at its influential apex, "The rhyme, rhythm, and imagery *are* meaning, and it is as important in reading Hopkins to observe the ironic rhyming of 'spark' and 'dark,' the change in speed of the sentences, from 'all is an enormous dark' to 'a heart's clarion![,]' and the several implications of 'dust,' 'bonfire,' and 'diamond,' as it is to know the eschatology of the resurrection of the body."[18] Much like Johnson himself, the best New Critics, especially when they are paying attention to work like Hopkins's that calls for just such intense analysis, observe carefully how various lexical and tempo differentiations within a developing poem enhance through poetic texture the semantic denotation and connotation of figures and ideas.[19]

Many of my most valuable graduate school discoveries about Hopkins's "Heraclitean Fire" resulted from a procedure that New Critics often to some degree practice: elucidation of ambiguity in the poem's lexicon. However, the thoroughness of Jakobson and Jones's linguistic structuralism first made me aware that a student of a poem's vocabulary should carefully seek all applicable definitions for a poet's chosen word and then test all those definitions in the poem's fuller context. One should thus probe a poem's vocabulary as it functions at both Saussurian-defined semantic levels where it operates: first, the "*paradigmatic*" level—of the individual word's total potential array of meanings when it is given no particular fixed context—and, then, the level of "*syntagmatic* . . . sequential relations"—where one studies the word's various allowable meanings in one discrete contextual locale.[20] As linguist Milroy has noted, "In some of Hopkins's derivatives (*overbend, onewhere*), the paradigmatic relations of the words are alone sufficient to account for their meanings; in others the contexts are necessary, and sequential relations in the text must be invoked."[21]

Intensively examining the vocabulary of "Heraclitean Fire," I found as a graduate student that, from the beginning, its ambiguous vocabulary demonstrated Hopkins's awareness of the kinetic flux which propels, and threatens, even a lustrously vibrant natural scene. Each word within even the mere opening segment of "Heraclitean Fire" can imply either frolic or violence. "Chevy," a verb derived from the eighteenth-century border skirmish at Chevy Chase, carries ambiguous meanings of "to chase" or "to scamper." "Roysterer" has come to mean "a swaggering or noisy reveller," but in historically earlier parlance it meant "a swaggering or blustering bully." Both meanings are appropriate to Hopkins's poetized "gay-gangs" of clouds that "throng"—potentially violent groups which press, move, or unify, and then further press, move, or unify. The "cloud[s]" of the poetic text quite fittingly "glitter," or "shine with a brilliant . . . tremulous light," for they dwell amid natural scenes that the adopted lexicon describes as frolicsome now but potentially threatening later.

All the above lexical definitions I derived in 1974 from the *Oxford English Dictionary*. Hopkins of course could not have derived his poem's lexicon from that same source, for only the first complete volume of the many in the final dictionary had appeared, with its compilation of words beginning with the letters *A* and *B*, by the year (1888) of this poem's composition.[22] Thus a Hopkins scholar can be absolutely certain of the poet's etymological knowledge of only those words that Hopkins actually discusses in his etymological diary entries or in other prose. Still, Milroy adds his linguist's knowledge to my instinctual sense that "overwhelmingly, the sources of Hopkins's lexicon lie, not in the classics, but in his observation of the patterns of current language, aided by knowledge derived from dictionaries and language scholarship. . . ."[23] Milroy presents this argument as part of his own convincing demonstration that

> . . . it was philology that helped to breathe life into Hopkins's poetry. . . . [T]he etymological notes and other linguistic comments in [his] undergraduate diaries are often well-informed by mid-[nineteenth-]century standards; the dialectal notes in [his] journal . . . and his contributions to Joseph Wright's *English Dialect Dictionary* show him sharing the attitudes of the early students of dialect.[24]

The diverse etymological sources of Hopkins's obviously rich and ambiguous lexicon have by force of their relevance to his art drawn the attention of many serious Hopkinsian interpreters. These include MacKenzie, in a journal article concerning "Spelt from Sibyl's Leaves";[25] Ellis, during her revealing discussions of vocabulary both in *The Wreck* and in Hopkins's sonnets;[26] and Mariani throughout his *Commentary*—as in such a revealing analysis as that which finds the word "rankle," "from *dracunculus*, the diminutive of *draco*, serpent," to be significantly used in "The Bugler's First Communion."[27]

However, vocabulary is not the only linguistic feature of poetry worthy of exegetes' consideration. Jakobson, in a key essay concerning linguistics and poetics, finds "no linguistic property of the verse design" irrelevant to study.[28] My first research on "Heraclitean Fire," inspired by Jakobson and Jones's methodologies, traced in the poem interrelations between strophes distanced from each other by "alternation (a b a b)" as well as "binary correspondences" in strophes conjoined through sequential "neighborhood (a a b b)."[29] For instance, I found that in the poem's strophic section 2, the verb "beat" ("Heraclitean Fire," 5) shows how both active wind and human footprints positively erase storm-creases from the earth. In the alternated strophic section 4 the verb "beat" ominously describes humankind and its "marks" while they are themselves being eroded ("beat[en] level") by Heraclitean time and death. Humankind thus partially controls as *subject* the beating action in the second stanza, while human beings are the beaten *object* of strophic section 4.

These dire transformations in mood, however, are soon thrust aside. As the poem turns in the thematic direction of resurrectional victory, in the next neighboring stanza (strophic section 5), Hopkins uses the verb "beam," a word phonemically and orthographically close to "beat." Foreshadowing later depictions of Christ's Cross-beam and the beaming "immortal diamond" of resurrectional eschatology, the softened final consonant of "beam" subtly modulates the poem's tone away from earlier harsh and terror-increasing uses of "beat."

Obviously, a full-fledged linguistic analysis of a caudated sonnet of only twenty-four lines has liabilities. It consumes much of the critic's time, even as it does not seem absolutely necessary for at least a basic understanding of the poem. It may also seem to produce an excessively amoebalike ever-expanding array of technical details. My original paper about "Heraclitean Fire" ran to twenty-eight pages with notes. And a monograph published several years later in the same critical tradition, Stephan Walliser's *"That Nature is a Heraclitean Fire and of the comfort of the Resurrection": A Case Study in G. M. Hopkins' Poetry*, totals 192 pages of analysis and notes and still does not duplicate all the same technical discoveries that I made.[30] Literary works like "Heraclitean Fire," it thus appears, are incredibly rich, never interpretively exhaustible.

Yet any one reader's truly careful phenomenological study of a poem, play, or novel also is likely to convince that reader rather strongly that literary works are also to some degree limited, that they are bounded phenomenological systems within themselves. While, according to a major phenomenological critic, "many interpretations are possible for one and the same work of art," these possible interpretations, he adds, must "arise from diverse understandings . . . permissible within limits set by the text."[31] It is surely true that close concentration on a particular text over a period of time will, at least to a very large degree, lead to the concentrating reader's "conscious . . . bracketing of experience," a "distancing" or "epochē" from intrusions by most ordinary daily concerns.[32] That reader can then, through "a special effort," "bring about a perception of the essential qualitative relationship of several cooperating, harmonizing, aesthetically relevant qualities" that are meshed within the work.[33] This necessary "bracketing," "distancing," "epochē" for aesthetic experiences, by which one seeks to "*mean* or *intend* the object and only the object as it essentially is,"[34] truly can prove to some degree a deceptive goal, if it too much emphasizes "a fictive—non-historical—reconstruction of nature according to model systems of science" and thus forgets the artist's and reader's primal "imagining," their search for always-"hidden," even "mythic," intuitional discoverings.[35] And yet epoche can surely contribute to intimacy with the artifact; this intimacy a phenomenologist literary theoretician considers possible and indeed absolutely required:

. . . [T]he primary function proper to the literary work of art consists in enabling the reader who has the correct attitude toward the work to

constitute an aesthetic object which belongs to the [potential] aesthetic objects permitted by the work. . . .[36]

Hopkins certainly knew that he had created complicated poetic structures. He told Bridges, on 15 February 1879, "I have of myself made
verse so laborious."[37] He appears, nonetheless, to have liked it that way.
At the very time when he wished his poem "Harry Ploughman" more
easily communicable to Bridges, and was thus fearing that he might
need to make "a confession of unintelligibility" or at least "prefix short
prose *arguments* to some of [his] pieces,"[38] he simultaneously was
fiercely defending his obscurity:

> . . . Plainly if it is possible to express a sub[t]le and recondite thought
> on a subtle and recondite subject in a subtle and recondite way and
> with great felicity and perfection, in the end, something must be
> sacrificed, with so trying a task, in the process, and this may be the
> being at once, nay perhaps even the being without explanation at all,
> intelligible. . . .[39]

Hopkins seems definitely perplexed here, for he so wants to communicate the meaning of his poem that he is willing even to launch his
future poetic efforts, from the very time of composition, with prose
glosses. Yet he would obviously have preferred to have a reader who
was able to penetrate the textual difficulties of any poem on his or her
own. A poem, for Hopkins, at least by this late period of his life, seems
to be like a chess victory.[40] It is given by the poet "one way only, in
three moves [three strophes? three argumentative sections?]," but
proper phenomenological readers' personal exegeses of that poem
should come "various ways, in many [moves]" (as in Ingarden's "many
interpretations [that] are possible," all those readings "permissible
within limits set by the text").[41]

Hopkins as a theorist for a more markedly speech-modeled poetry
could declare in his 1873 Roehampton lectures that poetry is "speech
framed to be heard for its own sake and interest even over and above its
interest of meaning,"[42] yet he still cared about conveying meaning. And
meaning, in the analysis of his especially dense works, only becomes
truly clear to readers who will spend time examining those works
through the "whispered . . . mental performance of the closet, the
study."[43] The rigorous practitioner of poetry Hopkins told Bridges, in a
letter of 21 May 1878 that dealt with Bridges's challenge to the poetic
worth of *The Wreck of the Deutschland,*

> Granted that *it needs study* and is obscure, for indeed I was not
> over-desirous that the meaning of all should be quite clear, at least
> unmistakable, you *might, without the effort that to make it all out*

would seem to have required, have nevertheless read it so that lines and stanzas should be left in the memory and superficial impressions deepened, and have liked some without exhausting all. I am sure I have read and enjoyed pages of poetry that way.[44]

Not "over-desirous" to communicate "quite clear . . . [or] unmistakable meaning," Hopkins was, at the same time, altogether desirous to communicate a *certain* amount of meaning. He also wanted a reader to devote enough attention to the poem so that he or she could have "superficial impressions deepened," although "without exhausting all." It seems likely that he emphasized a poetry for the ear as a way of registering upon an audience positive "superficial impressions," but that he hardly wanted the "impressions" to cease at that impressionistic point, without "deepen[ing]," through "study."[45]

Hopkins grew peevish with Bridges the imperfect reader because, as something of an aesthetic purist, he wanted his primary audience member to discover poetic meanings on his own. At first, certainly, he wanted Bridges to give the musical poem his receptive ear. But then, at a later stage, he also wished him to give "laborious" visual and mental attention to the poems' architectonic lexical-semantic designs and to their sacramental thematics, to the fully wrought structure of the dense "verse."[46] If he had, without apology, "made verse . . . laborious," he wanted audiences who would both carefully hear and watch all the structural strata of that "verse." Although convinced that "mere clarity" might seem to "shrink" his important key theme,[47] he certainly *did* want to communicate that theme—the calling to saintliness.

* * *

Hopkins surely wrote a poetry of both sound and sense. He thus desired, I am sure, both of the reactions he received from me when I first, as a college freshman, met his work. He wished to evoke awestruck pleasure in his lyrics' lustrous music and also to entice awestruck curiosity about defamiliarized semantics and the shocking spiritual experience that they suggest—a "wrestling with (my God!) my God" ("Carrion Comfort," 14). However much he wished to be honored as a formal poetic technician, Hopkins's ultimate goals were semantic and finally extraliterary. He wanted Bridges or any reader to find saintly inscape, and his sacramental thematics, he believed, could point to decisions for sanctity—at least if the poetic "utterance" of "religious experience" encountered "consent [in] its recipient."[48]

By the likely use of a pun on the word "convert," Hopkins rather confusedly blends, in the first of the two following quotations, his two goals—aesthetic and spiritual—for sharing his poetry with Bridges. The actual spiritual goal is more obvious in the second quotation, although

Hopkins here has to admit, and even to Bridges himself, that "literature" cannot easily provoke the desired spiritual transformation he wishes to see in his chief reader.

> I cannot think of altering anything. Why shd. I? I do not write for the public. You are my public and I hope to convert you.[49]

> When we met in London we never but once, and then only for a few minutes before parting, spoke on any important subject, but always on literature [alone?]. This I regret very much. . . . You understand of course that I desire to see you a Catholic or, if not that, a Christian or, if not that, at least a believer in the true God (for you told me something of your views about the deity, which were not as they should be). Now you no doubt take for granted that your already being or your ever coming to be any of these things turns on the working of your own mind, influenced or uninfluenced by the minds and reasonings of others as the case may be, and on that only. You might on reflection expect me to suggest that it also might and ought to turn on something further, in fact on prayer, and that suggestion I believe I did once make. Still under the circumstances it is one which it is not altogether consistent to make or adopt. But I have another counsel open to no objection and yet I think it will be unexpected. I lay great stress on it. It is to give alms. . . .[50]

Salmon writes, using the first of the quotations as part of her evidence, that the poet-priest Hopkins "had already [by 1877] given up on the idea of an extensive audience, but not the missionary urge."[51] The second of the quotations above shows him finding "literature" a difficult mode through which to urge spiritual "conver[sion]," and hence in itself not so "important" as that ultimate goal. Yet Salmon rightly maintains that he kept on trying to use "literature" for such "missionary" purposes, despite some sense on his part of what the deconstructionists today would call language's problematic distance from the metonymic spiritual wholeness he wished to teach.

In balancing artistic against spiritual purposes, then, Hopkins would seem to concur and *not* concur with the philosophical rigor of Ingarden, who argues that literature *can* have "positive or negative moral effect," but only as an extraliterary instrument:

> . . . All other functions which the literary work of art can perform in the cultural, or especially in the moral, atmosphere of a community, regardless of whether it has a positive or negative moral effect on the individual reader, are secondary and not specific to the literary work of art, however significant they may be in other respects and however much they can endow the work with new positive or negative values in addition to its artistic or aesthetic value.[52]

Hopkins's writing conflict between aesthetic and spiritual goals has also been identified by critics exactly opposite to Ingarden in their perspectives. While Ingarden judges spiritual purposes to be intrusive upon aesthetic values, moral-religious critics find aesthetic values intruding upon spirituality. For instance, Downes judges that the "mature poems" of Hopkins are "passionate and powerful . . . metaphors of Hopkins' rich, religious consciousness," and yet at the same time dangerous "self-expressions, self-assertions, a dazzling mosaic of inscapes of self."[53] Critic Downes is writing in the same tradition as the Benedictine Jean Leclercq. That scholar spiritually downgrades all art, even that with spiritual themes, if it "seek[s], more or less consciously," to be "admired."[54] And the Benedictine also wonders about the sincere spirituality of any writer who does not reveal "a simplicity of soul . . . reflected in a certain simplicity of artistry."[55]

Hopkins would seem eminently accusable by the principle that only "simplicity of artistry" can mark spiritual sincerity. By his complicated poetic method it is likely that he has himself inevitably caused some interpretations of his poems—especially his late poems—that he might abhor. The chaotic images and despairing surface tone of the "Terrible Sonnets" seem repeatedly to have confused the critics who sought for their meaning. Even good Hopkins scholars have felt compelled to rearrange the order of these six poems from that of the sequence Hopkins sent to Bridges, thus trying to find a sequential pattern or an image system which works for them more adequately than what they see as the original one.[56]

Yet Hopkins did provide the "kernel" of meaning that guides us to the most likely constructive code of the "Terrible Sonnets" as the cycle probably was intended to have sequential order. He did, to be sure, bury that "kernel" cue to meaning—"New Nazareths in us"—in the sixtieth line of his little-discussed poem "The Blessed Virgin compared to the Air we Breathe." That poem, unfortunately, at first sight no doubt looks to the average critic like innocuous piety and hence unimportant to Hopkins's total corpus. Yet it clearly seems to give dynamic focus to the semantics of many late Hopkins lyrics. Although one can hardly say, for instance, that the "Terrible Sonnets" become exactly easy poetry once one senses their "Blessed Virgin[al]" imagery of spiritual gestation, they do then at least become clearly cogent as a patterned sonnet cycle. And it is a cycle linked to many more Hopkins poems and to an entire Judaeo-Christian tradition, one that dates as far back in time as Isaiah.

It does not thus seem appropriate for us to distrust Hopkins's spiritual humility just because his art is generally *complex*. Indeed, it seems more important to ask how virtuous is that Hopkinsian art which seeks its spiritual goals too *simply*.

Philip Endean thinks that Hopkins's life in the active priesthood was centrally important to him, and that he therefore felt himself to be somewhat frivolous when he was writing poetry. To Endean, Hopkins's poetry surely is sometimes frivolous, or at least occasionally inept. A "patronizing" Hopkins, he says, bizarrely invokes "some sort of elemental presence" in the character of Felix Randal, while in The Wreck of the Deutschland "bold, fertile sacramentalism sits alongside an Ultramontane narrowness of outlook about the salvation of non-Catholics."[57]

Endean here makes several distinctly correct but complicatedly intermeshed points. The priesthood certainly was to Hopkins his most important of earthly vocations. Yet Endean, even though he quite rightly judges that "there are inherent difficulties in giving a sacramental vision . . . linguistic expression,"[58] does not seem to see that Hopkins collides with those "difficulties" most of all whenever he turns zealously to render a poem itself priestly altar or baptistry.[59] When Salmon wisely writes that proper "theological language strives to describe, not embody" human "participation in the Eucharist,"[60] it seems to me to be highly significant that she only makes this statement (if one judges by her footnotes) after she has been considering Augustine's paradigmatic Christian caution against would-be sacramentalist language.[61] All Hopkinsians might note Augustine's cautiousness.

In "The Windhover," "Hurrahing in Harvest," and the "Terrible Sonnets" (despite their textual complexity), Hopkins only "describe[s]" sacramental "participation," and any distorting deconstructive readings of those poems have not been the result of Hopkins's naïvely commanding sacramental participation on the reader's part. In the apparent "embod[ied]" Eucharist of "The Starlight Night," however, Hopkins seems anxious for all his readers to join him in what is likely to be for many of them at best a confused, because an unprepared, sacramental participation. The reader (e.g., Robinson) who deconstructively rejects either of these two poems' sacramental commands seems partly justified in doing so. The reader has apparently been asked to respond to the persona of a narrating priest who could well have addressed his audience member more sensibly, by drawing the reader more slowly and carefully into the poem's anagogical world.

It is true that "The Starlight Night" might yet reach any reader who knows Dante's Divine Comedy and thus can recognize the allusions to it that are hidden within the Hopkins lyric—just as any reader might best deal with the mysteries of the "Terrible Sonnets" if he or she knows Hopkins's "The Blessed Virgin" and the Pauline theology of the Mystical Body of Christ. Yet at least in the "Terrible Sonnets" Hopkins seemingly does admit, as he seems not to do in the "Starlight" poem, that he composes mere poetry. Albeit that he labels even the "Terrible Sonnets" spiritual "inspirations unbidden,"[62] Hopkins is surely not by 1885 audaciously mixing poet and priest roles. If he does mutely expect the reader of the post-1883 lyrics to pay attention to "The Blessed Virgin," he does not assault his reader as he seems to do in "The Starlight Night"; he does not appear to make the reader's conversion his central purpose, while at the same time assuming too much innate sacramentalist knowledge from that reader. We may misread the "Terrible Sonnets" because we struggle with difficult poetry and its hidden thematic code, and yet Hopkins elsewhere does kindly provide the codes that we need for understanding these poems. If we misread "The Starlight Night," we probably do so dominantly because we have never, or have only rarely, attended and/or studied the significance of a liturgical Eucharist. We thus are ignorant of the form of Eucharistic invitations and the contrition needed before we can properly greet them. Yet Hopkins *does not*, in this case, give us the interpretive codes we may need. His poetry can lead us to the sacramentalist experience he wishes to prepare for us, but it will more fully succeed in so doing the more clearly he guides us.

* * *

Of course, a reader should never feel permitted to avoid trying to find Hopkins's textual emphases, whatever limitations of knowledge he or she may begin with. First of all, Bump repeatedly and rightly does suggest that Hopkins uses the unified sound scheme of his verse with a purpose: he seeks to ease thereby a reader's encounter with intricate poetic argumentation about purposeful unity in a divinely created and sustained cosmos.[63]

Hopkins's attitude toward speech certainly supports a "connection between Hopkins's and Saussure's theories of language," one "based upon their common reading and training in the writings of some of the more prominent linguists of the second half of the nineteenth century."[64] Hopkins and Ferdinand de Saussure both came to believe, although separated by several decades of history, that "Speech is a language that is original and natural, the key to interpreting writing," and that "writing [is] subservient to speech," "not language [itself] but only represent[ing of] language graphically."[65] Certainly writing is thus for both Hopkins and Saussure removed from what they assumed to be language's "purity of . . . origin."[66] Nevertheless, they were not deconstructionists; for both, writing still is *like* speech, *linked* to a "purity of . . . origin."[67]

As an open-minded linguistic structuralist in the lineage of Hopkins and Saussure, I sympathize with poststructuralist positions asserting that the reader to some degree always "produces" a text's "meaning."[68] But I cannot easily become a full-fledged Derridan believer in écriture as a confused "field of dispersed signs," "ontologically unconditioned."[69] Saussure and even Hopkins may have believed, as I do, that "language perpetually changes and cannot be arbitrarily arrested in its development."[70] Nonetheless that fact does not make the vocabulary of an 1877 Hopkins poem, for instance, unlimited by the definitions historically and contextually available to its author. The "ooze of oil crushed" in "God's Grandeur" (2) will never refer to refined crude oil. That definition is not ruled out on a historical basis, for "struck oil" is an *OED* example for 1875 and even earlier, but crude oil is a definition ruled out of "God's Grandeur" by context, given that crude oil is not "crushed." Language changes, but it still has boundaries; it *can* be meaningfully *read*.

One can respect Salmon's partially poststructuralist approach to Hopkins's poetry, for she at least painstakingly examines the verbal texture of his works; she follows sincerely Sprinker's perhaps-insincere advice, for she truly "immerses [her]self in the text's language," as he claims also to do.[71] Yet Sprinker himself flagrantly avoids any real examination of the statements made in whole sestets of Hopkins's sonnets. He bases his readings on mere corners of the poems' entire systemic constructs. In this way he can glibly overemphasize[72] Hopkins's apparent deep doubts (his "cries like dead letters sent / To dearest him that lives alas! away" ["I wake and feel," 7–8]). He evidently feels that he need not analyze the poet's obvious Christian resolution at the sonnet's conclusion (although he does quote the appropriate lines, which he then proceeds to avoid: "I see / The lost are like this, and their scourge to be / As I am mine, their sweating selves; but worse" ["I wake and feel," 12–14]).

Poetry as intricate as Hopkins's (to say nothing of poetry even much simpler) cannot be intelligently read with inattention, whether or not that inattention claims to justify itself as fidelity to a contemporary theory of dispersed signification. "Defamiliarized" artifacts such as those that Hopkins composed[73] only naturally shocked his contemporary Bridges, the citizen of a traditionalist Victorian "interpretive community."[74] Bridges's first baffled reactions as a Hopkinsian reader were inevitable and largely forgivable. Yet Bridges eventually came (albeit that he did not do so until a full thirty years had passed) to demonstrate much deeper insight than at first into Hopkins's work. He must have striven over the preceding decades to make himself able to share, at least largely if not completely, Hopkins's own "interpretive community." Like other critics, however, the modern Sprinker not only skims poems superficially, as is hardly necessary with the advent of sophisticated exegetical methodologies, but he also (despite numerous references to them in his book) proves fairly inattentive to Hopkins's prose and intellectual history. He surely does not "immerse himself" in these words.

Sprinker, of course, behaves in this way because he has a myopic commitment to make Hopkins sound principally like an unwitting precursor of Derrida,[75] and thus he puts thoughts into the Jesuit's head that were never there, prophecies about the inevitable dissolution of all language into a far-too-completely relativistic Derridan écriture. For example, even if there is a definite surface resemblance between the sacramentally mysterious texture of Hopkins's late lyrics and the then-contemporary (and assuredly deconstructionist) hermeticism of Mallarmé's, Sprinker does not admit the real differences between the two writers.

While Mallarmé really is a Nietzschean forerunner of the modern Derrida, Hopkins truly stretches backward in history, to Origen's and Augustine's Christian hermeticism. Mallarmé's "Un coup de dés jamais n'abolira le hasard" is surely what Paul Valéry called it: "A text . . . all clarity and enigmas, as tragic or as indifferent as might be; that spoke and did not speak; woven of multiple meanings, assembling order and disorder; proclaiming a God as forcefully as it denied Him."[76] The deconstructive Mallarmé places equal metaphysical bets on two interpretations of the cosmos; to him it is either orderly "constellation" or disorderly "hasard," but who knows which? Hopkins's poems of supposed doubt, on the contrary, always practice the conscious conquest of irony. For him the answer to Mallarmé's query is certainly that the cosmos is much more "constellation" than apparent "hasard."

In a Hopkins "doubt" lyric, once the outer "husk" of superficial doubt collapses before the "kernel" of internally revealed divine triumph, the result is not the typical Mallarméan resurgence of doubt, but a prayer ("Mine, O thou lord of life, send my roots rain"—"Thou art indeed," 14) or a "yield[ing]" of declared fruitful "explanation" ("To R. B.," 14). Indeed, if Mallarmé believed chance ("le hasard") to be something one could never abolish, Hopkins proclaimed "Chance . . . incredible or impossible by . . . *a priori* consideration, but more strikingly . . . incredible from experience. It is never verified and the more examined the less it is verified, the more is it out of the question."[77]

As a reader-respondent, Sprinker unfortunately seems almost anxious for a "rupture" in "understanding," rather than avidly seeking a truly forthright "modification of the interests and concerns that are already in place."[78] Like all readers defined by Stanley Fish, Sprinker has his own "norms and values,"[79] and yet Sprinker's distorted "norms" of deconstructionism truly do appear anarchic when he blithely neglects so many previous "norms" functioning within the Hopkinsian "interpretive community."[80] Distinguished earlier interpreters' norms have already given us a far more consistent picture than does Sprinker of how this sacramental Jesuit Gerard Manley Hopkins became the most astute of all Victorian medievalists.

When Bridges published the first full-scale edition of Hopkins's poems in 1918, he still lamented, as he long had, over the poems' supposed lack of "continuous literary decorum."[81] Yet Bridges had ultimately come to appreciate, it appears, even much of Hopkins's most arcane style (for he alludes in the following poem to "Henry Purcell," a sonnet that Hopkins had needed repeatedly to gloss for him). And Bridges also had gained considerable sympathy for Hopkins's poetic thematics, even their encouraging of a sacramentalist response to life.

> Our generation already is overpast,
> And thy lov'd legacy, Gerard, hath lain
> Coy in my home; as once thy heart was fain
> Of shelter, when God's terror held thee fast
> In life's wild wood at Beauty and Sorrow aghast;
> Thy sainted sense trammel'd in ghostly pain,
> Thy rare ill-broker'd talent in disdain:
> Yet love of Christ will win man's love at last.
>
> Hell wars without; but, dear, the while my hands
> Gather'd thy book, I heard, this wintry day,
> Thy spirit thank me, in his young delight
> Stepping again upon the yellow sands.
>   Go forth: amidst our chaffinch flock display
> Thy plumage of far wonder and heavenward flight![82]

To be sure, Bridges was still expressing what Ritz terms "Anglican agnosticism" in *The Testament of Beauty*, a poetic collection issued just before Bridges's death twelve years after this 1918 dedicatory sonnet to Hopkins.[83] And Bridges, in addition, wrote to Hopkins's sister Kate, concerning this very dedicatory sonnet of 1918, that he was "rather afraid [she] might think it too sad."[84] He felt he could justify that sadness, however, because "the poems w[ould] disclose . . . that Gerard suffered dreadfully from a sort of melancholy—and I do not think there wd. be any advantage in not recognizing this—besides I shd. judge it a good thing to tell the truth about, and show that medievalizing does not always produce complete ease of mind."[85] There seems truth, then, to Harris's opinion that "Bridges bridled as he praised," judging that Hopkins in his stringent life "had wasted his exquisite charm and aesthetic sensibility."[86]

Yet Ritz has shown, in his marvelously controlled but sensitive biography about the Bridges-Hopkins friendship, how Harris's words here would much better fit a Bridges of thirty years earlier. In 1889, although he originally planned an immediate memoir about his just-deceased friend, Bridges eventually "shrank from the task of telling even his private readers of the unhappiness and failure of Hopkins as a man."[87] By 1918, however, he had approached closer to that fuller understanding of the essential Hopkinsian spirituality which Ritz believes he later memorialized in his own *Testament of Beauty*:

> Now in spiritual combat, altho' I must deem
> them the most virtuous who with least effort excell,
> yet, virtue being a conflict, moralizers hold
> that where conflict is hardest virtue must be at best. . . .[88]

It is not actually the likely line "Yet love of Christ will win man's love at last" ("Our generation. . . ," 8) that strikes me as the most revealing sign of a change in Bridges's view of Hopkins between 1889 and 1918. In 1889, just after Hopkins had died, Bridges had already recalled, as he did again in 1918, both his friend's "strange life" and the "spiritual consolation it is possible to have from the consideration of his single-hearted devotion."[89] He already then had, therefore, an appreciation for Hopkins's spirituality, and his appreciation was perhaps just as intermittent in 1918 as it had been earlier.

What impresses me more about Bridges's dedicatory sonnet is that the sonnet itself emulates Hopkins's sacramentally medievalist, rather than any strangulatingly "medievalizing," sense of life. It is true that Bridges may here only have stylized an allusion to Hopkins as a Dantesque figure "held" by "God's terror" in "life's wild wood" ("Our generation. . . ," 4–5). He also may not have sensed the Holy Ghost to be active in Hopkins's "ghostly pain" (6). But if the Dante of the selva oscura episode himself shares some of Hopkins's lamentably human "melancholy," an allusion to Dante naturally carries a contextual base that expands past the *Inferno* to the *Paradiso*. Therefore, such an allusion reminds us, as it must also have reminded Bridges, that out of human "melancholy" can arise the need and search for "l'amor che move il sole e l'altre stelle [the love that moves the sun and the other stars]" (*Paradiso* 33.145). That is a Dantesque-Hopkinsian definition of what Bridges, in 1916, called "spirituality" as "the basis and foundation of human life.[90]

Bridges also seems by 1918 to have understood more spiritually than have many later critics Hopkins's concern, in his final poem "To R. B.," with a "winter world." Himself associating a "wintry day" with "wars" fought by "Hell"-forces ("Our generation . . . ," 9–10), Bridges in this later sonnet speaks both literally of the contemporary First World War and symbolically of all demonic warfare. In truth, earthly demonic warfare was much like what Hopkins actually meant by "winter world" in "To R. B." (13). It is intriguing to make this discovery of Bridges's eventual interpretive skills after reading so much criticism by others that treats the "winter world" reference only as a reflection of Hopkins's apparent gloom and creative barrenness. We may very much need to stop accusing Robert Bridges of constant critical blindness.

Hopkins wrote, during his Beaumont retreat of 3–10 September 1883, "[T]oday I earnestly asked our Lord to watch over my compositions, not to preserve them from being lost or coming to nothing, for that I am very willing they should be, but [I asked they] not do me harm through the enmity or imprudence of any man or my own; that he should have them as his own and employ or not employ them as he should see fit."[91] In response to these Beaumont retreat notes, we certainly must act toward Hopkins and his work as Bridges eventually acted. One learns in criticism both from those who err and from those who unearth hidden ore. As one who both erred and unearthed the ore, Bridges can teach us not only the value of his "preserv[ing]" Hopkins's poems "from being lost"—an act that was in truth not the one for which Hopkins was at Beaumont expressing the most particular fervency. We must too, as Bridges eventually did, respect Hopkins's most fervent Beaumont wish—that his poems "not do [him] harm through [his own or others'] enmity or imprudence." We must carefully encounter the poems, and the man revealed behind them, as disciplined students of both their innate and their ever-developing reasonable textualities; we must, in essence, belong to the most inclusive "interpretive community" possible.[92] Bridges—who, as Ritz repeatedly remarks, did truly despise Hopkins's Jesuit loyalties[93]—can provide us hope that even those who do not fully agree with a man's personal theology still can faithfully greet his poetic craftmanship without distorting it. Such readers as the eventually matured Bridges help us continually to reconstruct, not inevitably and only to deconstruct, Hopkins's magnificent art.

* * *

In a 1970 review of several then-recent books about Hopkins, Mac-Kenzie praised, as have I, Johnson's *Gerard Manley Hopkins: The Poet as Victorian*. That book, MacKenzie declared, allows Hopkins as both a historical and literary figure to be revealed to us as "somewhat less of a stranger within his own age" than we (and he himself) might have thought him. Besides, MacKenzie added, "Where Boyle derived largely religious messages for Catholics" from his study of Hopkins, "Johnson belongs firmly to literary criticism."[94] Obviously, books emphasizing

Victorian historical contexts—books like Bump's, Ong's, Johnson's, Sulloway's, Downes's, Milroy's—have greatly assisted our scholarship; they have shown us, through much careful and evidence-rich literary criticism, Hopkins in his Victorian environment.

My own work here should demonstrate "firmly" my own personal commitment to careful "literary criticism," to a faith in reading. Yet, like Boyle, I have still also emphasized the "religious messages" in Hopkins's art—for such religious insights simply *are*, after all, that art's principal focus.[95] Unlike Boyle, however, I have included attention to some religious messages that united Hopkins in "his own age" as much to his Anglican upbringing, and to basics of all Christianity, as to his Roman Catholic Scotist-Jesuit adulthood. The Anglican and basic Christian doctrine of all-important sacramental readiness in the receptive soul clearly prepared Hopkins for his later Roman Catholic Scotist-Jesuit emphasis on a sacramentally readied elective will.

It is, after all, Hopkins's will to elect self-sacrificial faith that remains constant throughout the twenty-nine years of words by which we know him. He surely relied, like his predecessor and partial model Newman, far more on dogmatic theology than did Søren Kierkegaard. Yet Hopkins was always ready to tell himself—and to tell us through our experience of his verbally sacramental wordings—that something like a Kierkegaardian "leap" to "faith"[96] might sometimes seem to prove a necessity if darkness obscured consolatory visible signs. Despite his limited resemblances to Kierkegaard, however, I can hardly agree with those who appear to judge Hopkins's persistent elective faith "absurdist." I can see in Hopkins, the believer in a Eucharistic soul that promised him nonabsurdity, no "failure of grace."[97]

In studying Hopkins, I find myself at least an intellectual witness to the anagogically rich spiritual affectivity of a faith-electing poet. Hopkins surely did sense in his environment myriad objects that appeared to him "outward and visible sign[s] of an inward and spiritual grace." In just one typical example, the "meal-drift *moulded* ever and melted across skies" of "Hurrahing in Harvest" (4; emphasis Milroy's) "the poet manages to suggest by using meal-drift as the subject of an intransitive verb that it may be both actor and acted upon at the same time."[98] He essentially senses Christ to be sacramentally molding his Real Presence into the "inward" center of the molded "outward" clouds.

And Hopkins's clearly perceptible faith did not stop, or even reach its expressive apex, in his nature poetry of the 1870s. In the seemingly "dark" sonnets of the 1880s, Hopkins was still at least able to *imagine* how Christ could become Eucharistically present in the faith-electing

soul. That soul would then itself transubstantiate sacramental power—
for within it Christic Real Presence would assuredly dwell, even though
swathed (or swaddled?) in apparent external darkness.

Throughout his mature writing life, Hopkins both defines and illustrates in poetry his Origenian-Augustinian belief in the basic if nonetheless still-limited power of language. In verbal "overthought" and
"underthought," he shows that the outscapes of dim, imperfect or sin-
burdened human sadness, doubt, and uncertainty can be voiced simultaneously with the inscapes of faith in a God who transubstantiates
both nature and humanity. God's substance of infused inscape in essence is said to triumph over, but not on earth to remove, the outscaped
species of imperfection, sin, sadness, doubt, and uncertainty.

As a young Arminian receptionist Anglican ready to become an
Augustinian transubstantiationist Roman Catholic, Hopkins wrote one
fragmentary lyric that both Miller[99] and I[100] have considered a marked
prefiguring of his very latest work:

> Trees by their yield
> Are known; but I—
> My sap is sealed,
> My root is dry.
> If life within
> I none can shew
> (Except for sin),
> Nor fruit above,—
> It must be so—
> I do not love.
>
> Will no one show
> I argued ill?
> Because, although
> Self-sentenced, still
> I keep my trust.
> If He would prove
> And search me through
> Would he not find
> (What yet there must
> Be hid behind
>
> . . . . . .

This fragment of 1865 (P, 307) contrasts with "Thou art indeed just,
Lord" of 1889 (for which it may eventually have become a draft) by
emphasizing that God must "search" (17) a man or woman and "find"
(18) whether his or her receptionist election of faith remains "hid
behind" (20) even an apparent lack of spiritual fruits (1–10). "Trees by
their yield" is rather fully dominated by a receptionist sense that

human faith must produce visible outward signs through its own active Arminian strivings. In "Thou art indeed just, Lord," by contrast, God, "not I" (12), quietly does the interior "build[ing]" of faith (12) within a human being. God does so even though the human being has been rendered seemingly ineffectual—as if, by necessity, made into a passive sacramental vessel.

Yet there is already an Augustinian transubstantiationist coloring to "Trees by their yield." The early fragment implies that in the believer's soul some inner sacramentalization must be occurring (19); a "life within" exists (5, 7), even if "hid behind" apparent outer barrenness (20). And some receptionist fervor also remains in the more basically transubstantiationist "Thou art indeed just, Lord." That poem's persona, after all, does actively ask the "lord of life" to "send . . . roots rain" (14). Hopkins's life seems clearly to illustrate that principle which De Nicolas also finds operating in the life of the model Jesuit Loyola: "Faith is like life: one has to make it to receive it."[101]

And, in his study of Ignatius, De Nicolas shows us one more insight that illuminates our discussion of Hopkins. Saints' lives, this modern Spanish hermeneuticist declares, are "exemplary," not because of "external details of their lives" but because of what they show us of "our human capacities for creation."[102] In the end, I am certain, no earthly individual reader will ever recognize all that is "hid behind" Hopkins's words. Readers may come to see, however, as Canon Dixon did, that Hopkins's extraordinary sacramental impulse helps to transubstantiate all his words. Thus, even if they sometimes reveal the dark outscapes of an imperfect world, these words ultimately can unveil, for Dixon and for us as well as for Hopkins, an inscaped "terrible crystal" of divine revelation.[103]

Gerard Manley Hopkins's elective soul believed, like the soul of John the Baptist's father Zechariah before him, that the chief sacramental force empowering this world came from the Holy Spirit, "the dayspring from on high [which] has visited us" (Luke 1:78).[104] Another previous spiritual voice, that of a fifteenth-century Augustinian hymnist,[105] speaks of the Spirit-fed sacrament which we have found most steadily revealed in the nineteenth-century Jesuit poet before our attention. In Hopkins, the sacramentally receptive author of would-be sacramental words, we have sensed consistently burning the "morning sun," the "dayspring," of sacramentally kindled Christic substance:

Come down, O Love divine,
Seek thou this soul of mine,
And visit it with thine own ardor glowing;
O Comforter, draw near,

Within my heart appear,
And kindle it, thy holy flame bestowing.

. . . .

And so the yearning strong,
With which the soul will long,
Shall far outpass the power of human telling;
For none can guess its grace,
Till he become the place
Wherein the Holy Spirit makes his dwelling.[106]

Notes

Preface

1. Stanley Fish, *Is There A Text In This Class?: The Authority of Interpretive Communities* (Cambridge: Harvard University Press, 1980), 14.

Chapter 1. The Sacrament of the Soul

1. Anthony F. Alexander, *College Sacramental Theology* (Chicago: Henry Regnery Company, 1961), 24.
2. Augustine, cited in Jared Wicks, S.J., "The Sacraments: A Catechism for Today," in *The Sacraments: Readings in Contemporary Sacramental Theology*, ed. Michael J. Taylor, S.J. (New York: Alba House, 1981), 20.
3. Wicks, "The Sacraments," 21.
4. Ibid., 20.
5. Alexander, *College Sacramental Theology*, 30.
6. Ibid,, 27.
7. Augustine, quoted in Louis Bouyer, "Word and Sacrament," in *Sacraments: The Gestures of Christ*, ed. Denis O'Callaghan (New York: Sheed and Ward, 1964), 139.
8. Bouyer, "Word and Sacrament," 142.
9. Alexander, *College Sacramental Theology*, 30–31.
10. Ibid., 34.
11. Saint Paul, quoted in Alexander, *College Sacramental Theology*, 35.
12. G. M. A. Jansen, O.P., *The Sacramental We: An Existential Approach to the Sacramental Life* (Milwaukee, Wis.: The Bruce Publishing Company, 1968), 44–45.
13. Bernard Cooke, *Sacraments and Sacramentality* (Mystic, Conn.: Twenty-Third Publications, 1983), 70–71.
14. Ibid., 71.
15. Ibid., 73.
16. Wicks, "The Sacraments," 20–21; Alexandre Ganoczy, *An Introduction to Catholic Sacramental Theology*, trans. Willis Thomas, with the assistance of Alexander Sherman (New York: Paulist Press, 1984), 7–25, 41.
17. Augustine, *On Christian Doctrine*, trans. D. W. Robertson, Jr. (Indianapolis, Ind.: Bobbs-Merrill, 1958), 90.
18. Hopkins as poet images the human soul as the spiritual "kernel" within the outer "husk" of the human body or self; he also images Christ as the spiritual "kernel" transubstantiating the "husk" of the soul itself. The latter images do not of course fit with the traditional definition of the sacramental "husk" as something "sensible"; we cannot, after all, encounter an inner soul with our physical senses. But Hopkins was always innovative in his discussion and portrayal of sacrament and sacramentalization; his intuitive spirituality and intellect were willing to expand traditional definitions.
19. Jerome Bump, *Gerard Manley Hopkins* (Boston: Twayne, 1982), 59.
20. Gerard Manley Hopkins, *Sermons and Devotional Writings*, ed. Christopher Devlin, S.J. (London: Oxford University Press, 1959), 113. Hereafter S.
21. Bump, *Gerard Manley Hopkins*, 149.
22. See Augustine, *On Christian Doctrine*, 86.

In his third Rule for the Discernment of Spirits, Saint Ignatius Loyola writes that the soul experiencing "consolation," or "increase in hope, faith, and charity and any interior joy that calls and attracts to heavenly things," "consequently can love no created thing on the face of the earth for its own sake, but only in the Creator of all things" (quoted in Antonio T. De Nicolas, *Powers of Imagining / Ignatius de Loyola: A Philosophical Hermeneutic of Imagining through the Collected Works of Ignatius de Loyola, with a Translation of Those Works* [Albany: State University of New York Press, 1986], 164). The Jesuit retreatant and his spiritual guide, "both . . . looking for . . . signs that would enable decisions to be made," must judge, says De Nicolas, whether there is a "nod of God" to specific signs, or whether those signs contrastingly "come from . . . the bad angel"(55).

23. Andrew Greeley, "A Christmas Biography," in *The Wiley Reader: Designs for Writing*, ed. Caroline D. Eckhardt, et al. (New York: John Wiley and Sons, 1976), 360.

24. Ibid., 359.

25. Daniel A. Harris, *Inspirations Unbidden: The "Terrible Sonnets" of Gerard Manley Hopkins* (Berkeley: University of California Press, 1982), 134.

26. Rachel Salmon, " 'Wording it How': The Possibilities of Utterance in *The Wreck of the Deutschland*," *Hopkins Quarterly* 10 (1983–84): 95, 105.

27. Bump, *Gerard Manley Hopkins*, 69.

28. Ibid., 141.

29. Greeley, "A Christmas Biography," 360.

30. Ibid., 359.

31. John Keble, cited in Bump, *Gerard Manley Hopkins*, 91.

32. Bump, *Gerard Manley Hopkins*, 79.

33. Ibid., 168.

34. W. H. MacKean, *The Eucharistic Doctrine of the Oxford Movement: A Critical Survey* (London: Putnam, 1933), 2.

35. Bump, *Gerard Manley Hopkins*, 168.

36. J. Hillis Miller, *The Disappearance of God: Five Nineteenth-Century Writers* (Cambridge: Harvard University Press, 1963), 358.

37. David A. Downes, *The Great Sacrifice: Studies in Hopkins* (Lanham, Md.: University Press of America, 1983), 58.

38. Marylou Motto, *"Mined with a Motion": The Poetry of Gerard Manley Hopkins* (New Brunswick, N.J.: Rutgers University Press, 1984), 71.

39. Michael Sprinker, *"A Counterpoint of Dissonance": The Aesthetics and Poetry of Gerard Manley Hopkins* (Baltimore and London: The Johns Hopkins University Press, 1980), 131.

40. Robert Boyle, S.J., " 'Man Jack The Man Is': The *Wreck* from the Perspective of *The Shepherd's Brow*," in *Readings of "The Wreck": Essays in Commemoration of the Centenary of G. M. Hopkins' "The Wreck of the Deutschland*,*"* ed. Peter Milward, S. J. and Raymond Schoder, S. J. (Chicago: Loyola University Press, 1976), 104.

41. Boyle, " 'Man Jack the Man Is,' " 111.

42. Ibid.

43. James Finn Cotter, *Inscape: The Christology and Poetry of Gerard Manley Hopkins* (Pittsburgh, Pa.: University of Pittsburgh Press, 1972), 110.

44. *The Correspondence of Gerard Manley Hopkins and Richard Watson Dixon*, ed. Claude Colleer Abbott, second edition (London: Oxford University Press, 1956), 159–60; hereafter L 2; Jean-Georges Ritz, *Robert Bridges and Gerard Hopkins, 1863–1889; a Literary Friendship* (London: Oxford University Press, 1960), 142–43.

45. Downes, *Great Sacrifice*, 58.

46. Like the tradition of the mystics, the Jesuit meditative tradition founded by Saint Ignatius and followed by Hopkins seeks, says De Nicolas, the "secret of human communion," "the secret of how life is and has been (*Powers of Imagining*, 68).

47. Alison Sulloway, *Gerard Manley Hopkins and the Victorian Temper* (London: Routledge and Kegan Paul, 1972), 76.

48. Downes, *Great Sacrifice*, 88.

49. Harris, *Inspirations Unbidden*, 4.

50. Motto, *"Mined with a Motion,"* 105.

51. Wendell Stacy Johnson, *Gerard Manley Hopkins: The Poet as Victorian* (Ithaca: Cornell University Press, 1966), 26.

52. Ibid., 51, 57.

53. Robert Boyle, S.J., *Metaphor in Hopkins* (Chapel Hill: University of North Carolina Press, 1960), 84–89.

54. Wendell Stacy Johnson, "Halfway to a New Land: Herbert, Tennyson, and the Early Hopkins," *Hopkins Quarterly* 10 (1983–84): 116.

55. My study of the Jesuit Hopkins would emulate the principle of De Nicolas as a student of Loyola: "Hermeneutics demands of the philosopher that all human possibilities be first held evident. . . . [One] cannot be a common mortal, take a philosophical position, and read the world through that technology [alone]" (De Nicolas, *Powers of Imagining*, 86).

56. So also, again, with Ignatius: "The mysteries of Christian life which Ignatius used for meditation in his initial stages became finally centered around the Christian mandala of the Mass and the Eucharist, where the whole of Christian life arose simultaneously for Christian memory to 're-member' " (De Nicolas, *Powers of Imagining*, 11). By contrast, "As far as Ignatius was concerned, the whole system of Scholastic philosophy was heuristically ineffective," although worthy of "praise" as "part of the public system of social communion" (16).

57. Martin E. Marty, *A Short History of Christianity* (Philadelphia: Fortress Press, 1980), 313.

58. MacKean, *Eucharistic Doctrine*, 8–9; Marty, *History of Christianity*, 219.

59. MacKean, *Eucharistic Doctrine*, 2, 11–12.

60. Sulloway, *Victorian Temper*, 11–21.

61. MacKean (*Eucharistic Doctrine*, 55) writes that "For the most part the Tractarians were concerned rather with exalting the importance of the Sacrament than in dealing with its doctrine." Keble at first, as his 1828 poem for 5 November in *The Christian Year* indicates (58), was a receptionist who revered the Reformed Anglican theology of Hooker (59). Pusey in Tract 81 "rejected the Roman doctrine of 'the sacrifice of the Mass' " (62), while Newman in 1833 was deeming the doctrine of the Mass a great Roman error (72); to MacKean "it is difficult to decide what Newman's doctrine was" (76). Even after 1850, MacKean notes (116), Pusey "found the utmost difficulty in making up his mind on the adoration of Christ in the Sacrament, the reception by the wicked, and Transubstantiation." (Admittedly, MacKean himself opposes all Roman doctrines.)

62. Gerard Manley Hopkins, *Poems*, ed. W. H. Gardner and N. H. MacKenzie, 4th ed. (London: Oxford University Press, 1967), 28–29. Further quotations of Hopkins's poems will be inserted in the text with line numbers; references to editors' remarks will be denoted by P and a page number.

63. Johnson, "Halfway to a New Land," 121.

64. *New Catholic Encyclopedia* 1st ed., s.v. "Transubstantiation."

65. Downes, *Great Sacrifice*, 42.

66. As De Nicolas summarizes (*Powers of Imagining*, 54), it is to just such firm confirmational persons as Hopkins, "persons bent on a vocation looking for the will of God," that Saint Ignatius addresses his *Spiritual Exercises*. See Alison Sulloway's excellent "St. Ignatius Loyola and the Victorian Temper: Hopkins' Windhover as Symbol of 'Diabolic Gravity,' " *Hopkins Quarterly* 1 (1974–75): 43–51.

67. Boyle, *Metaphor in Hopkins*, 93–94.

68. Alfred Thomas, S.J., "G. M. Hopkins' 'The Windhover': Sources, 'Underthought,' and Significance," *Modern Language Review* 70 (1975): 504.

69. Ibid., 506.

70. This interpretation of "The Windhover" as an allusive commentary on Isaiah 40 is that of my student Cindy Holifield Waldron.

71. Robert Southwell, S.J., quoted in Thomas, "Hopkins' 'The Windhover,' " 504.

72. See Boyle, *Metaphor in Hopkins*, 93. My student Suzanne Sasser basically does agree with Boyle and finds the windhover that "rebuffed the big wind" ("The Wind-

hover," 7) to be a fit symbol of Christ, who, when "there arose a great storm of wind, and the waves bent into the ship," "rebuked the wind, and said unto the sea, Peace, be still" (Mark 4:37, 39).

73. Boyle, *Metaphor in Hopkins*, 93.

74. Quoted in Sulloway, *Victorian Temper*, 110–11.

75. Johnson, *Poet as Victorian*, 85.

76. Ibid., 103 (emphasis mine).

77. Ibid. (emphases mine).

78. Yngve Brilioth, *Eucharistic Faith and Practice: Evangelical and Catholic*, trans. A. G. Hebert (London: S.P.C.K., 1961), 15.

79. In a notable letter denying his father's accusation that he is becoming a Roman Catholic for mere aesthetic reasons, Hopkins writes, on 16 October 1866, that he is "surprised you sh[oul]d say fancy and aesthetic tastes have led me to my present state of mind: these w[oul]d be better satisfied in the Church of England, for bad taste is always meeting one in the accessories of Catholicism." See Gerard Manley Hopkins, *Further Letters, Including His Correspondence with Coventry Patmore*, ed. Claude Colleer Abbott, 2d ed. (London: Oxford University Press, 1956), 93; hereafter L 3.

80. Alfred Thomas, S.J., *Hopkins the Jesuit: The Years in Training* (London: Oxford University Press, 1969), 15–16.

81. Hopkins, L 3, 17.

82. Miller, *Disappearance of God*, 312.

83. Hopkins, L 3, 92.

84. Miller, *Disappearance of God*, 309.

85. Cotter, *Inscape*, 37.

86. Miller, *Disappearance of God*, 312–13.

87. Ibid., 311.

88. Gordon W. Lathrop, "A Rebirth of Images: On the Use of the Bible in Liturgy," *Worship* 7 (1984): 301.

89. Paul Mariani, *A Commentary on the Complete Poems of Gerard Manley Hopkins* (Ithaca and London: Cornell University Press, 1970), 233.

90. Lathrop, "Rebirth of Images," 303.

91. De Nicolas, *Powers of Imagining*, 33.

92. *New Catholic Encyclopedia*, 1st ed., s.v. "Transubstantiation."

93. Lathrop, "Rebirth of Images," 298.

94. Miller, *Disappearance of God*, 4.

95. Donald Gray, "The Real Absence: A Note on the Eucharist," in *Living Bread, Saving Cup: Readings on the Eucharist*, ed. R. Kevin Seasoltz, O.S.B. (Collegeville, Minn.: The Liturgical Press, 1982), 195.

96. Miller, *Disappearance of God*, 358.

97. Gray, "Real Absence," 191.

98. Miller, *Disappearance of God*, 352.

99. Hopkins, S, 262.

100. Ibid.

101. Ibid.

102. Ibid. In quoting these lines, Miller (*Disappearance of God*, 357) somewhat dishonestly weights the evidence toward negativism by quoting, after the passage of prayer for aid, the words "Helpless loathing" from a retreat note entry of two days later (3 January 1888). The prayer, although not ended with a period, completes the entry for 1 January, and even the 3 January entry (Hopkins, S, 263) mentions Hopkins's leaving his loathing in order to say the Te Deum and to summon forth "amendment of life."

103. The Eucharistic poems are "Barnfloor and Winepress," "Easter Communion," "The Half-way House," and, with a less dominant emphasis on the Eucharist, "New Readings," "Easter," and "He hath abolished the old drouth." Joining the Holy Orders poems in a strong emphasis upon renunciatory suffering are four additional poems of this early period: "Myself unholy, from myself unholy," "See how Spring opens with disabling cold," "My prayers must meet a brazen heaven," and "Let me be to Thee as the circling bird." "Heaven-Haven" also treats the aspirations toward inner spiritual life of a

vocational religious, although its subject is a nun, not technically a member of Holy Orders.

104. See Miller, *Disappearance of God*, 352, 355. One must say at least that Hopkins's poems are not willing to show grace failing and (when read other than superficially) do not show it to fail. One would be more willing to admit as potential here "the tragedy of the failure of the work of art" (Miller, *Disappearance of God*, 14), for Hopkins's poems, of course, cannot *prove* that his God lives. Yet they also do not *disprove* his existence, especially for Hopkins.

105. These are the Anglican definitions of a sacrament, added first to the 1604 version of *The Book of Common Prayer* (see Massey Hamilton Shepherd, *The Oxford American Prayer Book, with Commentary* [New York: Oxford University Press, 1950], 578A, 581). They are also essentially Calvin's definitions (Brilioth, *Eucharistic Faith and Practice*, 165). Even if he abandoned the Protestantism in which these definitions were uttered, it does seem that Hopkins, reared with these definitions, would never have forgotten them completely. And, in any case, they essentially verbalize the same ideas as Roman Catholic definitions of sacrament.

106. Downes, *Great Sacrifice*, 32.

107. Ibid.

108. Bernard Bergonzi, *Gerard Manley Hopkins*, Masters of World Literature (New York: Macmillan, 1977), 154.

109. Harris, *Inspirations Unbidden*, 124.

110. Paul Mariani, *A Usable Past: Essays on Modern and Contemporary Poetry* (Amherst: University of Massachusetts Press, 1984), 144.

111. Ibid.

112. Downes, *Great Sacrifice*, 42.

113. Ibid.

114. Ibid.

115. Ibid.

116. Cotter, *Inscape*, 34–41.

117. Ignatius, similarly, produced in the "*Spiritual Exercises* a string of memory-points in the history of salvation using the images of the life of Christ" (De Nicolas, *Powers of Imagining*, 13).

118. David A. Downes, *Gerard Manley Hopkins: A Study of His Ignatian Spirit* (New York: Bookman Associates, 1959), 26–51.

119. De Nicolas finds one distinctive feature of early Christianity to be "its assertion that . . . the life of every human . . . was part of a plan of a . . . supernatural will . . . [which] had created out of nothing, but . . . at the cost of a self-sacrifice in the Second Person of the Trinity, the historical Jesus. . . . Men and women were free to repeat that act of creation at the cost of cancelling their own natural worlds, through the mediation of Christ" (De Nicolas, *Powers of Imagining*, 9). This spiritual task of recapturing Christic Creation by self-sacrifice De Nicolas finds to be at the center of Jesuit spirituality (11–12).

120. At the very least, "Hopkins continues to recognize and envy the vitality of the physical world outside of his suffering self," a world that for him is "objective[ly] . . . charged [with Christ]" (Margaret R. Ellsberg, *Created To Praise: The Language of Gerard Manley Hopkins* [New York and Oxford: Oxford University Press, 1987], 70). Or, as Christopher Devlin, S.J., avers ("Time's Eunuch," *The Month*, 1 [May 1949]: 312), "From the beginning to the end, what bound [Hopkins] to Scotus was his longing to see unconscious nature redeemed, to make a distinct and gracious word of that inchoate word of natural mysticism which is a genuine echo in the Church's liturgy. . . ."

121. Hopkins, S, 127–28: "On *Principium sive Fundamentum*," 20 August 1880.

122. Sprinker, "*Counterpoint of Dissonance*," 86.

123. Hopkins, S., 283.

124. Miller, *Disappearance of God*, 315.

125. Downes, *Great Sacrifice*, 112.

126. Geoffrey Hartman, "Poetry and Justification," in *Hopkins: A Collection of Critical Essays* (Englewood Cliffs, N.J.: Prentice-Hall, 1966), 14.

127. Ibid.

128. John M. Warner, "Belief and Imagination in 'The Windhover,'" *Hopkins Quarterly* 5 (1978–79): 134–35.

129. Hartman, *Collection*, 3.

130. Ibid.

131. Augustine, *On Christian Doctrine*, 90.

132. Hartman, *Collection*, 2.

133. L 3, 252; letter of 14 January 1883.

134. Ibid., 17–18; letter of 6 January 1865.

135. Hopkins does refer to Augustinian scriptural exegesis for the kenosis passage of Philippians 2:5–11 in a letter to Bridges of 26 March 1883 (Gerard Manley Hopkins, *The Letters of Gerard Manley Hopkins to Robert Bridges*, ed. Claude Colleer Abbott, 2d ed. [London: Oxford University Press, 1955], 177; hereafter L 1). No reference to Augustine appears as early as Hopkins's Oxford years, however; the first actual Augustinian work to which he refers is the *De Musica*, mentioned in the 1873 Roehampton lecture "Rhythm and the Other Structural Parts of Rhetoric—Verse" (Gerard Manley Hopkins, *Journals and Papers*, ed. Humphry House and Graham Storey [London: Oxford University Press, 1959], 273; hereafter J). Still, one suspects that Hopkins as an Oxford undergraduate had already gained much of that knowledge of Augustine which he eventually often displayed. See Cotter, *Inscape*, 115.

136. My analysis here would show that I can almost agree with Jacob Korg in "Hopkins' Linguistic Deviations," *PMLA* 92 (1977): 977–86: "Each poem draws its material from a landscape. But the poetic whole that emerges corresponds not [so much] with the physical facts on which it is based, but with the linguistic means used to embody a spiritual condition" (984). I cannot, however, concur with Korg's claim that Hopkins ever came to believe "that words are, after all, no more than self-reflecting improvisations, unrelated to the external world or to God, mere 'dead letters'" (977).

137. Although she does not specifically discuss Hopkins's transubstantial (or any other) sacramental doctrines, nor mention his sources in either Augustine or Origen, Virginia Ridley Ellis, in her valuable 1969 Brandeis University dissertation "'Authentic Cadence': The Sacramental Method of Gerard Manley Hopkins," does note his early and lifelong search for God as "the 'one spot' at the world's center" (19; see Hopkins, "The Alchemist in the City" [1865], 32; P, 24–25, 250). The chief difference between Ellis's and my views of Hopkinsian sacramentalism is that her perspective emphasizes its ultimate "cadence," while mine emphasizes its originative and omnipresent "dayspring."

138. Augustine, *On Christian Doctrine*, 94.

139. In a recent comment on his observations of the Hopkins manuscripts, Norman White proposes that the poems which critical tradition has read as "Terrible Sonnets" and has dated (according to remarks in Hopkins letters) from late 1885 may actually have variant datings as late as 1887 (Norman White, "Review of Harris's *Inspirations Unbidden*," *Hopkins Quarterly* 11 [1984–85]: 89). I follow the traditional 1885 dating in my study of these poems, but welcome White's freeing of the poems' dating from a rigid biographical time frame, given that my own interpretation of the sonnets in question does not see them primarily as personal autobiographical laments.

140. For Hopkins the word "strain" always seems to have meant simultaneously (in poems such as "Spring," "The Handsome Heart," and "Thou are indeed just, Lord") "song," "aspiration," "distillation," and "struggle."

Chapter 2. Hopkins at Highgate and Oxford

1. Juan de la Cruz, quoted in De Nicolas, *Powers of Imagining*, 63–64.

2. De Nicolas, *Powers of Imagining*, 36.

3. Conrad of Hirsau, quoted in Jean Leclercq, O.S.B., *The Love of Learning and the Desire for God: A Study of Monastic Culture*, trans. Catherine Misrahi (New York: Fordham University Press, 1982), 118.

4. Hopkins, L. 3, 252; letter of 14 January 1883.

5. Cotter, *Inscape*, 115.

6. Augustine, *On Christian Doctrine*, 90.

7. Leclercq, *Monastic Culture*, 94, 97.

8. Origen, *Origen: Spirit and Fire—A Thematic Anthology of His Writings*, ed. Hans Urs Balthasar, trans. Robert J. Daly, S.J. (Washington, D.C.: The Catholic University of America Press, 1984), 105.

9. Ibid., 103.

10. Ibid., 341.

11. Hopkins, *L* 3, 17.

12. De Nicolas, *Powers of Imagining*, 74, seems to be thinking of mentalities like Origen's when he speaks positively of the "mystics" who optimistically see a "hidden text" of potential "divine restoration" built into human life. By contrast, he labels as "not Christian, but Greek" the Augustinian "concept" of "nature" under the doom of "original fall" (72–73). Such an Augustinian concept, however, remains partly Hopkins's, too, despite his Origenian mystical strain.

13. Augustine, *On Christian Doctrine*, 85–86.

14. Origen, *Anthology*, 341–42.

15. In his excellent article "The Science of a Sacrament" (*Hopkins Quarterly* 4 [1977–78]: 63), James Leggio also sees in Hopkins's ardor for the sacramental doctrine of transubstantiation his reaction against nonbiological scientific theories: "The language with which Hopkins describes the Incarnation and the Blessed Sacrament suggests that he sensed in them a theological counter to the predictions of the new astrophysics; the transformation of bread and wine into body and blood provided a model for change that served as an alternative to the physicists' model of thermodynamic decline. In transubstantiation there was change from a lower to a higher state of charge instead of the reverse; therein lay the action of grace." Ellsberg (*Created to Praise*, 57–59) discusses and slightly expands Leggio's argument.

16. Paddy Kitchen, *Gerard Manley Hopkins* (New York: Atheneum, 1979), 24.

17. Sulloway, *Victorian Temper*, 19–21, 26, 42–46, 50, 56–62; Ritz, *Bridges and Hopkins*, 30–44.

18. Howard Fulweiler, *Letters from the Darkling Plain: Language and the Grounds of Knowledge in the Poetry of Arnold and Hopkins* (Columbia: University of Missouri Press, 1972), 93–96.

19. David A. Downes, *Victorian Portraits: Hopkins and Pater* (New York: Bookman Associates, 1963), 28.

20. Hopkins, *L* 3, 74.

21. The poem's ethereal tone, along with its alternating shifts of trochaic and iambic meter, makes it seem a mere literary imitation of Dante Gabriel Rossetti's similar tone and technique. Yet Hopkins significantly chose to imitate Rossetti's chaste and otherworldly "Mary's Girlhood" (also subtitled "For a Picture"), rather than to mimic the laments over lost earthly joy of "The Blessed Damozel" (see Cecil Y. Lang, *The Pre-Raphaelites and Their Circle* [Boston: Houghton Mifflin, 1968], 1–5, 7–8). In general, as Bump amply demonstrates (*Gerard Manley Hopkins*, 43–52), the more ascetic and traditionally Christian Christina Rossetti had a far more penetrating impact on Hopkins's themes than did her brother.

22. Norman MacKenzie, *A Reader's Guide to Gerard Manley Hopkins* (Ithaca and London: Cornell University Press, 1981), 23.

23. The angel first says that the flowers came from some distant earthly region, "starry water-meads" toward which sailors coursed themselves by starlight ("For a Picture," 17). But the region gradually comes to be known as Heaven, with its very special "starry water-meads."

24. MacKenzie, *Guide to Hopkins*, 27.

25. Bump, *Gerard Manley Hopkins*, 69.

26. Ibid., 69–70.

27. Ibid., 68.

28. Ibid., 75–77.

29. Ibid., 73–74.

30. De Nicolas writes of how "a fourfold harmony . . . of the strings, of the body and soul, of the state, of the starry sky" came forward from Pythagoras (*Powers of Imagining*,

21) through the "musical map" of Plato (22) to "reappear . . . almost whole in the church fathers" (23). He cites (25) Augustine's *De Musica*, which, as we have already noted, was known to Hopkins.

31. Ellsberg sees a marked difference between the mainly visual emphasis of the Romantics (*Created to Praise*, 75–76) and the practice of Hopkins, who believed that "Christ entered the world . . . as *word* . . ." (77). She later calls Hopkins a "Jesuit emblematist" in the "baroque" tradition (107), participating in "an *esprit* of poetic discourse that represents and says at the same time" (106).

32. Sulloway, *Victorian Temper*, 54.

33. Downes, *Hopkins: Ignatian Spirit*, 20.

34. Downes (*Hopkins: Ignatian Spirit*, 77) reminds us that a resultant "act of sacrifice" is necessary to full participation in sacrament as an Ignatian like Hopkins would perceive it, and as he clearly does perceive it in the 1882 "Golden Echo": "Give beauty back . . . back to God, beauty's self and beauty's giver" (19).

35. In the words of John Seland, in his 1976 University of California at Riverside dissertation "Hopkins and the Eucharist," the Eucharist came to mean for Hopkins "certain evidence that there existed at least one bright, divine light in an otherwise dark, sordid world, full of materialistic values and smoke-polluted cities" (2). Kitchen, in a less charitable reading of Hopkins's motives, argues that the "sordid" which he was most trying to escape by his religious faith was his own troublesome human libido (*Gerard Manley Hopkins*, 80).

36. Shepherd, *Oxford American Prayer Book* 293A. See also Ellsberg, *Created to Praise*, 49.

37. Peter Brooks, *Thomas Cranmer's Doctrine of the Eucharist: An Essay in Historical Development* (New York: The Seabury Press, 1965), 5.

38. Ibid., 54–55.

39. MacKean, *Eucharistic Doctrine*, 55–129.

40. Thomas Cranmer, quoted in Brooks, *Cranmer's Doctrine of the Eucharist*, 3.

41. Brooks, *Cranmer's Doctrine of the Eucharist*, 19.

42. Ibid., 8.

43. Ibid., 24–34.

44. Ibid., 20. This interpretation of the Eucharist by Cranmer and Luther seems to make even the term *consubstantiation* inappropriate to their theology, although history has labeled Luther a believer in such a doctrine because of one brief speculation he makes in his early *De Captivitate Babylonica* (Brooks, *Cranmer's Doctrine of the Eucharist*, 18–19).

45. Henry, after all, brought Anglicanism into existence not because of any particular doctrinal qualms against Roman Catholic sacraments (he had written anti-Lutheran tracts, after all). In his princely greed, however, he wanted both to acquire a male heir (seemingly necessitating a new wife and a papally disapproved divorce from the old one) and to confiscate church lands and monasteries. See Jasper Ridley, *Thomas Cranmer* (Oxford: Clarendon Press, 1962), 25, 31–38, 95–97; Lacey Baldwin Smith, *Henry VIII: The Mask of Royalty* (Boston: Houghton Mifflin, 1973), 36–37, 108–10, 117; Brooks, *Cranmer's Doctrine of the Eucharist*, 45.

46. Thomas Cranmer, quoted in Brooks, *Cranmer's Doctrine of the Eucharist*, 45–46.

47. Cranmer, quoted in Brooks, *Cranmer's Doctrine of the Eucharist*, 48.

48. MacKean, *Eucharistic Doctrine*, 20.

49. Cranmer, quoted in Brooks, *Cranmer's Doctrine of the Eucharist*, 49.

50. Brooks, *Cranmer's Doctrine of the Eucharist*, 51.

51. Marty, *History of Christianity*, 167–70.

52. Seland judges, I think rightly, that Hopkins was at first "exhilarated at the aspect of the Eucharist as *presence*," although he later saw "the sacraments more in terms of the power they conferred . . . to heal and strengthen the soul" ("Hopkins and the Eucharist," 3). Hopkins indeed might always at heart have wanted to share Loyola's reported visions of Christ and Mary as pure substance, "without distinguishing the members" of their accidental species (Loyola, *Autobiography*, 29, quoted in De Nicolas, *Powers of Imagin-*

ing, 12). But he came to relax his demands for any such visions while he yet remained on earth.

53. See Stanley Fish's strong chapter on Herbert in *Self-Consuming Artifacts: The Experience of Seventeenth-Century Literature* (Berkeley: University of California Press, 1972), 156–223.

54. *A Greek-English Lexicon*, ed. Henry George Liddell and Robert Scott, with Sir Henry Stuart Jones and Roderick McKenzie, 9th ed. (Oxford: Clarendon Press, 1940), 1150, 1427.

55. Cotter, *Inscape*, 5.

56. Hopkins, *J*, 4.

57. Ibid.; entry of 1863.

58. Ibid., 125.

59. Ibid.

60. Christopher Devlin, S.J., "The Image and the Word, I," *The Month*, n.s., 3 (1950): 115.

61. Bump calls the "multivalence" of "meaning" in Hopkins's poetry part of the "incredibly high 'bond density' between . . . words" that can "heighten the emotional impact of his images and reinforce their parallels, . . . creat[ing] a powerful supralogical atmosphere of harmony" and "mak[ing] the phonic harmony of a poem its ultimate 'message'" (*Gerard Manley Hopkins*, 64, 88). While recognizing the power of this "phonic harmony" at the primary level of Hopkins's lyrics, I still also emphasize the poems' semantic messages, or themes, which enhance this "phonic harmony" with intellectual theological content.

62. Hopkins, *J*, 4–5, 12, 25.

63. Ibid., 4.

64. James Milroy, *The Language of Gerard Manley Hopkins* (London: André Deutsch, 1977), 59.

65. Ibid., 52.

66. Ibid., 45.

67. Ibid., 68.

68. Ibid., 45.

69. Salmon, "'Wording it How,'" 104.

70. One suspects that Hopkins also knew Donaldson's *The New Cratylus, or Contributions towards a more accurate knowledge of the Greek Language*, a common textbook for students of philology at Oxford during the 1860s (see Michael Allsopp, "Hopkins at Oxford, 1863–1867: His Formal Studies," *Hopkins Quarterly* 4 [1977–78]: 169).

71. Plato, *Cratylus, Parmenides, Greater Hippias, Lesser Hippias*, ed. H. N. Fowler (Cambridge: Harvard University Press, 1926), 7.

72. Hopkins, *J*, 5.

73. Plato, *Cratylus*, 7.

74. Ibid., 51.

75. Plato, *Euthyphro, Apology, Crito, Phaedo, Phaedrus*, ed. H. N. Fowler (Cambridge: Harvard University Press, 1917), 391.

76. Plato, *Cratylus*, 191.

77. Hopkins, *L* 3, 267.

78. Sprinker, "*Counterpoint of Dissonance*," 53.

79. Hopkins, *L* 3, 266 (emphasis mine).

80. Margaret W. Ferguson, "Saint Augustine's Region of Unlikeness: The Crossing of Exile and Language," *Georgia Review* 29 (1975): 856.

81. Hopkins, *J*, 31.

82. Sulloway, *Victorian Temper*, 13.

83. Johnson, *Poet as Victorian*, 104.

84. Stella Brook, *The Language of 'The Book of Common Prayer'* (London: André Deutsch, 1965), 47.

85. Miller, *Disappearance of God*, 278–81, 308–11.

86. The poem really seems much more theologically ambitious in its symbolism than

Seland implies in his biographical reading, which interprets the "bat" to represent Hopkins "departing" from Anglicanism in order to become the "bird" that is "circling" toward a Roman Catholic goal ("Hopkins and the Eucharist," 91).

87. One cannot here deny that Hopkins's use of terms such as "infallibly," "authentic," and "changeless" may at least partly refer to his migration toward Romanism (Seland, "Hopkins and the Eucharist," 115), although biography does not limit those words' meanings. To Ellis (" 'Authentic Cadence,' " 17), the "authentic cadence" is, more generally, God.

88. John Robinson, *In Extremity: a study of Gerard Manley Hopkins* (Cambridge: Cambridge University Press, 1978), 95–96, 98–99.

89. Sulloway, *Victorian Temper*, 20.

90. Downes, quite sensibly, avers that Hopkins "has to some extent dramatized the religious happening in the first part of the poem to balance the drama of the shipwreck in the second part" (*Great Sacrifice*, 96). Still, Ellsberg judges that Hopkins's words throughout *The Wreck* "are not the words of a creature at docile ease with the image of God as a tender shepherd" (*Created to Praise*, 27).

91. Kitchen, *Gerard Manley Hopkins*, 70–71.

92. Hopkins, L 3, 95.

93. Kitchen, *Gerard Manley Hopkins*, 59–60.

94. Hopkins, L 3, 18.

95. Bump, *Gerard Manley Hopkins*, 55–56.

96. Hopkins, L 3, 18.

97. Seland, "Hopkins and the Eucharist," 76, again sees the Hopkinsian biographical tension between Anglican and Romanist loyalties as motivating this seeming self-portrait.

98. Sulloway, *Victorian Temper*, 12–19.

99. Ibid., 55.

100. Ibid., 17.

101. Origen, *Anthology*, 65.

102. MacKenzie, *Guide to Hopkins*, 26–27.

103. *Tennyson's Poetry: Authoritative Texts, Juvenilia and Early Responses, Criticism*, ed. Robert W. Hill, Jr. (New York: Norton, 1971), 188.

104. Thomas Carlyle, *Sartor Resartus: The Life and Opinions of Herr Teufelsdröckh*, ed. Charles Frederick Harrold (New York: The Odyssey Press, 1937), 188.

105. Sulloway, *Victorian Temper*, 14.

Chapter 3. Hopkins's Preparation and Early Priesthood

1. Hopkins, S, 122.

2. Downes, *Great Sacrifice*, 103.

3. Ibid., 48.

4. Saintly inscape seems a forming of sacramental unity, in the human being, with God's Being. It develops not by an "affective will" (wherein one can only perceive, acknowledge God's *Being in natural things*); it rather is developed in the "elective will" of one's arbitrium, the "personality or individuality" where one is not, as with the use of the "affective will," "incapable . . . of an infinite object and . . . [of] tend[ing] towards it" (Hopkins, S, 138–39; comments of 3 and 5 September 1883).

5. De Nicolas, *Powers of Imagining*, 53.

6. The message of ecology's importance had, of course, already been featured in "God's Grandeur" and "The Sea and the Skylark," of 1877. But one key poem opposing industrial destruction of the natural environment is "Binsey Poplars" of 1879 (P, 272), with its lament "O if we but knew what we do / When we delve or hew [trees]" (9–10)—a passage echoing Christ's words from the cross about sinners who "know not what they do" as they crucify him (Luke 23:34). Cf. the revered "wildness and wet" (15) of "Inversnaid" (1881; P, 280).

7. Norman MacKenzie, "Hopkins, Robert Bridges, and the Modern Editor," in *Editing British and American Literature, 1880–1920*, ed. Eric W. Domville (New York: Garland, 1976), 29; Mariani, *Commentary*, 178.

8. I do think this more likely a later poem (for it does not seem to suggest the 1877 theological universalism of "The Lantern out of Doors"). Yet it surely resembles the 1877 poems rather strongly also.

9. Thomas, *Hopkins the Jesuit*, 23–86.

10. Thomas (ibid., 31–32) quotes John Hungerford Pollen and R. F. Clarke, English Jesuit novices only a few years later in the 1870s than Hopkins, in order to demonstrate the rigors that the novitiate demanded: "no talking" during most of the morning; no personal choice of companions during recreation hours; "deeds, not words." Ellsberg reminds us, however, of how this sort of rigor especially matched with Hopkins's own personal "restraint, . . . search for personal justification and perfection, his hectoring character . . . " (*Created to Praise*, 8).

11. Hopkins, *L* 3, 231.

12. Ibid., 228–29.

13. Hopkins, *J*, 138 (entry of 1 June 1866).

14. Ibid., 164–65.

15. Ibid., 537–38.

16. Hopkins, *L* 2, 14.

17. Hopkins, *J*, 538.

18. Hopkins, *L* 1, 24.

19. Elisabeth Schneider, *The Dragon in the Gate: Studies in the Poetry of G. M. Hopkins* (Berkeley and Los Angeles: University of California Press, 1967), 48–60.

20. Studies of Hopkins's journals include the analyses by Patricia M. Ball, *The Science of Aspects: The Changing Role of Fact in the Work of Coleridge, Ruskin, and Hopkins* (London: The Athlone Press, 1971), 115–32; Stephan Walliser, *"That Nature is a Heraclitean Fire and of the comfort of the Resurrection": A Case-Study in G. M. Hopkins' Poetry* (Bern: Francke, 1977), 125–44; Bump, *Gerard Manley Hopkins*, 31–42; Milroy, *Language of Hopkins*, 163–74.

21. Hopkins, *S*, 125 (20 August 1880): "Nothing finite . . . can either begin to exist or eternally have existed of itself. . . . And this is above all true of that inmost self of mine which has been said to be and to be felt to be, to taste, more distinctive than the taste of clove or alum . . . more distinctive, more selved, than all things else and needing in proportion a more exquisite determining, selfmaking, power." Ellsberg (*Created to Praise*, 86–87) and Walter J. Ong, S.J. (*Hopkins, the Self, and God* [Toronto, Buffalo, and London: University of Toronto Press, 1986], 41–45) both illuminate how ideal "selving" for Hopkins involved an embracing of one's primal divine creaturehood, but how he also saw the free will given humanity by God as potentially allowing them to become *selfish* Satanic rebel selves.

22. Miller, *Disappearance of God*, 337, with reference to Hopkins, *S*, 200–201: "But first I suppose that Christ, in his first stead of angelic being, led off the angel choir . . . calling on all creatures to worship God as by a kind of *Venite adoremus*. They obeyed the call, which indeed was a call into being. . . . [But the] song of Lucifer's was a dwelling on his own beauty, an instressing of his own inscape, and like a performance on the organ and instrument of his own being; it was a sounding, as they say, of his own trumpet and a hymn in his own praise. Moreover it became an incantation: others were drawn in; it became a concert of voices, a concerting of selfpraise, an enchantment, a magic, by which they were dizzied, dazzled, and bewitched. They would not listen to the note which summoned each to his own place (Jude 6.) and distributed them here and there in the liturgy of the sacrifice; they gathered rather closer and closer home under Lucifer's lead and drowned it, raising a countermusic and countertemple and altar, a counterpoint of dissonance and not of harmony."

23. Plato, *Cratylus*, 129.

24. Robert Boyle, S.J., "Hopkins, Brutus, and Dante," *Victorian Poetry* 24 (1986): 12.

25. Allen Tate, "Tension in Poetry," in *The Modern Critical Spectrum*, ed. Gerald Jay and Nancy Marmer Goldberg (Englewood Cliffs, N.J.: Prentice-Hall, 1962), 87.

26. In "The Loss of the Eurydice" Hopkins laments the drowned sailors as "Unchrist, all rolled in ruin" (96), and he speaks also there of how "hell knows [not] redeeming" (117). But he also avers, like a would-be universalist, that "for souls sunk in seeming /

Fresh, till doomfire burn all, / Prayer shall fetch pity eternal" (118–20). One can say that Hopkins surely had precedent, in that Pauline passage on kenosis which was of such vital impact on his own nineteenth-century theology, for believing (with Origen long before him) that "every tongue should [shall?] confess that Jesus Christ is Lord" (Philippians 2:11). And as major Roman Catholic theologians argue today, "in view of the cross of Christ, it is false and un-Christian to act as though hell was in fact the normal outcome of world history" (Karl Rahner and Karl-Heinz Weger, *Our Christian Faith: Answers for the Future* [New York: Crossroad, 1981], 121). Yet these recent writers also caution against "a premature optimism" (120). As his life went on, Hopkins (who, even at the time of *The Wreck*, feared that at least non-Romanists were inevitably damned), expressed less and less "premature optimism" but instead "seriously consider[ed] the opposite: final damnation" (121).

27. Schneider, *Dragon in the Gate*, 23–34.

28. Cotter, *Inscape*, 110–11.

29. I tend to read these passages as universalist in tone because Hopkins elsewhere in the ode speaks of Christ as the Logos (cf. John 1:1) who "worded" the time and space that are now his extended "word" (st. 29, 5–6). It thus seems likely that the "best or worst / Word" with which Hopkins claims "We lash . . . / . . . last!" (st. 8, 2–3) must also be the Logos. I recognize, however, that others, such as my students Danielle DuRant and Sonya Houston, could argue with fervor, and with no necessary error, that the "best . . . / Word" is a "Yes!" to Christ, while the "worst / Word" is a "No!" to him. Perhaps Hopkins indeed intended ambiguity in interpretation, however likely seems the universalist reading.

30. Peter Milward, S.J., " 'On A Pastoral Forehead in Wales': The Composition of Place of *The Wreck*," in Milward and Schoder, *Readings*, 70.

31. Cotter, *Inscape*, 107–111.

32. Milward, in Milward and Schoder, *Readings*, 74–75.

33. Downes, *Great Sacrifice*, 99.

34. Boyle, in Milward and Schoder, *Readings*, 103.

35. Ibid.

36. Ellis, " 'Authentic Cadence,' " 121.

37. Boyle, in Milward and Schoder, *Readings*, 103.

38. Hopkins, *L* 3, 51.

39. MacKenzie, *Guide to Hopkins*, 231.

40. Downes, *Hopkins: Ignatian Spirit*, 32.

41. Ibid., 38.

42. Lyle H. Smith, Jr., "Beyond the Romantic Sublime: Gerard Manley Hopkins," *Renascence* 34 (1982): 183.

43. Ibid.

44. Thomas, *Hopkins the Jesuit*, 149–86.

45. Robinson, *In Extremity*, 85.

46. Downes, *Great Sacrifice*, 34.

47. Even Ellsberg, in her fine recent book, would claim in Hopkins "after 1874 . . . a tacit assumption of total sacramentality" in "pure and stainless" nature (*Created to Praise*, 95–96). Yet Downes (*Hopkins: Ignatian Spirit*, 38), cites the historian of philosophy S. J. Curtis on the Scotist "distinction [of God from creatures] . . . [as] being *per se* and being *per participationem*." Hopkins in his 17 November 1881 prose meditation on the Incarnation speculates that "in Adam unfallen there was venial sin strictly possible or even actual," "in the Holy Angels . . . imperfection" (Hopkins, *S*, 170). He certainly does, like Augustine, "associate man's inability to know a whole with the Fall" (Ferguson, "Augustine's Region of Unlikeness," 859). And he seems to sense (unlike some of his critics) that Scotus's doctrine of univocal being may help support anagogical imagery of divine unity with creaturehood, but that Scotus does not thereby deny creatures' limitations. While to Scotus their being may be "common" with God's, it hardly equals God's being (*The Encyclopedia of Philosophy*, s. v. "Duns Scotus, John").

48. Mariani, *Commentary*, 100–101.

49. Sulloway, *Victorian Temper*, 110.

50. Downes, *Great Sacrifice*, 100.

51. Ibid., 85 (emphasis mine).

52. Ibid., 104.

53. Ibid., 36 (emphasis mine).

54. Mariani, *Commentary*, 100.

55. Harris, *Inspirations Unbidden*, 42–43.

56. Ibid., 43.

57. White, "Review," 93.

58. Robert Kaske, "Chaucer's Marriage Group," in *Chaucer the Love Poet*, ed. Jerome Mitchell and William Provost (Athens: University of Georgia Press, 1973), 55–56.

59. Peter Dronke, *The Medieval Lyric*, 2d ed. (Cambridge: Cambridge University Press, 1977), 67.

60. Maxwell S. Luria and Richard L. Hoffman, eds., *Middle English Lyrics: Authoritative Texts, Critical and Historical Backgrounds, Perspectives on Six Poems* (New York: Norton, 1974), 186.

61. For medieval source information concerning the "glassy peartree" image I thank my colleague Pamela Clements; for the idea of the "fling[ing]" lambs as ignorant of their role in sacrifice I thank my student Joanne Fabish.

62. Ferguson, "Augustine's Region of Unlikeness," 861.

63. Downes, *Great Sacrifice*, 106.

64. Harris, *Inspirations Unbidden*, 89.

65. Ibid. Harris emphasizes oxymoronic richness in Hopkins's pairing of the temporal adverbs I have emphasized in my text ("*then now*").

66. Humankind, Hopkins says, very rarely has emulated Moses' barefoot awe before theophanous revelations in nature. Instead, wearing shoes, "Generations have trod, have trod, have trod" ("God's Grandeur," 5). My student Allyse Robertson Turner senses here an allusion to Hebrews 10:29: "If a man disregards the Law of Moses, he is put to death without pity on the evidence of two or three witnesses. Think how much more severe a penalty that man will deserve who has trampled under foot the Son of God, profaned the blood of the covenant by which he was consecrated, and affronted God's gracious spirit!"

67. The thought that sea and lark do "ring right out our sordid turbid time, / Being pure!" ("The Sea and the Skylark," 10–11) may, however, suggest that cosmic sacred history circles earthly time and judges it with the "ring" of an eschatological clarion trump.

68. Harris, *Inspirations Unbidden*, 80.

69. Hopkins's moral self-portrait in *The Wreck of the Deutschland*, st. 4, 1–4, is worth remarking: "I am soft sift / In an hourglass—at the wall / Fast, but mined with a motion, a *drift, / And it crowds and it combs to the fall*" (emphasis mine).

70. Robinson, *In Extremity*, 85.

71. Mariani, *Commentary*, 99. See also Ellsberg, *Created to Praise*, 64–65.

72. Harris, *Inspirations Unbidden*, 138.

73. Robinson, *In Extremity*, 86.

74. Edward Proffitt, "Tone and Contrast in Hopkins' 'The Starlight Night,'" *Hopkins Quarterly* 5 (1978–79): 47–49.

75. Robinson, *In Extremity*, 86.

76. Despite her marked appreciation for "The Starlight Night," Ellis does disagree with the many who judge it "readily accessible and comprehensible"; she finds it "a most complicated example of [Hopkins's] method of fusing the natural and spiritual . . ." ("'Authentic Cadence,'" 161). My own experience as a teacher is that students, including those in upper-division classes, seem to find it far less vitally "accessible" than even the apparently much more difficult "Windhover."

77. Downes, *Great Sacrifice*, 102.

78. Ibid., 103.

79. Ibid., 34.

80. Ibid., 113.

81. Bump, *Gerard Manley Hopkins*, 144–45.

82. If Hopkins has at all reminded readers of their sin, it is in the very brief reference to the "farmyard scare" of Eden's Fall (or, as my students Susan Bunn and Kevin Sughrue

suggest, the Flood, which involved Noah's "farmyard" ark and, later, a prophetic "Flake-dove"). Also, some very obscure Dante allusions may suggest not only that the night scene contains the stars of the *Paradiso* saints, but also that it reveals the infernal "grey lawns cold where gold" has imprisoned the greedy ("The Starlight Night," 5). Also recalled here seem to be the "dim woods" (4) of the Dantesque "selva oscura," where Dante (like this Hopkins poem's most properly sacramentalist reader) could begin his pilgrimage toward the "diamond delves" (4) of a starlit paradise. In that paradise, his saintly predecessors, like "airy [Abels]," already dwell, according to my punster student William Chivers.

83. Downes, *Great Sacrifice*, 10.

84. Peter Milward, S.J. with Raymond V. Schoder, S.J., *Landscape and Inscape: Vision and Inspiration in Hopkins's Poetry* (Grand Rapids, Mich.: Eerdmans, 1975), 35.

85. The Psalms of nature not mentioned in my text are Psalms 8, 47, 89, 93, 113, and 148 (Psalms 8, 46, 88, 92, 112, and 148 in the Douay version).

86. Hopkins, *J*, 254.

87. Ibid., 31.

88. Bump, *Gerard Manley Hopkins*, 10.

89. While Miller has briefly mentioned that "In one sense the dappledness of things is a sign of their deficiency from the wholeness of God" (*Disappearance of God*, 304), he sees "Pied Beauty" basically as a "Scotist" poem about common inscape in "dappled things [that] have visibly the relation of likeness in difference which makes them echo and chime" (299). Both our readings seem equally arguable, to a point; which reading is truly closer to the literal level, which the more symbolic, seems uncertain. He does, however, rather seem to fear answering the question about moral dappledness that to me seems obviously asked by Hopkins, and his interpretation of a morally suggestive word like "counter" as only meaning "counter to one another, original" (299) seems to me limited.

90. Since all the Christian sacraments are memorials of God's mercy, perhaps we can now sense the biblical Psalms celebrating memorials of distantly recalled mercy (now itself seeming absent) as sometimes the most profoundly sacramental. Dermot Ryan notes how Psalms 77, 104, 105, and 135 all recall God's "saving activity . . . on behalf of his own people," although he also notes in Psalm 135 "an acclaim 'which greets not only God's saving activity in Israel's history but every work of his creation" ("Sacraments Fore-shadowed," in *Sacraments: The Gestures of Christ*, ed. Denis O'Callaghan [New York: Sheed and Ward, 1964], 8, 10).

91. Hopkins, *J*, 168.

92. Ibid., 125.

93. Hopkins, *L* 2, 147; letter of 23 October 1886.

94. Alan Heuser, *The Shaping Vision of Gerard Manley Hopkins* (London: Oxford University Press, 1958), 106.

95. Miller, *Disappearance of God*, 282.

96. Hopkins, *L* 3, 284.

97. Cotter, *Inscape*, 20–21. V. de S. Pinto ("Letter—'Hopkins and the Trewnesse of the Christian Religion,'" *Times Literary Supplement*, 10 June 1955, 317) has cited Sir Philip Sidney's and Arthur Golding's use of the term *inshape* as early as 1587, when they translated Philippe de Mornay's "The Trewnesse of the Christian Religion." To them the term meant the world's "Pattern or Mould," God's "knowledge of himselfe," and, most succinctly, "very essence."

98. John Ruskin, *Modern Painters* (New York: John Wiley and Sons, 1883), 2:105.

99. Thomas Zaniello, "The Tonic of Platonism: The Origins and Use of Hopkins' 'Scape,'" *Hopkins Quarterly* 5 (1978–79): 10–15.

100. *Encyclopedia of Philosophy*, s.v. "Duns Scotus, John."

101. Ruskin, *Modern Painters*, 2:50.

102. Ibid.

103. Ibid., 51.

104. John Ruskin, *Diaries* ed. Joan Evans and J. B. Whitehouse (London: Oxford University Press, 1956–59) 1:103 (entry of 4 November 1840).

105. Ruskin, *Modern Painters*, 1:258.

106. John Ruskin, *Praeterita: Outlines of Scenes and Thoughts Perhaps Worthy of Memory in my Past Life*, intro. by Kenneth Clark (London: Rupert Hart-Davis, 1949), 297.

107. Ruskin, *Modern Painters*, 2:89.

108. Ibid., 90.

109. Ibid.

110. Ibid., 111–12.

111. Ibid., 116.

112. Hopkins, *J*, 24.

113. Ibid., 134.

114. Miller, *Disappearance of God*, 291.

115. Hopkins, *J*, 21.

116. Ibid., 184.

117. Hopkins, *S*, 60.

118. Bump, *Gerard Manley Hopkins*, 129.

119. G. B. Tennyson, "The Sacramental Imagination," in *Nature and the Victorian Imagination*, ed. U. C. Knoepflmacher and G. B. Tennyson (Berkeley: University of California Press, 1977), 371.

120. Bump, *Gerard Manley Hopkins*, 82–87.

121. Ibid., 59.

122. Ibid., 81–82.

123. Ibid., 39.

124. Ruskin, *Modern Painters*, 2:4.

125. M. B. McNamee, S.J., "The Ignatian Meditation Pattern in the Poetry of Gerard Manley Hopkins," *Hopkins Quarterly* 2 (1975–76): 21.

126. Hopkins, *J*, 199.

127. Cotter, *Inscape*, 24.

128. Ibid.

129. Bump, *Gerard Manley Hopkins*, 149.

130. Ibid., 144–45.

131. Ibid., 129.

132. For all that "The Windhover" does surely force one to examine Hopkins's tactics as a poet who formed its complex structure, it intends and does far more than simply say "I am a poem" and reflect its author's merely aesthetic "*askesis*" (Sprinker, "*Counterpoint of Dissonance,*" 7, 14).

133. William Empson, "From *Seven Types of Ambiguity*," in *Gerard Manley Hopkins / 'The Windhover'*, ed. John Pick, The Merrill Literary Casebook Series (Columbus, Ohio: Charles E. Merrill, 1969), 13.

134. Boyle, "Hopkins, Brutus, and Dante," 3.

135. Ibid., 4–5.

136. Bump, *Gerard Manley Hopkins*, 138.

137. Ibid., 135.

138. The interpretation concerning the Harrowing of Hell I owe to my student Debbie Mitchell; the interpretation concerning the invasion of souls derives from Bump's Hopkins criticism but also resembles the major theme of Flannery O'Connor's Roman Catholic fiction.

139. Warner, "Belief and Imagination," 129; see also 129–31.

140. Hopkins, *S*, 283.

141. Warner, "Belief and Imagination," 133.

142. Quoted in Emily K. Yoder, "Evil and Idolatry in 'The Windhover,'" *Hopkins Quarterly* 2 (1975–76): 35.

143. Quoted in Yoder, "Evil and Idolatry," 34–35.

144. Quoted in Sulloway, *Victorian Temper*, 110–11, and in Yoder, "Evil and Idolatry," 34.

145. Bump, *Gerard Manley Hopkins*, 141.

146. Ibid., 138.

147. Hopkins, *S*, 60, 63, 90–91.

148. This definition is cited in Yoder, "Evil and Idolatry," 35.

149. If Hopkins indeed means to suggest that the windhover, like any creature, might—through what Scotus deems creatures' "intrinsic limitation"—become distanced from its source in the "wind" of the Spirit, there seems supreme logic in the words of Hopkins's next poetic line. If "the hurl and gliding [of the bird] / Rebuffed [scorned] the [Spirit's] big wind" (6–7), it is no wonder that the properly spiritual "heart in hiding" of the speaker (7) should immediately have "Stirred for a bird" (8)—now no mere creaturely kestrel but the Spirit itself: "the achieve of, the mastery of the thing!" (8).

150. See Yoder, "Evil and Idolatry," 33.

151. J. D. Thomas, "*Explicator*, XX [December 1961], Item 1035," in Pick, *Hopkins / 'The Windhover,'* 116.

152. Warner, "Belief and Imagination," 130.

153. Ibid., 132.

154. Yvor Winters, "From *Hudson Review*, I [Spring 1949]," in Pick, *Hopkins / 'The Windhover,'* 49.

155. Joris-Karl Huysmans, *La cathédrale*, Vol. 14, part 2 of *Oeuvres complètes*, ed. Charles Grolleau and Lucien Descaves (Paris: Crés, 1931), 198.

156. To be sure, this diving gesture also is central to the more anagogical interpretation of the poem, for the bird's dive would expose its flame-colored chest, symbolic of its inscape (with thanks again to Debbie Mitchell's in-class explications, and to Bump, *Gerard Manley Hopkins*, 132).

157. Ellis writes, "If 'Buckle' does not mean among other things 'fall,' if Hopkins is merely saying 'Let me be heroic, active, like the bird,' he could not possibly also say 'No wonder of it: sheer plod makes plough down sillion / Shine': there would be great wonder of it, since the contrast is sharply pointed between soaring bird and plodding man. To my mind, in short, the windhover is not a full symbol of Christ but like so many other aspects of nature in Hopkins' poems, a splendid partial revelation of him, pointing beyond itself to its source, sacramental in that it bespeaks, is informed by, and yet does not wholly contain, divinity. . . " ("'Authentic Cadence,'" 228).

158. The color scheme here very much resembles the gold and vermilion blend of colors that dominates "A Dream of the Rood," a medieval poem which in its theme of Christ's mighty battle on the cross is surely of background influence upon "The Windhover." The Cross of the dream is "Now wet and stained | with the Blood outwelling, / Now fairly jeweled | with gold and gems" (24–25).

159. In "Hopkins' Ember Poems: A Liturgical Source," *Renascence* 17 (1964): 32–33, Ronald Bates notes that the 30 May 1877 compositional date of "The Windhover" follows just after three liturgical Ember Days "set apart for special prayer and fasting, and *for the ordination of the clergy.*" Hopkins, who was to be ordained at the September Ember Days, therefore may perhaps fuse in his "embers" imagery thoughts of his own sacramental confirmation and his loyalty to Holy Orders—meanwhile treating both these sacramental commitments as expressions of a personal Eucharist.

160. Mariani, *Commentary*, 77–78.

161. Although I sense in Hopkins's poetry a more definite development toward emphasis on elective will than does she, Rachel Salmon very effectively argues that Hopkins always, from beginning to end of his poetic canon, was stimulating both affective and elective wills simultaneously. See "Poetry of Praise and Poetry of Petition: Simultaneity in the Sonnet World of Gerard Manley Hopkins," *Victorian Poetry* 22 (1984): 383–406.

162. Hopkins, L 1, 92.

163. Ibid.

164. W. H. Gardner, after reading these words, accused Hopkins of Hamlet-like morbidity (*Gerard Manley Hopkins (1844–1889): A Study of Poetic Idiosyncrasy in Relation to Poetic Tradition* [London: Oxford University Press, 1958], 2:296). It is true that Hopkins told Bridges (L 1, 92) that he almost wished the boy would die in war. He was evidently no theological universalist, as he feared that the boy's continued service in the armed forces would cause him to lose his moral resolve if he remained alive. See Wendell Stacy Johnson's "Sexuality and Inscape," *Hopkins Quarterly* 3 (1976–77): 61.

165. Through observation of the Hopkins Oxford manuscripts, Ellis finds that Hopkins in "Felix Randal" at first intended to emphasize further, by accentuation, his own

personal role in the sacramental guidance of the dying Felix: "since I had our swéet repríeve and ránsom / Tendered to him" ("Felix Randal," MS. B, 7–8). ("'Authentic Cadence,'" 203). Yet Ellis concludes, much as I have in discussing the bugler poem, that "the real reason for that stressed 'I'" is Hopkins's "wonder" over "the comforting and saving power" of the "sacraments" (204).

166. Sigurd Burkhardt, "Poetry and the Language of Communion," in Hartman, *Collection*, 163. See, in general, Hartman, *Collection*, 160–63.

167. Mariani, *Commentary*, 175–76.

168. Hopkins, L 1, 225; L 2, 25, 113. See Jeffrey B. Loomis, "As Margaret Mourns: Hopkins, Goethe, and Shaffer on 'Eternal Delight,'" *Cithara* 22 (1982): 22–29.

169. Hopkins did not deliberately accent in his text as we have it the words "What heart heard" or "ghost guessed," yet Dixon accents them in a letter to Hopkins of 24 January 1881, suggesting that Hopkins may have accented them in an earlier version of the poem sent to his friend (L 2, 44).

170. Mariani, *Commentary*, 170–71.

171. Indeed, such service has "endear[ed]" his own life ("Felix Randal," 9). It has sacramentalized that life, made it more rich with transubstantial Christic power, uniting it further with the Christ who to Hopkins, as to Herbert before him, is "my dear" ("The Windhover," 13).

172. Hopkins, S, 195 (emphasis mine).

173. Donald Baillie, *The Theology of the Sacraments, and Other Papers* (New York: Charles Scribner's Sons, 1957), 50.

174. Augustine, quoted in Baillie, *Theology of the Sacraments*, 50.

175. Hopkins, S, 253.

176. Ibid., 122.

177. Ibid.

178. Ibid., 123.

179. Ibid., 122.

180. Ellis judges that Hopkins "apparently felt that 'The Lantern out of Doors' required an answering poem which would emphasize, with some severity, the responsibility of the individual man toward his own salvation" ("'Authentic Cadence,'" 263).

181. Mariani, *Commentary*, 145–46.

182. The reading I am offering here obviously interprets the phrase "truckle at the eye" ("The Candle Indoors," 4) in terms of the whole sonnet's context, which suggests that Hopkins's persona feels himself wishing wrongly to invade the lives of others whom he sees behind windows closed to him on the street. However, in terms only of its immediate quatrain's context, the line probably means that the "beams" from the others' eyes "truckle" or "are subservient" (*OED*) before the narrator's own eyes—in an exchange of genial, and yet also reverential, interpersonal communication. It is only later that Hopkins's narrator seems to feel that he is too attentive to the others, invasively so, and not attentive enough to his own moral situation.

183. These lines might be the words addressed to "Jessy or Jack" and their spiritual needs, words of which Hopkins as persona seemed to be contemplating the writing in "The Candle Indoors." It therefore seems all the more significant that such apparently other-directed lines strike one as just as much directed by the poet to himself.

Chapter 4. Hopkins's Final Decade: The Taming of Tempests

1. Jean-Georges Ritz, *Le poète Gérard Manley Hopkins, s.j. (1884–1889): l'homme et l'oeuvre* (Paris: Didier, 1963), 198.

2. Robinson, *In Extremity*, 131.

3. Hopkins, L 1, 90, 135; letters of 8 October 1879 and 16 September 1881.

4. Hopkins, L 2, 33; letter of 14 May 1880.

5. Hopkins, L 1, 83–84, 170–71.

6. John Ruskin, *The Two Paths*, vol. 16 of *Works*, ed. Alexander Wedderburn and E. T. Cook (London: George Allen, 1903–12), 269–70.

7. Christopher Devlin, S.J., n. 138, in Hopkins, S, 290.

8. Ibid.

9. Hopkins, it is true, does not speak of this redemptive action in the epigraph, but his poem's ambiguous words do suggest it. He can thus be blamed for overextending aesthetic texture, if he wishes no such readings. He did not, it is true, offer any such readings even outside the epigraph, in the 1879 and 1883 glosses sent to Bridges. Yet we should recall that he had always had extraordinary difficulty in convincing Bridges that his poems had a recognizable meaning of any type. He would not likely have dared to suggest the possibility of multiple layers of meaning.

10. Miller, *Disappearance of God*, 333.

11. Ibid., 329.

12. Hopkins once wrote to his friend Alexander Baillie about "two strains of thought," "counterpointed," that existed in poetry: the "overthought," "that which everybody, editors, see," and the "underthought," "conveyed chiefly in the choice of metaphors etc used and often only half realised by the poet himself" (Hopkins, L 3, 252—letter of 14 January 1883). We shall come to see that this concept proves to have important sacramentalist significance for Hopkins.

13. Hopkins, L 1, 83.

14. Alluding to Hopkins, S, 200–201, Patricia A. Wolfe discusses this "age-old anvil" and the similar "song of Lucifer" in "The Paradox of Self: A Study of Hopkins' Spiritual Conflict in the Terrible Sonnets," *Victorian Poetry* 6 (1968): 95.

15. Sulloway, *Victorian Temper*, 113.

16. Joris-Karl Huysmans, quoted in Pie Duployé, O. P. "Huysmans en 1968," *La Table Ronde* 243 (April 1968): 73.

17. See Francis Keegan, S.J., "Gerard Manley Hopkins at Mount St. Mary's College, Sprinkhill, 1877–1878," *Hopkins Quarterly* 6 (1979–80): 22–26.

18. I myself truly concur with Wendell Stacy Johnson when he writes that the two "Leaden Echo" and "Golden Echo" choruses "hardly require in themselves more explication," for "Reading them aloud expressively is explicating them" ("Reading Oneself into Hopkins," in *The Victorian Experience: The Poets*, ed. Richard Levine [Athens, Ohio: Ohio University Press, 1982], 175).

19. Miller, *Disappearance of God*, 334.

20. Ibid., 336.

21. Hopkins, L 1, 231; letter of 13 October 1886; quoted in Harris, *Inspirations Unbidden*, 131.

22. Hopkins, L 2, 95—letter of 1 December 1881; L 1, 66—letter of 15 February 1879; see Harris, *Inspirations Unbidden*, 131–32.

23. Cf. Devlin's comments on the Dublin retreat notes of January 1889: "In these last notes all is juice sucked from the words of the gospel [:] nothing is spun from fancy" (Hopkins, S, 221).

24. Thomas K. Beyette, "Hopkins' Phenomenology of Art in 'The shepherd's brow,'" *Victorian Poetry* 11 (1973): 210.

25. George Eliot, quoted in Cotter, *Inscape*, 239.

26. Cf. 2 Corinthians 3:3, 18, where, using the fiery-browed Moses of Sinai as prototype, Saint Paul argues for realized sanctity as of far more value than any human writing: ". . . [Y]e are manifestly declared to be the epistle of Christ ministered by us, written not with ink, but with the Spirit of the living God; not in tablets of stone, but in fleshly tables of the heart. . . . [W]e all, with open face beholding as in a glass the glory of the Lord, are changed into the same image from glory to glory, even as by the Spirit of the Lord."

27. Cotter, *Inscape*, 267; Mariani, *Commentary*, 312–13; Boyle, *Metaphor in Hopkins*, 133–34.

28. The Holy Spirit seems defined as a participant in cosmic creation in Job 26:13: "By his winds the heavens were made fair." Hopkins's attribution to· that Spirit of inspirational power for all poetic making may, however, derive just as likely from the words of the Nicene Creed that define the Spirit as that Person of the Trinity "who spake by the prophets." De Nicolas writes that "in the absence of the Father and the Son, the Spirit is the only text Christians are left with" (*Powers of Imagining*, 52).

29. Hopkins, *L* 1, 222; letter of 1 September 1885.

30. Geoffrey Chaucer, "Retraction" to *The Canterbury Tales*, in *Works*, ed. F. N. Robinson, 2d ed. (Boston: Houghton Mifflin, 1961), 265.

31. Miller, *Disappearance of God*, 324–27.

32. Harris, *Inspirations Unbidden*, 20.

33. Bump, *Gerard Manley Hopkins*, 167–69.

34. Hopkins, *S.* 90.

35. Ibid., 63 (sermon of 25 January 1880).

36. Ibid., 60 (sermon of 18 January 1880).

37. Mariani, *Commentary*, 200.

38. Even in this poem, nonetheless, Hopkins hints that nature also reveals inscape, as "tool-smooth bleak light"—despite the persona's fear of eternal punishment, which causes him to see Satan imposed on the panorama as "the beakleaved boughs dragonish | damask the tool-smooth bleak light; black, / Ever so black on it" (9–10). And Ellis notes that Hopkins revised in line 12 the phrase "black, white; | wrong, right" to "black, white; | right, wrong." By chiasmus he destroyed absolute parallelism of thought on either side of the caesura, and he has received negative criticism for doing so. But, says Ellis, he also "thrust . . . into the center of the phrase the words which 'rhyme' in moral meaning as in sound . . . [,] focus[ing] our attention exactly where it must be morally rivetted. . ." ("'Authentic Cadence,'" 216). Hopkins indeed thus focused once again a sacramental kernel of command to self-sacrificial penance.

39. Cotter, *Inscape*, 231.

40. Ellis already finds Hopkins offering hope for humankind in word choice by which he foreshadows their buried selves as "Squadroned masks and manmarks" ("Heraclitean Fire," 8). She implicitly thus declares understanding of his "husk-kernel" transubstantial theology as she interprets that to him "the physical marks man leaves on earth, the life-masks, as it were, the moulds of his physical self, are only outward, and perhaps deceptive, signs of his selfhood, are not after all the only reality—there is his spirit too to be considered" ("'Authentic Cadence,'" 250).

41. MacKenzie, *Guide to Hopkins*, 173.

42. Avrom Fleishman, *Figures of Autobiography: The Language of Self-Writing in Victorian and Modern England* (Berkeley: University of California Press, 1983), 112.

43. Jerome Hamilton Buckley, *The Turning Key: Autobiography and the Subjective Impulse Since 1800* (Cambridge: Harvard University Press, 1984), 5, 145–46.

44. See Hopkins, *L* 1, 222; letter of 1 September 1885. Albeit that the episode occurred at an earlier stage of his spiritual life than did Hopkins's 1885 despondency, Saint Ignatius Loyola did, at Manresa in 1522–23, "find no remedy in men, nor in any creature," and, "[w]hile lost in these thoughts, . . . fe[el] very strong temptations to throw himself through a large hole that was there in his room, next to the place where he was praying" (Loyola, *Autobiography* 3. 23–24, in De Nicolas, *Powers of Imagining*, 258).

45. Hopkins, *L* 1, 219; letter of 7 May 1885; *L* 1:221; letter of 1 September 1885.

46. See Hopkins, *S*, 170. As Ellis so rightly perceives, "Hopkins' meditation notes reveal [that] the sources of [his] desolation seem not to have included any genuine doubt of God's existence, but the reverse; he is tormented by his failures to meet God's demands, to submit his will to God, to live up to his vocation and the end for which he was created" ("'Authentic Cadence,'" 277). More recently, Ellsberg declares, similarly, that "images of wretchedness, wrestling, and struggle in the last poems . . . suggest not an absence of God, but an engagement of two wills" (*Created to Praise*, 114).

47. Boyle (*Metaphor in Hopkins*, 113) notes the nesting image without linking it to a developing Hopkinsian image pattern of Christic gestation in the human soul.

48. When the Hopkinsian soul-persona in "Carrion Comfort" speaks of "now done darkness" I cannot but hear echoed the triumphantly punning last stanza of John Donne's "To Christ": "Sweare by thy self that at my Death, thy Sunn / Shall shine as it shines nowe, & heretofore; / And having done that, thou hast done, / I have noe more" (15–18; emphases mine). See John Donne, *Poetical Works*, ed. Sir Herbert Grierson (London: Oxford University Press, 1933), 338.

49. Every statement Hopkins makes in his prose concerning "pitch" seems to indicate

that it is at least approximately a synonym for inscape in the individual. In his meditation of 20 August 1880 on Loyola's "*Principium sive Fundamentum*," he speaks of each human being as "a pitch of the universal" (Hopkins, S, 128): "my mind would be one selving or pitch of a great universal mind" (125). Therefore, "Pitched past pitch of grief" ("No worst," 1) may mean "pitched" *nearer* to God or "the universal," after having endured the "pitch of grief," rather than being "pitched" further away from him, in a yet-deeper despair. Hopkins, however, has rather aptly allowed for dramatic suspense in the ambiguous poetic words. See Ellsberg, *Created to Praise*, 91.

50. Michael D. Moore, "Newman and the Motif of Intellectual Pain in Hopkins' 'Terrible Sonnets,'" *Mosaic* 12 (1978–79): 30–31.

51. Hopkins, one once again recalls, was highly scornful of the "rascal" or "scoundrel" Goethe (L 2, 25; letter of 27 February 1879), and Goethe's Werther is one of the most striking literary sufferers from *Weltschmerz*.

52. Downes, *Great Sacrifice*, 47–57.

53. Harris, *Inspirations Unbidden*, 116.

54. See Hopkins, S, 174 (emphasis Hopkins's own). Cotter focuses his important book *Inscape* on the Hopkinsian concept of gnosis at which this quotation hints.

55. Harris, *Inspirations Unbidden*, 124.

56. Ibid., xv.

57. Boyle sees here an allusion to "The kingdom of heaven . . . [as] a handful of yeast which a housewife mixes with three measures of flour, to work there till the whole mass has risen" (Matthew 13:33). He adds, ". . . The action of the Spirit is toward God, and lifts the whole mass, bones, flesh, and blood, to a sweet and vivified loaf. But when the activity of the spirit in a man is toward self and not toward God, then there is no rising, no working through the mass, and that yeast which should be the principle of life and sweetness rots and becomes the principle of sourness and corruption" (*Metaphor in Hopkins*, 155).

58. Hopkins, L 2, 137–38—"See how the great conquerors were cut short, Alexander, Caesar. . . . Above all Christ our Lord: his career was cut short and, whereas he would have wished to succeed by success . . . nevertheless he was doomed to succeed by failure; his plans were baffled, his hopes dashed, and his work was done by being broken off undone. However much he understood all this he found it an intolerable grief to submit to it. He left the example: it is very strengthening, but except in that sense it is not consoling."

59. The beehive imagery has further metaphoric aptness because, like the actual Virgin Mary, who has left the Marian soul as her working embodiment within Hopkins, the queen bee lays the eggs of the worker bees in a hive and then leaves them to do the work themselves.

60. Luria and Hoffman, *Middle English Lyrics*, 13–14.

61. My medievalist colleague Pamela Clements helped me perceive in "To R. B." the allusion to "Winter wakeneth all my care."

62. Boyle, *Metaphor in Hopkins*, 203.

63. Alexander, *College Sacramental Theology*, 35.

64. Wolfgang Riehle, *The Middle English Mystics*, trans. Bernard Standring (London: Routledge and Kegan Paul, 1981), 150.

65. Meister Eckhart, "Eternal Birth," in *Medieval Culture and Society*, ed. David Herlihy (New York: Harper Torchbooks, 1968), 398.

66. Ibid., 397.

67. Ibid., 394–95.

68. Ibid., 394.

69. Ibid., 396.

70. Ibid., 398. As De Nicolas observes, the Ignatian *Spiritual Exercises*, which Hopkins so well knew, do attempt at least to mimic the mystical "dark night of the soul." At "some time around the third week [of the exercises] . . . all the careful, agonic dedication to sharpening the will, remembering, and imagining accumulate on the retreatant with such force" as to produce a "new life . . . that sensitizes the retreatant from the inside out rather than from the outside in" (*Powers of Imagining*, 44). Do the "Terrible

Sonnets" then perhaps themselves attempt to mimic an Ignatian experience of this third week, the week of Passion, as well as of the fourth week of Resurrection, which sees how "justice, goodness, pity, mercy, etc., descend from above just as the rays from the sun" (*Spiritual Exercises*, 237, in De Nicolas, *Powers of Imagining*, 146)—"light[ing] a lovely mile" ("My own heart," 14)? See Downes, *Hopkins: Ignatian Spirit*, 146.

71. Caroline Walker Bynum, *Jesus as Mother: Studies in the Spirituality of the High Middle Ages* (Berkeley: University of California Press, 1982), 129.

72. Thomas, *Hopkins the Jesuit*, 237.

73. Hopkins, *L 3*, 17–18.

74. Cotter, *Inscape*, 107–111.

75. Origen, *Anthology*, 268–70.

76. Ibid., 279.

77. Edmund Gosse, quoted in Hopkins, *L 3*, xxxiv.

78. Hopkins, *L 3*, xxxvii.

79. Coventry Patmore, quoted in Hopkins, *L 3*, xxxvi.

80. Hopkins, *L 1*, 219.

81. Miller, *Disappearance of God*, 352. Ellsberg, like me although more mildly, critiques the Miller who would be "too easy" in his "overlook[ing of] the possibility of an imm[a]nent God present in history" (*Created to Praise*, 114).

82. Hopkins, *S*, 151; quoted in Miller, *Disappearance of God*, 345.

83. Hopkins, *L 1*, 219.

84. Ibid., 221.

85. Bump, *Gerard Manley Hopkins*, 195; see Ellsberg, *Created to Praise*, 90, for a surprising discounting of Hopkins's allusiveness.

86. Bump, *Gerard Manley Hopkins*, 193–94.

87. Ibid., 193.

88. Ibid., 194.

89. Mary Ann Rygiel, "Hopkins and Herbert: Two Meditative Poets," *Hopkins Quarterly* 10 (1983–84): 45–54.

90. Moore, "Motif of Intellectual Pain," 35–36.

91. Mariani, *Commentary*, 229.

92. Hopkins, *S*, 170.

93. John Henry Newman, "Righteousness not of us, but in us," in *Public and Parochial Sermons* 5, vol. 27 of *Works* (London: Longmans, Green, 1907), 132.

94. Fulweiler, *Arnold and Hopkins*, 96.

95. Hopkins, *L 1*, 219.

96. Peter Milward, S.J., *A Commentary on the Complete Sonnets of Gerard Manley Hopkins* (London: C. Hurst, 1970), 137.

97. *A New Latin Dictionary Founded on a Translation of Freund's Latin-German Lexicon*, ed. E. A. Andrews, rev. Charlton T. Lewis and Charles Short (New York: American Book Company, 1894), 593. See also the *OED* entry for "contend."

98. Donald McChesney, *A Hopkins Commentary: An Explanatory Commentary on the Main Poems, 1876–1889* (New York: New York University Press, 1968), 178.

99. Bertrand F. Richards, "Meaning in 'Carrion Comfort,'" *Renascence* 27 (1974): 45–50.

100. Hopkins, *S*, 263; notes of 5 January 1888.

101. Hopkins, *L 1*, 270; letter of 12 January 1888. See Ellsberg's discussion of "Thou art indeed just, Lord" (*Created to Praise*, 41–45).

102. See Frederick William Faber, *A Father Faber Heritage*, ed. Sister Mary Mercedes S.N.D. de Namur (Westminster, Md.: The Newman Press, 1958), 343. Thomas notes that several of Father Faber's London Oratorian devotional writings, especially *Bethlehem*, were used as refectory reading during Hopkins's Jesuit studies at both Stonyhurst and Roehampton (*Hopkins the Jesuit*, 235, 239).

103. Faber, *Father Faber Heritage*, 332–33.

104. Hopkins, *S*, 260.

105. Faber, *Father Faber Heritage*, 332.

106. Ibid., 333.

107. Ibid.

108. Mariani, *Usable Past*, 146, 149.

109. Ibid., 139.

110. De Nicolas, *Powers of Imagining,*, 39.

111. William Butler Yeats, quoted in Bergonzi, *Gerard Manley Hopkins*, 132.

112. The Rev. Daniel Riggall long ago showed me that the "fruits of the spirit" passage was of relevant intertextual background for Hopkins's writing, especially for "Thou art indeed just, Lord."

113. It is fitting to offer a counterargument from Fulweiler, a rather sane voice from among those who (largely because they read the late sonnets too literally) judge Hopkins in "conflict" with no satisfactory "resolve": "Hopkins was not paralyzed by despair; rather, he attempted to overcome it. [But] he was certainly held in the grip of an overscrupulous conscience. There is no doubt that he struggled, not necessarily with Christianity, but with a rationalized form of it" (*Arnold and Hopkins*, 156–57). My own argument would be that Hopkins's sacramentalist practice eventually gave him a level of inner spiritual confidence which could overcome all problems resulting from rationalistic overemphases.

114. This undated Hopkins translation is of a Latin prayer by Father Condren of the French Oratory of Saint Philip Neri (*P*, 324).

Chapter 5. Hymns, Oblations, Sighs to The Lord of Life

1. Cotter, *Inscape*, xvi.

2. Bergonzi (*Gerard Manley Hopkins*, 134–37) gives a good account of Hopkins's situation at this time, especially emphasizing his discomfort with being an English Roman Catholic priest in Ireland, where the Roman Catholic citizenry were fervently anti-English. He quotes Hopkins's lament that "the Catholic Church in Ireland and the Irish Province in it and our College in that are greatly given over to a partly unlawful cause" (*S*, 262). A similar analysis is that of Bridges, quoted by Ritz from Bridges's notice to a selection of Hopkins poems he submitted to the 1893 edition of A. H. Miles's *Poets and Poetry of the Century*: "He seems to have entirely satisfied the Society [of Jesus] as classical examiner at Dublin. That drudgery, however, and the political dishonesty which he was there forced to witness, so tortured his sensitive spirit that he fell into a melancholy state" (quoted in Ritz, *Bridges and Hopkins*, 159).

3. I intend here wordplay on Geoffrey Hartman's 1975 titular essay for *The Fate of Reading*. Even as he depreciates formalistic or linguistic "structure" criticism in which I have greater faith than he (Hartman, *The Fate of Reading, and Other Essays* [Chicago: University of Chicago Press, 1975], 256), Hartman seems to share some of my respect for the linguistic structuralism of Roman Jakobson, although "not sufficiently convinced" that it is a real "technique" (273). I would surely not call Jakobson's methodology a mere "style," as Hartman suggests that it is, but I would concur with Hartman that linguistic structuralism cannot show us all that it is valuable to learn from literature. I would, for instance, agree with his positive citation of Lionel Trilling's view that literature is the complex "expression" of a personal "will," indeed an "objectification of will" (256). Much of my focus in this book involves demonstrating that Hopkins's *sacramentalist* art is an "objectification" of his *sacramentalist* will.

4. Milroy, *Language of Hopkins*, 229. See also Ellsberg, *Created to Praise*, 81.

5. Milroy, *Language of Hopkins*, 157.

6. Ibid., 11.

7. J. Hillis Miller, "Nature and the Linguistic Moment," in Knoepflmacher and Tennyson, *Nature and Victorian Imagination*, 449.

8. Ibid.

9. Hopkins, *J*, 125.

In what appears to be his own calm rebuttal to inevitable deconstructionist cynicism about language and its metaphors, De Nicolas sees the "earthy images" of "Christian art" to "appear, then melt away and vanish. To the Christian eye they are not valuable in themselves, but only as memory points to lead to their original background, the Creator.

Metaphors, as in the old Greek and Latin authors like Cicero, lose their double directions. Metaphors for a Christian are realities of true fusion" (*Powers of Imagining*, 24–25).

10. Richard Gunter, "Grammar, Semantics, and the Poems of Gerard Manley Hopkins," *Hopkins Quarterly* 1 (1974–75): 35. Gunter indeed dares express such interpretive confidence even when dealing with Hopkins's most tortuously structured poem, "Tom's Garland."

11. Jeffrey B. Loomis, "Chatter with a Just Lord: Hopkins' Final Sonnets of Quiescent Terror," *Hopkins Quarterly* 7 (1980–81): 56–58, 60, 62–63n. 26.

12. A statement expressing gratitude to an influential teacher may seem, at this late point in a lengthy scholarly study, to be naïve and misplaced. In the literary critical wars of the 1980s, however, such a statement may be at heart a muted battle cry. In an era when Jonathan Culler tells us that we should be teaching interpretive skills to our students but meanwhile should devote our own energies chiefly to literary theoretical debates, one does gratefully recall professors who, even while teaching detailed courses in literary theory, still made clear their primary commitment to interpretation. See Jonathan Culler, *The Pursuit of Signs: Semiotics, Literature, Deconstruction* (Ithaca: Cornell University Press, 1981), 16–17.

13. Roman Jakobson and Lawrence G. Jones, *Shakespeare's Verbal Art in 'Th 'Expence of Spirit'* (The Hague; Mouton, 1970), 32.

14. Ibid., 31.

15. Ibid., 32.

16. Ibid., 31.

17. Ibid., 32.

18. Johnson, *Poet as Victorian*, 160.

19. Mariani, *Commentary*, 288.

20. Milroy, *Language of Hopkins*, 160–62.

21. Ibid., 162.

22. P, 293; *Oxford English Dictionary*, compact edition (New York: Oxford University Press, 1971), viii.

23. Milroy, *Language of Hopkins*, 155.

24. Ibid., 39.

25. Norman MacKenzie, "Gerard Manley Hopkins' 'Spelt from Sibyl's Leaves,'" *Malahat Review* 26 (1973): 218–28.

26. Ellis, "'Authentic Cadence,'" 105–6, 116, 185, 206, 214, 232.

27. Mariani, *Commentary*, 133–34, 144–45, 149.

28. Roman Jakobson, "Closing Statement: Linguistics and Poetics," in *Style in Language*, ed. Thomas Sebeck (Boston: MIT Press, 1960), 365.

29. Jakobson and Jones, *Shakespeare's Verbal Art*, 10.

30. Walliser's excellent book is worthy of much more attention than it has received.

31. Roman Ingarden, *The Cognition of the Literary Work of Art*, trans. Ruth Ann Crowley and Kenneth R. Olsen (Evanston, Ill.: Northwestern University Press, 1973), 72.

32. Roman Ingarden, *The Literary Work of Art: An Investigation on the Borderlines of Ontology, Logic and Theory of Literature*, trans. George C. Grabowicz (Evanston, Ill.: Northwestern University Press, 1973), lx–lxi.

33. Ingarden, *Cognition*, 88.

34. Eugene H. Falk, *The Poetics of Roman Ingarden* (Chapel Hill: University of North Carolina Press, 1981), 7.

35. De Nicolas, *Powers of Imagining*, 34, 81.

36. Ingarden, *Cognition*, 83–84.

37. Hopkins, L 1, 66.

38. Ibid., 265; letter of 6 November 1887.

39. Ibid., 265–66. See Ellsberg's defense of these sorts of letters by Hopkins as showing "wit, resilience, charm, affection" despite their fervent "eccentricities" of artistic "confidence" (*Created to Praise*, 5).

40. Hopkins, L 1, 266.

41. Ingarden, *Cognition*, 72.

42. Hopkins, J, 289.

43. Quoted in Bump, *Gerard Manley Hopkins*, 75; 1885 letter of Gerard to Everard Hopkins (his brother).

44. Hopkins, *L* 1, 50 (emphasis mine). Ellsberg rightly instructs us that "Hopkins' own discussion of his artistic 'methods' is less helpful and ultimately less important than his advice, 'Pay attention' [*L* 1, 46], by which he meant, read this poetry with the capacity to listen carefully, with the most receptive intelligence" (*Created to Praise*, 24).

45. To Ellis Hopkins never claims "that poetry can or should be merely a pleasing pattern of sounds *without* meaning, but [only] that it must offer the mind, the ear, all the aesthetic senses, some interest 'even over and above its interest of meaning' " (" 'Authentic Cadence,' " 56). Like Walliser (*Case-Study*, 69), she correctly emphasizes the centrality for Hopkins of his semantics by treating his sprung rhythm accents as cues to meaning rather than as mere metrical effects. In "As kingfishers catch fire" (9), Ellis says, the phrase "Í say more" is accented so as to declare Hopkins's own commitment to the primacy of elective spiritual will (198).

46. Hopkins, *L* 1, 66.

47. Ellis, " 'Authentic Cadence,' " 61.

48. Salmon, " 'Wording it How,' " 105.

49. Hopkins, *L* 1, 46; letter of 21 August 1877. Ellsberg comments, "Presumably [Hopkins] meant to convert [Bridges] to his literary theories, though already these were inseparable from his Catholicism" (*Created to Praise*, 30).

50. Hopkins, *L* 1, 60; letter of 19 January 1879.

51. Salmon, " 'Wording it How,' " 95.

52. Ingarden, *Cognition*, 84.

53. Downes, *Great Sacrifice*, 102.

54. Leclercq, *Monastic Culture*, 262.

55. Ibid., 263.

56. Mariani, *Commentary*, 212–241; Downes, *Hopkins: Ignatian Spirit*, 138–45.

57. Philip Endean, S. J., "The Spirituality of Gerard Manley Hopkins," *Hopkins Quarterly* 8 (1981–82): 126. I agree with Endean about *The Wreck*, but not about "Felix Randal."

58. Ibid., 128.

59. Ellis, by contrast to Endean, rightly notes of "Henry Purcell" that "the whole seems somewhat at odds with itself," because "Hopkins is straining to effect with his own hands, with his poetry, the redemption of a heretic . . . " (" 'Authentic Cadence,' " 192).

60. Salmon, " 'Wording it How,' " 92.

61. Ibid., 107.

62. Hopkins, *L* 1, 222.

63. Bump, *Gerard Manley Hopkins*, 71–78.

64. Sprinker, "Counterpoint of Dissonance," 69.

65. Ibid., 70.

66. Jacques Derrida, quoted in Sprinker, "Counterpoint of Dissonance," 70.

67. Culler notes that Saussure, while he generally surely believes that "[t]he linguistic sign is arbitrary," does allow for "onomatopoeia, where the sound of the signifier seems in some way mimetic or imitative," as well as "secondary motivation," which at least in a single language can take root words like *type* and *writer* and combine their sounds and meanings into the new word *typewriter*. See Jonathan Culler, *Ferdinand de Saussure*, rev. ed. (Ithaca: Cornell University Press, 1986), 28–30.

68. Sprinker, "Counterpoint of Dissonance," 71.

69. Ibid., 70, 72.

70. Ibid., 71.

71. Ibid.

72. Ibid., 136–37.

73. In his 1917 essay "Art as Technique," Victor Shklovsky, the central theorist of Russian formalism, argues that because "art exists [in order] that one may recover the sensation of life . . . [and] feel things," it must resist " 'algebrization,' the over-automatization of an object," and instead demonstrate descriptive "defamiliarization," making "the

familiar seem strange" (see Lee T. Lemon and Marion J. Reis, *Russian Formalist Criticism: Four Essays* [Lincoln: University of Nebraska Press, 1965], 12–13).

74. "Interpretive community" is a term of Stanley Fish in *Is There a Text in This Class?: The Authority of Interpretive Communities* (Cambridge: Harvard University Press, 1980), 14. He writes that "since the thoughts an individual can think and the mental operations he can perform have their source in some or other interpretive community, he is as much a product of that community (acting as an extension of it) as the meanings it enables him to produce" (14).

75. Cf. Richard F. Giles's concluding comments as he castigates Sprinker's book in a review for *Victorian Poetry* 20 (1982): "Sprinker wants to picture Hopkins as a myopic Romantic poseur. I do not think Hopkins was this, and I would argue my belief on the basis of the words he has left us; Sprinker feels justified in dispensing with Hopkins' words because they do not suit his schema as well as his own words, or those of Harold Bloom, J. Hillis Miller, Jacques Derrida, or Paul de Man, do" (216).

76. Paul Valéry, quoted in Sprinker, "*Counterpoint of Dissonance*," 44.

77. Hopkins, *S*, 123–24; 20 August 1880 meditation on *Principium sive Fundamentum*.

78. Fish, *Text*, 316.

79. Ibid., 319.

80. Ibid, 14, 318.

81. Robert Bridges, quoted in Milroy, *Language of Hopkins*, 3.

82. Gerard Manley Hopkins, *Poems*, ed. Robert Bridges and W. H. Gardner, 3d ed. (London: Oxford University Press, 1948), 4.

83. Ritz, *Bridges and Hopkins*, 50, 149.

84. Ibid., 50.

85. Bridges, quoted in Ritz, *Bridges and Hopkins*, 163; letter of 18 February 1918.

86. Harris, *Inspirations Unbidden*, 11.

87. Ritz, *Bridges and Hopkins*, 158.

88. Robert Bridges, "Ethick," 732–43; quoted in Ritz, *Bridges and Hopkins*, 156.

89. Bridges, quoted in Ritz, *Bridges and Hopkins*, 154; letter to Mrs. Catherine Hopkins, 19 June 1889.

90. Bridges, quoted in Ritz, *Bridges and Hopkins*, 155.

91. Hopkins, *S*, 253–54.

92. In *Does Deconstruction Make Any Difference?: Poststructuralism and the Defense of Poetry in Modern Criticism* (Bloomington: Indiana University Press, 1985), 118, Michael Fischer answers his titular question negatively out of belief that "conventions of interpretation may be enabling as well as constraining." He also writes that "when an interpretive community embraces multitudes, like the community that terms *Macbeth* a tragedy, it probably is right" (51).

93. Ritz, *Bridges and Hopkins*, 42, 63, 160.

94. Norman MacKenzie, "The Dragon's Treasure Hoard Unlocked," *Modern Language Quarterly* 31 (1970): 242.

95. Leclercq writes with firm assurance, obviously not limiting himself to the perspective of aesthetic criticism alone, that "*There is no spiritual literature without spiritual experience: it is the experience which gives rise to literature, not the reverse*" (*Monastic Culture*, 264). Ellsberg concurs that "spiritual aspects of a writer's achievement" must be treated if that writer is a Hopkins "whose language is so entangled with his deepest metaphysical involvements" (*Created to Praise*, 18).

96. Søren Kierkegaard, *Fear and Trembling* (Princeton: Princeton University Press, 1973), 47, 51. It is technically true, of course, that Hopkins never needs to take a specifically Kierkegaardian "leap" to "faith," for he really does not encounter what precedes that "leap": a close-to-despairing resignation of the world, resulting from a sense of that world's total spiritual inefficacy.

97. Miller, *Disappearance of God*, 352, 355.

98. Milroy, *Language of Hopkins*, 226.

99. Miller, *Disappearance of God*, 273.

100. Loomis, "Chatter," 59–60.

101. De Nicolas, *Powers of Imagining*, 33.

102. Ibid., xix.

103. See *L* 2, 80; letter of 26 October 1881.

E. E. Duncan-Jones, in "Dixon's Terrible Crystal," *Notes and Queries* 3 (1956): 267, has identified the source of the phrase "terrible crystal" as Ezekiel 1:22: "And over the heads of the living creatures was the likeness of the firmament, as the appearance of crystal terrible to behold, and stretched out over their heads above." That allusive context suggests that Dixon was most of all discussing Hopkins's nature theophany sonnets, as would be appropriate in a letter dated as early as 1881, although by that date such poems of nature theophany included the rather more somber vision of a darkening nature in "Spring and Fall" (sent to Dixon in January 1881; *L* 2, 174).

104. Ellis ("'Authentic Cadence,'" 128, 140) indirectly reminds us that Hopkins clearly agreed with Zechariah. He wrote, for instance, about the "elevating" grace of Pentecost, "which lifts the receiver from one cleave of being to another and to a vital act in Christ" (*S* 158). Pentecostal "elevating" grace has, Hopkins believed, greater potency for human transformation than either "quickening, stimulating" grace, which stirs the affective will, or the "corrective" grace that primally leads the elective will to proper self-"determining" (*S*, 158).

105. In *Companion to the Hymnal: A handbook to the 1964 Methodist Hymnal*, ed. Fred D. Gealy et al. (Nashville and New York: Abindgon Press, 1978), 489, Young writes that "Bianco da Siena (b. Anciolina, in the Val d'Arno, date unknown; d. Venice, Italy, c. 1434) in 1367 entered the order of Jesuates, the unordained men of the St. Augustine discipline. Little more is known of his life. His *Laudi Spirituali* was edited and published in 1851 by Telesforo Bini, at Lucca. These hymns in the vernacular are contemporary with efforts of the *laudisti*, a religious order . . . active in the fourteenth and fifteenth centuries that specialized in devotional verse."

106. Bianco da Siena, d. 1434; trans. R. F. Littledale. I am quoting the hymn from *The Hymnal 1940, According to the use of the Episcopal Church* (New York: The Church Hymnal Corporation, 1940), 376. While I greatly admire the principle of nonsexist language in the same denomination's *Hymnal 1982* (New York: The Church Hymnal Corporation, 1985) and have indeed firmly sought to follow that principle in my own language throughout this volume, the male pronouns of the earlier version seem more appropriate when applied to Hopkins.

Bibliography

Alexander, Anthony F. *College Sacramental Theology*. Chicago: Henry Regnery Company, 1961.

Allsopp, Michael. "Hopkins at Oxford, 1863–1867: His Formal Studies." *Hopkins Quarterly* 4 (1977–78): 161–76.

Andrews, E. A., ed. *A New Latin Dictionary Founded on a Translation of Freund's Latin-German Lexicon*. Revised by Charlton T. Lewis and Charles Short. New York: American Book Company, 1894.

Augustine. *On Christian Doctrine*. Translated by D. W. Robertson, Jr. Indianapolis, Ind.: Bobbs-Merrill, 1958.

Baillie, Donald. *The Theology of the Sacraments, and Other Papers*. New York: Charles Scribner's Sons, 1957.

Ball, Patricia. *The Science of Aspects: The Changing Role of Fact in the Work of Coleridge, Ruskin, and Hopkins*. London: The Athlone Press, 1971.

Bates, Ronald. "Hopkins' Ember Poems: A Liturgical Source." *Renascence* 17 (1964): 32–37.

Bergonzi, Bernard. *Gerard Manley Hopkins*. Masters of World Literature. New York: Macmillan, 1977.

Beyette, Thomas K. "Hopkins' Phenomenology of Art in 'The shepherd's brow.'" *Victorian Poetry* 11 (1973): 207–14.

Bouyer, Louis. "Word and Sacrament." In *Sacraments: The Gestures of Christ*, edited by Denis O'Callaghan. New York: Sheed and Ward, 1964.

Boyle, Robert, S. J. "Hopkins, Brutus, and Dante." *Victorian Poetry* 24 (1986): 1–12.

———. *Metaphor in Hopkins*. Chapel Hill: University of North Carolina Press, 1960.

Brilioth, Yngve. *Eucharistic Faith and Practice: Evangelical and Catholic*. Translated by A. G. Hebert. London: S.P.C.K., 1961.

Brook, Stella. *The Language of 'The Book of Common Prayer.'* London: André Deutsch, 1965.

Brooks, Peter. *Thomas Cranmer's Doctrine of the Eucharist: An Essay in Historical Development*. New York: The Seabury Press, 1965.

Buckley, Jerome Hamilton. *The Turning Key: Autobiography and the Subjective Impulse Since 1800*. Cambridge: Harvard University Press, 1984.

Bump, Jerome. *Gerard Manley Hopkins*. Boston: Twayne, 1982.

Bynum, Caroline Walker. *Jesus as Mother: Studies in the Spirituality of the High Middle Ages*. Berkeley: University of California Press, 1982.

Carlyle, Thomas. *Sartor Resartus: The Life and Opinions of Herr Teufelsdröckh*. Edited by Charles Frederick Harrold. New York: The Odyssey Press, 1937.

Chaucer, Geoffrey. *Works*. Edited by F. N. Robinson. 2d ed. Boston: Houghton Mifflin, 1961.

Cooke, Bernard, *Sacraments and Sacramentality*. Mystic, Conn.: Twenty-Third Publications, 1983.

Cotter, James Finn. *Inscape: The Christology and Poetry of Gerard Manley Hopkins.* Pittsburgh, Pa.: University of Pittsburgh Press, 1972.

Culler, Jonathan. *Ferdinand de Saussure.* Rev. ed. Ithaca: Cornell University Press, 1986.

———. *The Pursuit of Signs: Semiotics, Literature, Deconstruction.* Ithaca: Cornell University Press, 1981.

Dante. *La Divina Commedia / The Divine Comedy.* Edited and translated by John D. Sinclair. New York: Oxford University Press, 1972.

De Nicolas, Antonio T. *Powers of Imagining / Ignatius de Loyola: A Philosophical Hermeneutic of Imagining through the Collected Works of Ignatius de Loyola, with a Translation of These Works.* Albany: State University of New York Press, 1986.

Devlin, Christopher, S.J. "Time's Eunuch." *The Month,* n.s., 1 (1949): 303–12.

———. "The Image and the Word, I." *The Month,* n.s., 3 (1950): 114–27.

Domville, Eric, ed. *Editing British and American Literature, 1880–1920.* New York: Garland, 1976.

Donne, John. *Poetical Works.* Edited by Sir Herbert Grierson. London: Oxford University Press, 1933.

Downes, David A. *Gerard Manley Hopkins: A Study of His Ignatian Spirit.* New York: Bookman Associates, 1959.

———. *The Great Sacrifice: Studies in Hopkins.* Lanham, Md.: University Press of America, 1983.

———. *Victorian Portraits: Hopkins and Pater.* New York: Bookman Associates, 1963.

Dronke, Peter.*The Medieval Lyric.* 2d ed. Cambridge: Cambridge University Press, 1977.

Duncan-Jones, E. E. "Dixon's Terrible Crystal." *Notes and Queries* 3 (1956): 267.

Duployé, Pie, O.P. "Huysmans en 1968." *La Table Ronde* 243 (April 1968): 63–73.

Eckhart, Meister. "Eternal Birth." In *Medieval Culture and Society,* edited by David Herlihy. New York: Harper Torchbooks, 1968.

Ellis, Virginia Ridley, " 'Authentic Cadence': The Sacramental Method of Gerard Manley Hopkins." Ph. D. diss., Brandeis University, 1969.

Ellsberg, Margaret R. *Created To Praise: The Language of Gerard Manley Hopkins.* New York and Oxford: Oxford University Press, 1987.

Endean, Philip, S.J. "The Spirituality of Gerard Manley Hopkins." *Hopkins Quarterly* 8 (1981–82): 107–29.

Faber, Frederick William. *A Father Faber Heritage.* Edited by Sister Mary Mercedes S.N.D. de Namur. Westminster, Md.: The Newman Press, 1958.

Falk, Eugene H. *The Poetics of Roman Ingarden.* Chapel Hill: University of North Carolina Press, 1981.

Ferguson, Margaret W. "Saint Augustine's Region of Unlikeness: The Crossing of Exile and Language." *Georgia Review* 29 (1975): 842–64.

Fischer, Michael. *Does Deconstruction Make Any Difference?: Poststructuralism and the Defense of Poetry in Modern Criticism.* Bloomington: Indiana University Press, 1985.

Fish, Stanley. *Is There a Text in This Class?: The Authority of Interpretive Communities.* Cambridge: Harvard University Press, 1980.

———. *Self-Consuming Artifacts: The Experience of Seventeenth-Century Literature.* Berkeley: University of California Press, 1972.

Fleishman, Avrom. *Figures of Autobiography: The Language of Self-Writing in Victorian and Modern England.* Berkeley: University of California Press, 1983.

Fulweiler, Howard. *Letters from the Darkling Plain: Language and the Grounds of Knowledge in the Poetry of Arnold and Hopkins.* Columbia: University of Missouri Press, 1972.

Ganoczy, Alexandre. *An Introduction to Catholic Sacramental Theology.* Translated by Willis Thomas, with the assistance of Alexander Sherman. New York: Paulist Press, 1984.

Gardner, W. H. *Gerard Manley Hopkins (1844–1889): A Study of Poetic Idiosyncrasy in Relation to Poetic Tradition*. 2 vols. 1944 and 1948. Reprint. London: Oxford University Press, 1958.

Gealy, Fred, et al., eds. *Companion to the Hymnal: A handbook to the 1964 Methodist Hymnal*. Nashville and New York: Abingdon Press, 1978.

Giles, Richard F. "Review of Sprinker's 'A Counterpoint of Dissonance,'" *Victorian Poetry* 20 (1982): 209–16.

Grant, William, and David D. Murison, eds. *Scottish National Dictionary*. Edinburgh: Scottish National Dictionary Association, 1976.

Gray, Donald. "The Real Absence: A Note on the Eucharist." In *Living Bread, Saving Cup: Readings on the Eucharist*, edited by R. Kevin Seasoltz, O.S.B. Collegeville, Minn.: The Liturgical Press, 1982.

Greeley, Andrew. "A Christmas Biography." In *The Wiley Reader: Designs For Writing*, edited by Caroline D. Eckhardt et al. New York: John Wiley and Sons, 1976.

Gunter, Richard, "Grammar, Semantics, and the Poems of Gerard Manley Hopkins." *Hopkins Quarterly* 1 (1974–75): 23–36.

Harris, Daniel A. *Inspirations Unbidden: The "Terrible Sonnets" of Gerard Manley Hopkins*. Berkeley: University of California Press, 1982.

Hartman, Geoffrey. *The Fate of Reading, and Other Essays*. Chicago: University of Chicago Press, 1975.

———, ed., *Hopkins: A Collection of Critical Essays*. Englewood Cliffs, N.J.: Prentice-Hall, 1966.

Herbert, George. *Poems*. London, New York, and Toronto: Oxford University Press, 1961.

Heuser, Alan. *The Shaping Vision of Gerard Manley Hopkins*. London: Oxford University Press, 1958.

Hopkins, Gerard Manley. *The Correspondence of Gerard Manley Hopkins and Richard Watson Dixon*. Edited by Claude Colleer Abbott. 2d ed. London: Oxford University Press, 1956. (L 2)

———. *Further Letters, Including His Correspondence with Coventry Patmore*. Edited by Claude Colleer Abbott. 2d ed. London: Oxford University Press, 1956. (L 3)

———. *The Journals and Papers of Gerard Manley Hopkins*. Edited by Humphry House and Graham Storey. London: Oxford University Press, 1959. (J)

———. *The Letters of Gerard Manley Hopkins to Robert Bridges*. Edited by Claude Colleer Abbott. 2d ed. London: Oxford University Press, 1955. (L 1)

———. *Poems*. Edited by W. H. Gardner and N. H. MacKenzie. 4th ed. London: Oxford University Press, 1967. (P)

———. *Poems*. Edited by Robert Bridges and W. H. Gardner. 3d ed. London: Oxford University Press, 1948.

———. *Sermons and Devotional Writings*. Edited by Christopher Devlin, S.J. London: Oxford University Press, 1959. (S)

Huysmans, Joris-Karl. *La cathédrale*. Vol. 14 of *Oeuvres complètes*. Edited by Charles Grolleau and Lucien Descaves. Paris: Crès, 1931.

Hymnal, 1940, According to the use of the Episcopal Church. New York: The Church Hymnal Corporation, 1940.

Hymnal, 1982, According to the use of the Episcopal Church. New York: The Church Hymnal Corporation, 1985.

Ingarden, Roman. *The Cognition of the Literary Work of Art*. Translated by Ruth Ann Crowley and Kenneth R. Olsen. Evanston, Ill.: Northwestern University Press, 1973.

———. *The Literary Work of Art: An Investigation on the Borderlines of Ontology, Logic and Theory of Literature*. Translated by George C. Grabowicz. Evanston, Ill.: Northwestern University Press, 1973.

Jakobson, Roman. "Closing Statement: Linguistics and Poetics." In *Style in Language*, edited by Thomas Sebeck. Boston: MIT Press, 1960.

Jakobson, Roman, and Lawrence G. Jones. *Shakespeare's Verbal Art in 'Th'Expence of Spirit.'* The Hague: Mouton, 1970.

Jansen, G. M. A., O.P. *The Sacramental We: An Existential Approach to the Sacramental Life.* Milwaukee, Wis.: The Bruce Publishing Company, 1968.

Johnson, Wendell Stacy. "From Ruskin to Hopkins." *Hopkins Quarterly* 8 (1981–82): 89–106.

——. *Gerard Manley Hopkins: The Poet as Victorian.* Ithaca: Cornell University Press, 1966.

——. "Halfway to a New Land: Herbert, Tennyson, and the Early Hopkins." *Hopkins Quarterly* 10 (1983–84): 115–23.

——. "Reading Oneself into Hopkins." In *The Victorian Experience: The Poets,* edited by Richard Levine. Athens: Ohio University Press, 1982.

——. "Sexuality and Inscape." *Hopkins Quarterly* 3 (1976–77): 59–65.

Kaske, Robert. "Chaucer's Marriage Group." In *Chaucer the Love Poet,* edited by Jerome Mitchell and William Provost. Athens: University of Georgia Press, 1973.

Keegan, Francis, S.J. "Gerard Manley Hopkins at Mount St. Mary's College, Spinkhill, 1877–1878." *Hopkins Quarterly* 6 (1979–80): 11–34.

Kierkegaard, Søren. *Fear and Trembling.* Princeton: Princeton University Press, 1973.

Kitchen, Paddy. *Gerard Manley Hopkins.* New York: Atheneum, 1979.

Knoepflmacher, U. C., and G. B. Tennyson, eds. *Nature and the Victorian Imagination.* Berkeley: University of California Press, 1977.

Korg, Jacob. "Hopkins' Linguistic Deviations." *PMLA* 92 (1977): 977–86.

Lang, Cecil Y. *The Pre-Raphaelites and Their Circle.* Boston: Houghton Mifflin, 1968.

Lathrop, Gordon W. "A Rebirth of Images: On the Use of the Bible in Liturgy." *Worship* 57 (1984): 291–304.

Leclercq, Jean, O.S.B. *The Love of Learning and the Desire for God: A Study of Monastic Culture.* Translated by Catherine Misrahi. New York: Fordham University Press, 1982.

Leggio, James. "The Science of a Sacrament." *Hopkins Quarterly* 4 (1977–78): 55–67.

Lemon, Lee T., and Marion J. Reis. *Russian Formalist Criticism: Four Essays.* Lincoln: University of Nebraska Press, 1965.

Liddell, Henry George, and Robert Scott, eds. *A Greek-English Lexicon.* 9th ed. Oxford: Clarendon Press, 1940.

Loomis, Jeffrey B. "As Margaret Mourns: Hopkins, Goethe, and Shaffer on 'Eternal Delight.' " *Cithara* 22 (1982): 22–38.

——. "Birth Pangs in Darkness: Hopkins's Archetypal Christian Biography." *Texas Studies in Literature and Language* 28 (1986): 81–106.

——. "Chatter with a Just Lord: Hopkins' Final Sonnets of Quiescent Terror." *Hopkins Quarterly* 7 (1980–81): 47–64.

——. "A Defense of Hopkins' 'Brothers,' " *Hopkins Quarterly* 11 (1984–85): 35–42.

——. "Hopkins' 'To R. B.' " *The Explicator* 42 (1984): 23–26.

——. "Review of Michael Sprinker's 'A Counterpoint of Dissonance' and Donald Walhout's *Send My Roots Rain*." *West Virginia Association of College English Teachers' Bulletin,* n.s., 8 (1983): 50–52.

Luria, Maxwell S., and Richard L. Hoffman, eds. *Middle English Lyrics: Authoritative Texts, Critical and Historical Backgrounds, Perspectives on Six Poems.* New York: Norton, 1974.

McChesney, Donald. *A Hopkins Commentary: An Explanatory Commentary on the Main Poems, 1876–1889.* New York: New York University Press, 1968.

MacKean, W. H. *The Eucharistic Doctrine of the Oxford Movement: A Critical Survey.* London: Putnam, 1933.

MacKenzie, Norman. *A Reader's Guide to Gerard Manley Hopkins.* Ithaca: Cornell University Press, 1981.

———. "The Dragon's Treasure Hoard Unlocked." *Modern Language Quarterly* 31 (1970): 236–44.

———. "Gerard Manley Hopkins' 'Spelt from Sibyl's Leaves.'" *Malahat Review* 26 (1973): 218–28.

———. *Hopkins.* Writers and Critics Series. Edinburgh and London: Oliver and Boyd, 1968.

McNamee, M.B., S.J. "The Ignatian Meditation Pattern in the Poetry of Gerard Manley Hopkins." *Hopkins Quarterly* 2 (1975–76): 21–28.

Mariani, Paul. *A Commentary on the Complete Poems of Gerard Manley Hopkins.* Ithaca and London: Cornell University Press, 1970.

———. *A Usable Past.* Amherst: University of Massachusetts Press, 1984.

Martin, Philip. *Mastery and Mercy: A Study of Two Religious Poems—"The Wreck of the Deutschland" by G. M. Hopkins and "Ash Wednesday" by T. S. Eliot.* London: Oxford University Press, 1957.

Marty, Martin E. *A Short History of Christianity.* Philadelphia, Pa.: Fortress Press, 1980.

Miller, J. Hillis. *The Disappearance of God: Five Nineteenth-Century Writers.* Cambridge: Harvard University Press, 1963.

Milroy, James. *The Language of Gerard Manley Hopkins.* London: André Deutsch, 1977.

Milton, John. *Complete Poems and Major Prose.* Edited by Merritt Y. Hughes. New York: The Odyssey Press, 1957.

Milward, Peter, S.J. *A Commentary on the Complete Sonnets of Gerard Manley Hopkins.* London: C. Hurst, 1970.

———, with Raymond V. Schoder, S.J. *Landscape and Inscape: Vision and Inspiration in Hopkins's Poetry.* Grand Rapids, Mich.: Eerdmans, 1975.

———, and Raymond Schoder, S.J., eds. *Readings of "The Wreck": Essays in Commemoration of the Centenary of G. M. Hopkins' "The Wreck of the Deutschland."* Chicago: Loyola University Press, 1976.

Moore, Michael D. "Newman and the Motif of Intellectual Pain in Hopkins' 'Terrible Sonnets.'" *Mosaic* 12 (1978–79): 29–46.

Motto, Marylou. *"Mined with a Motion": The Poetry of Gerard Manley Hopkins.* New Brunswick, N.J.: Rutgers University Press, 1984.

Newman, John Henry. *Public and Parochial Sermons 5.* Vol. 27 of *Works.* London: Longmans, Green, 1907.

O'Connor, Flannery. *The Complete Stories.* New York: Farrar, Strauss, and Giroux, 1979.

Ong, Walter, J., S.J. *Hopkins, the Self, and God.* Toronto, Buffalo, and London: University of Toronto Press, 1986.

Origen. *Origen: Spirit and Fire—A Thematic Anthology of His Writings.* Edited by Hans Urs Balthasar. Translated by Robert J. Daly, S.J. Washington, D.C.: The Catholic University of America Press, 1984.

Oxford English Dictionary. Compact ed. New York: Oxford University Press, 1971.

Pick, John, ed. *Gerard Manley Hopkins / 'The Windhover.'* The Merrill Literary Casebook Series. Columbus, Ohio: Charles E. Merrill, 1969.

Pinto, V. de S. "Letter—'Hopkins and The Trewnesse of the Christian Religion.'" *Times Literary Supplement,* 10 June 1955, 317.

Plato. *Cratylus, Parmenides, Greater Hippias, Lesser Hippias.* Edited by H. N. Fowler. Cambridge: Harvard University Press, 1926.

———. *Euthyphro, Apology, Crito, Phaedo, Phaedrus.* Edited by H. N. Fowler. Cambridge: Harvard University Press, 1917.

Proffitt, Edward. "Tone and Contrast in Hopkins' 'The Starlight Night.'" *Hopkins Quarterly* 5 (1978–79): 47–49.

Rahner, Karl, and Karl-Heinz Weger. *Our Christian Faith: Answers for the Future.* New York: Crossroad, 1981.

Richards, Bertrand F. "Meaning in 'Carrion Comfort.'" *Renascence* 27 (1974): 45–50.

Riddle, Florence K. "Hopkins' Dramatic Monologues." *Hopkins Quarterly* 2 (1975–76): 51–66.

Ridley, Jasper. *Thomas Cranmer.* Oxford: Clarendon Press, 1962.

Riehle, Wolfgang. *The Middle English Mystics.* Translated by Bernard Standring. London: Routledge and Kegan Paul, 1981.

Rilke, Rainer-Maria. *Das Marien-Leben (The Life of the Virgin Mary).* Edited and translated by Stephen Spender. London: Vision Press, 1951.

———. *Poetry.* Vol. 2 of *Selected Works.* Translated by J. B. Leishman. London: The Hogarth Press, 1976.

Rimbaud, Arthur. *Oeuvres complètes.* Edited by Antoine Adam. Paris: Gallimard, 1972.

Ritz, Jean-Georges. *Le poète Gérard Manley Hopkins, s.j. (1884–1889): l'homme et l'oeuvre.* Paris: Didier, 1963.

———. *Robert Bridges and Gerard Hopkins, 1863–1889; A Literary Friendship.* London: Oxford University Press, 1960.

Robinson, John. *In Extremity: a study of Gerard Manley Hopkins.* Cambridge: Cambridge University Press, 1978.

Ruskin, John. *Diaries.* Edited by Joan Evans and J. H. Whitehouse. 3 vols. London: Oxford University Press, 1956–59.

———. *Modern Painters.* 6 vols. New York: John Wiley and Sons, 1883.

———. *Praeterita: Outlines of Scenes and Thoughts Perhaps Worthy of Memory in my Past Life.* London: Rupert Hart-Davis, 1949.

———. *The Two Paths.* Vol. 16 of *Works.* Library ed. Edited by Alexander Wedderburn and E. T. Cook. London: George Allen, 1903–12.

Ryan, Dermot. "Sacraments Foreshadowed." In *Sacraments: The Gestures of Christ,* edited by Denis O'Callaghan. New York: Sheed and Ward, 1964.

Rygiel, Mary Ann. "Hopkins and Herbert: Two Meditative Poets." *Hopkins Quarterly* 10 (1983–84): 45–54.

Salmon, Rachel. "Poetry of Praise and Poetry of Petition: Simultaneity in the Sonnet World of Gerard Manley Hopkins." *Victorian Poetry* 22 (1984): 383–406.

———. "'Wording it How': The Possibilities of Utterance in *The Wreck of the Deutschland.*" Hopkins Quarterly 10 (1983–84): 87–108.

Schneider, Elisabeth. *The Dragon in the Gate: Studies in the Poetry of G. M. Hopkins.* Berkeley and Los Angeles: University of California Press, 1967.

Seland, John. "Hopkins and the Eucharist." Ph. D. diss., University of California at Riverside, 1976.

Shakespeare, William. *The Tempest.* Edited by Northrop Frye. Baltimore: Penguin, 1959.

Shepherd, Massey Hamilton. *The Oxford American Prayer Book, with Commentary.* New York: Oxford University Press, 1950.

Smith, Lacey Baldwin. *Henry VIII: The Mask of Royalty.* Boston: Houghton Mifflin, 1973.

Smith, Lyle H., Jr. "Beyond the Romantic Sublime: Gerard Manley Hopkins." *Renascence* 34 (1982): 173–84.

Sprinker, Michael. *"A Counterpoint of Dissonance": The Aesthetics and Poetry of Gerard Manley Hopkins.* Baltimore and London: The Johns Hopkins University Press, 1980.

Sulloway, Alison. *Gerard Manley Hopkins and the Victorian Temper.* London: Routledge and Kegan Paul, 1972.

———. "St. Ignatius Loyola and the Victorian Temper: Hopkins' Windhover as Symbol of 'Diabolic Gravity.'" *Hopkins Quarterly* 1 (1974–75): 43–51.

Tate, Allen. "Tension in Poetry." In *The Modern Critical Spectrum.* Ed. Gerald Jay and Nancy Marmer Goldberg. Englewood Cliffs, N. J.: Prentice-Hall, 1962.

Tennyson, Alfred. *Tennyson's Poetry: Authoritative Texts, Juvenilia and Early Responses, Criticism.* Ed. Robert W. Hill, Jr. New York: Norton, 1971.

Thomas, Alfred, S. J. "G. M. Hopkins' 'The Windhover': Sources, 'Underthought,' and Significance." *Modern Language Review* 70 (1975): 497–507.

———. *Hopkins the Jesuit: The Years in Training.* London: Oxford University Press, 1969.

Walhout, Donald. *Send My Roots Rain: A Study of Religious Experience in the Poetry of Gerard Manley Hopkins.* Athens, Ohio: Ohio University Press, 1981.

Walliser, Stephan. *"That Nature is a Heraclitean Fire and of the comfort of the Resurrection": A Case-Study in G. M. Hopkins' Poetry.* Bern: Francke, 1977.

Warner, John M. "Belief and Imagination in 'The Windhover.'" *Hopkins Quarterly* 5 (1978–79): 129–37.

Weyand, Norman, S.J., ed. *Immortal Diamond: Studies in Gerard Manley Hopkins.* London: Sheed and Ward, 1949.

White, Norman. "Review of Harris's *Inspirations Unbidden.*" *Hopkins Quarterly* 11 (1984–85): 87–96.

Wicks, Jared, S.J. "The Sacraments: A Catechism for Today." In *The Sacraments: Readings in Contemporary Sacramental Theology,* edited by Michael J. Taylor, S.J. New York: Alba House, 1981.

Wolfe, Patricia A. "The Paradox of Self: A Study of Hopkins's Spiritual Conflict in the Terrible Sonnets." *Victorian Poetry* 6 (1969): 86–103.

Yoder, Emily K. "Evil and Idolatry in 'The Windhover.'" *Hopkins Quarterly* 2 (1975–76): 33–46.

Zaniello, Thomas. "The Tonic of Platonism: The Origins and Use of Hopkins' 'Scape.'" *Hopkins Quarterly* 5 (1978–79): 5–16.

Index